*Native to the Nation*

# BORDERLINES

*For more books in the series, see p. vi.*

# Native to the Nation

*Disciplining Landscapes and Bodies in Australia*

**ALLAINE CERWONKA**

BORDERLINES, VOLUME 21

University of Minnesota Press

Minneapolis

London

The photographs in the book were taken by the author.

Published by the University of Minnesota Press
111 Third Avenue South, Suite 290
Minneapolis, MN 55401-2520
http://www.upress.umn.edu

Library of Congress Cataloging-in-Publication Data

Cerwonka, Allaine.
    Native to the nation : disciplining landscapes and bodies in Australia / Allaine Cerwonka.
        p.    cm. — (Borderlines ; v. 21)
    Includes bibliographical references and index.
    ISBN 0-8166-4348-2 (hc : alk. paper) — ISBN 0-8166-4349-0 (pb : alk. paper)
    1. National characteristics, Australian. 2. Multiculturalism—Australia. 3. Natural landscaping—Australia. 4. Australia—Ethnic relations. 5. Australia—Race relations. 6. Australia—Emigration and immigration. 7. Australia—Politics and government. I. Title. II. Borderlines (Minneapolis, Minn.) ; v. 21.
    DU121.C47 2004
    305.8'00994—dc22

                                                        2004004492

Printed in the United States of America on acid-free paper

The University of Minnesota is an equal-opportunity educator and employer.

12 11 10 09 08 07 06 05 04        10 9 8 7 6 5 4 3 2 1

*For my parents*
*Diana and Ron Cerwonka*

# BORDERLINES

# Contents

# Acknowledgments

This book and the corresponding intellectual journey have been enormously enriched by the assistance, intelligence, and goodwill of many people. I am glad to have the opportunity to publicly acknowledge my sincere gratitude to them.

My largest debt is to the staff of the Fitzroy Police Station and to members of the East Melbourne Garden Club, who made this project possible with their generosity and insights about Australia. I appreciate the financial support of the Fulbright Foundation and the University of California Humanities Research Institute (UCHRI), which provided me with big chunks of time to research and write. I thank the Women's Studies Institute at Georgia State University for financing two very helpful assistants, Roxanne Guillory and Maria Hansen, whose talents benefited this project. I also gained in many ways from ongoing discussions and friendships of the UCHRI group members (Brook Thomas, Dana Takagi, Liz Constable, Terry Threadgold, Sneja Gunew, John Liu, Nan Seuffert, Chris Newfield, and Jim LaSpina) and from Deborah Massey Sanchez, the assistant director, for her many forms of help.

The informal mentoring of some talented people gave me many tools to write this book; I thank John Cash, Jim Ferguson, Mark Poster, Patricia O'Brien, Robyn Wiegman, Chris Lee, and Linda Bell. Gaby Schwab and Tracy Strong provided excellent insight and direction on earlier drafts of this project and have been important examples of creative, thoughtful scholarship. I appreciate the professionalism and talent of the staff at the University of Minnesota Press and of Carrie Mullen, Julie DuSablon, and Mike Stoffel in particular. The support and insights of Simon Philpott, David Campbell, and Michael J. Shapiro have been especially valuable.

Much of this book grows out of several years in Melbourne, Australia. Some of the curiosity that underwrote the project started when I was an American Field Service exchange student in 1984 and was further developed in later trips to Australia in 1988 and 1994. I am grateful to the Burgess family, who did not realize that they had signed on for an exchange student who would keep showing up at their door. Thank you to Lis, Claire, Sue, Wayne, Max, and Roma. I also thank Charles Richardson, Richard Allsop, Diane Therese, Robyn Clancy (and Paul), Gyorgy Scrinis, Heather Leatham, and Bill Doogue. My sincere thanks to Mathilde Lochert for generosity and friendship during my years in Australia, which have taught me a lot about living. This project was enriched additionally by the kindness and excellent insights of Prue Forester, Valerie and Bill Cannington, Elizabeth Hall, Violet and Len Cheffers, Len Ledwich, Dorothy Wakefield, Lillian Hall, Lee Tregloan, Joan Mercer, Arthur Turner, Charmaine Young, Ed Bourke, and Pat Allen.

I have also had plenty of support in the northern hemisphere. My family has been a vital resource—Dara, Eggy, Brian, Eric, Barbara, Donna, Evan, Colin, Meredith, Abigail, Homer, and my parents, Ron and Diana. Diana has been especially important to this project, providing transcription, editing, formatting, and an enthusiasm that only a mother could drum up. Several friends also provided support and intellectual stimulation. I am grateful to the following people for knowing when to engage in conversation about the manuscript and when to distract me from it: Amy Hutson, Eric Bilodeau, Cristin Searles, Monica Hulsbus, and Kate (Liguori) Merryweather. I appreciate the support of Jim Devlin, who shared my year of research in Australia and much of the intellectual journey of the book. My intellectual community in Atlanta has also sustained the project: Elizabeth Beck, Susan Talburt, Emanuela Guano, Peter Lindsay, Al Yee, Layli Phillips, Charlene Ball, Julie Kubala, Andrew Valls, and Kit Wellman. A special thank you to David Weberman for his editing of the introduction, many helpful insights, and most important keeping me whole.

I was fortunate to conceptualize this project within a community of amazing women academics who made me work harder and laugh harder than I thought myself capable. An enormous thank you to Kristen Hill Maher and Thu-huong Nguyen-Vo: many of the better ideas were theirs. Also crucial to this project was the insightful feedback and intellectual companionship of Deborah Mindry, Erica Bornstein, and Edna Levy.

Finally, I extend heartfelt appreciation to Liisa Malkki and Mark Petracca. Mark's faith and solid intellectual engagement at every stage of the project were enormously important for me. Liisa not only provided direction with the scholarly literature and ethnographic fieldwork but helped me experience the pleasures of the intellectual journey.

Without the significant contribution of this collection of people, this book would never have been written. I count myself enormously fortunate.

# Introduction
## Roots, Dislocations, and Origin Stories

In a suburb of Melbourne, a group of settler Australians[1] spends a mild autumn Saturday afternoon as volunteers, working to clear the Dandenong Ranges of offensive exotic (nonindigenous) species such as blackberries and willow trees, introduced to Australia during European settlement. In a few weeks, this voluntary community group will build boardwalks and plant "natives" (indigenous species), such as nodding salt bush *(Einadia nutans)* ground cover and a grove of silver banksia *(Banksia marginata)* trees, which have been "just taken over" by the exotics, creating an ecological imbalance. Volunteers and their supporters frame their activities as an effort to redress the effects of British colonization in Australia. They work to counter a destructive British imperialism that reshaped the Australian natural environment for a European agricultural economy and to suit the picturesque aesthetic of British colonials.

Contemporary spatial practices are one way some settler Australians reject the "colonialist mentality" of earlier generations who tried to grow camellias and "homesick gardens" in the Outback out of nostalgia for an imagined British homeland most Australians had never seen. Many contemporary Australians now draw on what they view as an Aboriginal model of stewardship and love for the Australian landscape. They use the natural environment to imagine a political and aesthetic break with British colonialism in Australia and to define the link between settler Australians, culture and national territory.

Mundane activities, such as weeding and planting, represent one way in which nations are legitimated and people "root" themselves in the face of increased deterritorialization. The transnational flows resulting from late capitalism, mass migration, and shifting post-colonial political structures have internationalized many countries, much like they have Australia. People, products, capital, and ideologies circulate between nation-states more frequently and in larger numbers. While nation-states have never been hermetically sealed, distinctive cultural spaces as popularly perceived, transnational flows across nation-state borders have disrupted any easy narration of a distinct national identity. Arjun Appadurai identifies "disjunctures" between economy, culture, and politics in the increased flows of late capitalism. He explains:

> People, machinery, money, images, and ideas now follow increasingly nonisomorphic paths; of course, at all periods in human history, there have been some disjunctures in the flow of these things, but the sheer speed, scale and volume of each of these flows are now so great that the disjunctures have become central to the politics of global culture. (1996, 37)

Given contemporary challenges and threats of the deterritorialization and displacement of people as well as the reassertion of tradition, it is important to understand better new forms of identification with place and the construction of "rootedness."

In his analysis of the terms by which nations originally became significant political communities, Benedict Anderson notes that nations are constituted through an imagined organic connection between people, culture, and place. Historically, this imagined organic connection was achieved through the development of maps, museums, and the census, all of which helped delineate a "people" and narrate its cultural and historical connection with the territory claimed by the nation-state (1993). Such an organic connection between a people, a unified culture, and the physical territory they claim is harder to imagine in the face of diasporic populations, multicultural nation-states, and global capital. The transnational flows prompted by postcolonial politics and late capitalism mean that more and more people are deterritorialized insofar as their national and cultural identities are "displaced" from a designated homeland. In turn, larger numbers of people find themselves emotionally, economically, and physically bound to more than one nation-state and culture.

In response to these social shifts in the late twentieth century, scholars have turned their attention to understanding how homeland, belonging, and identity are constructed by deterritorialized groups—whether diasporas (Leonard 1992; Ong and Nonini 1997), refugees (Malkki 1995), migrant workers (Rouse 1991), or other groups that engage in new forms of imagined homelands and political communities. In many cases even people who do not physically cross borders have been deterritorialized since the increasing ethnic, racial, and cultural diversity in their local landscape challenges their sense of their nation-state as a cultural whole with a cohesive "people" (see Bhabha 1990b). Transnational flows of images and products also challenge the experience of a distinct national culture of those who never leave their local community. National mythologies, perhaps always a fiction of sorts about a unified culture within an uncontested national homeland, are becoming increasingly more difficult for people to sustain. Gupta and Ferguson note:

> For even people remaining in familiar and ancestral places find the nature of their relation to place ineluctably changed, and the illusion of a natural and essential connection between the place and the culture broken. "Englishness," for instance, in contemporary, internationalized England is just as complicated and nearly as deterritorialized a notion as Palestinian-ness or Armenian-ness, since "England" ("the real England") refers less to a bounded place than to an imagined state of being or moral location. (1992, 10)

Scholars have paid less attention to the deterritorialization of people who "remain in place." While those who "remain in place" are not removed from their imagined homelands, as are members of a diaspora or refugees, my study draws attention to their need to reconstitute their imagined connection to place. This book examines the strategies of those who previously saw themselves at the center of nation and culture and who are increasingly challenged to (re)imagine the connection between themselves and the culture and land they claim for their nation-state. I put forth the processes by which people territorialize the nation in the face of a crisis of identity and cartography. And specifically, I inquire as to how people imagine a link between themselves and a cohesive culture in relation to a physical territory.

Spatial practices, such as the cultivation of native gardens in Australia, are a way of reimagining an alternative national subjectivity for deterritorialized Australian nationals. These spatial practices create and ground an identity for settler Australians in a "post-imperial" moment. They must be understood in terms of contemporary global shifts as well as a history in which settler Australians sought to locate Australia centrally in the British Empire and in "the West." Contemporary spatial practices also function to create new land claims for settler Australians at a time when the legitimacy of European colonization of the continent has been seriously challenged by successful Aboriginal land rights litigation. Thus, this study examines the processes by which nations are territorialized in the context of formidable political and cultural questions concerning land and resources.

This project aims to denaturalize and historicize state geography in order to show how it is an important ongoing mechanism of hegemony. But in addition to rendering state geography more vulnerable, this study explores the ways in which the geography of states is invariably already a site of construction and contestation.

Drawing on ethnographic material, I approach these issues by examining how people establish or imagine organic links between themselves, culture, and place through spatial practices. By spatial practices I mean the cultural practices by which people construct or define place. This term grows out of Michel de Certeau's concept of the everyday practices by which people "consume" the world. De Certeau argues that we need to understand more than the operations and representations of power but also the consumption inherent in practices related to urban spaces, memory, reading, and language use. De Certeau's analysis of urban spatial practices has been a helpful starting point. While he is interested in the "logic" of a wide range of practices, I focus on social practices that function to define *space* and how they are embedded in a wide range of power relations. My primary interest is in spatial practices that ultimately tie into the production of national territory.

Spatial practices take the form of actually moving physical earth, but they also include less obvious practices such as mapping and bureaucratically tracking people in the landscape, decorating one's home, performing certain behaviors within a space as well as the narrative practices de Certeau describes. While any social practice might qualify as a spatial practice, classifying something as such depends on whether the practice produces place or territorializes people and culture. For instance, under most circumstances, drinking a cup of tea would not be sensibly regarded as a spatial activity. But if drinking a cup of tea were part of an elaborate Australian ritual of coding their cottage garden as an authentically British spatial extension of the British Empire, then it could reasonably be read as a spatial practice. Ethnographic research has allowed me to read social practices in a larger political and cultural context in terms of the meanings they hold for the people involved. Consequently, I have been able to undertake a richer consideration of nonnarrative spatial practice than afforded to studies that look exclusively at text or narrative.

Looking at the spatial practices within two Australia communities—the East Melbourne Garden Club and the Fitzroy Police Station—I trace how settler Australians redefine and legitimate their claim to the land. They reimagine and reterritorialize the settler nation in response to a number of social and political issues that have deterritorialized white Australians. These issues involve the racial and cultural diversity of a multicultural Australia, Aboriginal land rights, and the pressures since the 1970s to form closer ties with economically successful Asian countries. I integrate the ethnographic material with historical analysis and theory not to make general claims about Australians, but rather to understand the processes by which political communities are imagined spatially and relegitimated in an era of globalization. I also trace how these local spatial practices are connected to "elsewhere" insofar as they correspond to past and present transnational discourses that function to construct imagined supranational communities.

Instead of presuming organic links among people, culture, and territory—"Texans are individualistic and bold because of the rugged, open landscape" or "Tasmanians are reserved because they are located so close to the cold winds of Antarctica"—we must instead ask how such common sense is produced. By analyzing how the imagination shapes and delimits the physical world, we gain insight into the political work achieved by assumptions about environmental determinism and into how spatial practices in turn generate certain social and political orders.

Although the processes discussed are not unique to Australia, the Australian context provides an especially rich field for understanding how political orders and culture are spatialized. Historically, Australia has been imagined in relation to geography. Its history testifies to how colonization largely depended on spatial practices that shaped the landscape. Details of the Australian context illuminate how race, civilization, and national identity are imagined through geography. Settler Australians expended a great deal of effort imagining their nation as coterminous with Great Britain; they did so through legislation such as the White Australian Policy (1901–73) and through more informal cultural practices like eating roasted turkey and Christmas pudding in an enactment of a "proper" British Christmas, despite the hot summer temperatures in Australia in December. Locating Australia in Britain and later in "the West" was a means of circumventing the physical proximity of Asia, long viewed as a threat to Australians' status as white and civilized. Both the historical and contemporary ethnographic analyses here, while particular to Australia, underscore more generally how invented geographies produce political community in relation to ideas of race and civilization.

Further, an ethnographic study of contemporary spatial practices in Australia and their links to history enables us to see how hegemony must be constantly rewon (Gramsci 1989). It gives us perspective on how nation-states are reterritorialized in response to political and social changes that have deterritorialized the nation. Combining ethnography with an analysis of history and the political debates in which they are embedded, we can better see how processes of reterritorializing the nation also reproduce other social and political categories such as modernity, "the West," and gender.

This study contributes to the ongoing social theories with which it engages. Perhaps most importantly, it pushes our understanding beyond how nations are produced through narrative to explore how nations are imagined through nonnarrative spatial practices. Indeed, to fully understand the production and hegemony of nation-states, we need to understand how claims to territory and the power of the state are intertwined with space. Spatial practices naturalize the nation. Australia was constituted as an "empty land" *(terra nullius)* not just through imperial edict. For instance, the classification of the Australian landscape as uncultivated "weeds," in turn, framed Aboriginal people as uncivilized and ultimately disqualified them from political rights to the land. Likewise, European ownership was naturalized and its culture rooted through spatial practices like agriculture and the cultivation of English cottage gardens. Such spatial practices produced Australia as a European, Western, civilized space and were thereby key to colonizing it. The ethnographic details of this study consider how contemporary political cosmologies are naturalized and how political belonging continues to be defined through the disciplining of natural landscapes as well as through the regulation of multicultural populations in the urban landscape.

Additionally, by taking space seriously, this ethnographic study highlights how contemporary state power depends on the disciplining of territory. Modern political subjectivity involves the production of "docile bodies" (Foucault 1979) through the surveillance and ordering of bodies in the social and physical landscape. Modern state power also depends on making alternative spatial meanings

Figure 1. The Australian bush, perceived to be "weeds" and "hostile" by Anglo-Celtic settlers in its uncultivated form. The process of colonization of the continent involved converting the Australian bush to agricultural land and grazing land for sheep farming, which in turn stripped the land of nutrients.

and practices, such as Aboriginal spatial practices, visible and thus more controllable by the state.

Finally, this study offers insight into how the imagining of community and the spatial construction of local landscapes relate to larger transnational regional identities and communities. It considers how the local, far from being a space of authenticity and purity, is often articulated in relation to transnational phenomena or identities. Indeed, global processes play out on the intimate landscape of the body. Through their spatial practices, people in local contexts like the Fitzroy Police Station produce supralocal landscapes and categories such as "the West" and "Asia." White Australians police the bodies of Vietnamese immigrants, marking their danger and disorder, as a means of asserting larger geopolitical differences between East and West and in order to reinscribe the whiteness of Australians at a historical moment when white Australians feel dependent on Asian economies.

The next section introduces three issues that have most significantly impacted white settler Australians' monopoly on the land and resources of the continent and their sense of Australia as Western and white. My description attends to only the most central elements of these aspects of Australian politics.

## UNSETTLING THE SETTLER NATION: CONTEMPORARY POLITICAL CONTEXTS

Three political issues of particular significance for unsettling the territorialization of the Australian nation-state became especially pressing in the 1980s, though having a much longer history. They reverberate in direct and indirect ways in the spatial practices of East Melbourne Garden Club members and Fitzroy police officers. These three political issues have been analyzed a great deal in relation to Australian national identity. However, they provide an important context to the theoretical and ethnographic questions here because each of these issues—Aboriginal land rights, Australia's redefined relationship with Asia, and multiculturalism—challenges the imagined connection between people, place, and culture upon which the settler nation-state has been premised. These issues animate the spatial practices described here because they have unsettled settler claims to Australia and have prompted a response from a white majority made to feel on the margins of the nation. In particular, the Keating (ALP)[2] and Howard (Liberal) governments in particular have constructed different rhetoric and policy on these issues, signaling the magnitude of deterritorialization with which the country has been confronted since the 1980s. Furthermore, as Anthony Burke suggests in his analysis of security in Australian politics (2001), despite some policy differences, both leaders sought to secure a unified Australian nation and consolidate the power of the settler state in the face of challenges.

By sketching these political contexts I am not positing a neat causal relationship or suggesting that people always self-consciously responded to these issues in their everyday practices. My point is that people were prompted to renarrate and reshape the nation's geography and the link between white Australians, the hegemonic culture, and the territory of Australia because that connection has been under significant transformation in the past thirty years. I have sometimes marked direct links between these three political debates and the spatial practices in East Melbourne and Fitzroy. At other times, the three political fields function as a general background to shifts that have unsettled political and geographical identity in Australia.

## ABORIGINAL LAND RIGHTS

The presence of Aboriginal people in Australia required settler Australians to work actively to legitimate their claim to the continent right from the earliest days of colonial contact.[3] The legal fiction of *terra nullius* should be read as an early attempt to territorialize Australia as a British colony by declaring the land unoccupied, literally, "empty." Further, the many narratives about Aboriginal barbarism, immorality, and ignorance have been the means of explaining and legitimating why white Australians have a valid claim to the land despite the presence of other societies in Australia before British colonization who have consistently laid claim to the land. Tom Griffiths's work examines the practices of amateur naturalists and historians in the nineteenth century as a means of working through the colonial dispossession of Aboriginal people. Griffiths argues that they were attempts to "foster emotional possession of the land" (1996, 4). Thus, settler Australians have always been engaged at some level with articulating a rationale for the dispossession of Aboriginal people.

Since initial colonization Aborigines have challenged the claim white Australians made to the continent, whether in the form of physical violence or a general lack of cooperation. In the second half of the twentieth century, Aboriginal people and sympathetic white Australians pursued a number of tacks for gaining political and human rights. Their demand for rights has challenged the legitimacy of the settler Australian nation because it asserts Aboriginal claims to the continent and resources as the basis of enhanced political rights within the nation-state. One of the most vibrant avenues of Aboriginal political activism has been litigation for land rights.

As in many places around the world, claims for minority rights gained much momentum in the 1960s and 1970s. During this time in Australia, the federal government (under Prime Minister Holt) established the Council for Aboriginal Affairs with a small budget. By 1972 frustrated Aborigines set up the Aboriginal tent embassy (which continues today) outside of the old Parliament House in protest of the federal government's land rights policies. Although the McMahon government announced its intention to establish funds for the purchase of land by Aboriginal groups outside of existing Aboriginal reserves, it did not establish a way for Aboriginal people to gain land rights to Aboriginal reservations based on their tradi-

*Figure 2. Aboriginal tent embassy.*

tional association with the land. During the 1960s, as a consequence of years of political work, some Aboriginal people regained ownership of their traditional lands. The Gurindji people, whose seven-year battle began when a group walked off the Vestey's Wave Hill station in protest of pay and working conditions, won land rights over traditional lands. And the Yolngu people, also in northern Australia, gained land rights in the 1960s. However, these victories were hard fought, exceptional, and legally idiosyncratic. It was not until the High Court Mabo decision in 1992 and then later the High Court Wik decision in 1996 that Aboriginal people established a strong legal foundation for their long-standing claims to their traditional lands.

The Mabo and Wik decisions were highly significant in unsettling the settler state's moral and legal claims to the Australian continent. The Mabo decision (1992) was the resolution of a court battle spearheaded by Eddie Mabo, a Murray Islander who argued for recognition of continued native title to his land. He based his claim on the fact that his people had maintained uninterrupted possession of the land from before British settlement to the present. Further, with the support of anthropological research documenting the presence of gardens in traditional Aboriginal culture, Mabo's legal case demonstrated that his community had cultivated the land. This case was significant because it contested the terms of *terra nullius* that denied Aborigines and Torres Strait Islanders legal land rights based on the European understanding that indigenous people had no history of cultivating the land before European contact.

The Mabo decision also had profound ramifications in that it prompted Keating's Labor Government to craft legislation (the Native Title Act 1993) to define further the parameters of land rights demands by indigenous people. This legislation expanded the terms of the original High Court decision by allowing for claims not necessarily based on the cultivation of the land by indigenous people. The Native Title Act allowed Aboriginal groups to make claims to land based on its (uninterrupted) spiritual significance, which a number of groups have since done successfully. But, as many commentators have pointed out, the Mabo decision and the Native Title Act also left significant limitations on the terms of Aboriginal land rights claims. One significant limitation of the Mabo decision, its irrelevance to pastoral leases, was challenged by the Wik decision.

The decision still left Aborigines forcibly removed from their land and communities disqualified from making land claims.

In the 1996 Wik decision, the Australian High Court ruled that in cases where native title was not inconsistent with a later grant of interest in land (such as a government pastoral lease) the two titles could coexist. Prime Minister Howard responded with a "ten point plan" that attempted to dull most of the power of both the Mabo and Wik decisions. To promote his plan, he appeared on television to appeal to settler Australians' anxieties by displaying a map in which 78 percent of the land in Australia could be subject to Aboriginal veto, a largely inflated estimation of where Aborigines would be able to establish native title (Burke 2001, 200). Subsequent negotiations diminished some of the power of Howard's plan. However, the amendments passed in July 1998 still gave states the power to deny Aboriginal rights to negotiate with miners over infrastructure projects in order to protect spiritually significant territories. Needless to say, Aboriginal leaders were disappointed with the outcome of the amendments.

In addition to legal battles over land rights, a number of political developments undermined the moral legitimacy of the Australian nation-state, in particular, the findings of the Royal Commission into Aboriginal Deaths in Custody (1991), which found that Aboriginal people were incarcerated and died in police custody at a significantly larger rate than non-Aboriginal Australians. Following the findings of this commission, the *Bringing Them Home* report was published in 1996 and drew national and international attention to the assimilation practices of the Australian state and federal governments from the 1930s through the 1970s. A dire consequence of these policies, as delineated by the *Bringing Them Home* publication, was a generation of Aboriginal people cut off from their families, communities, and culture. In addition to the personal devastation many people experienced as a result of governmental policies for the forced removal of children from their communities, the children have had less opportunity to benefit from political gains in land rights since most of them have been permanently severed from their ancestral lands.

Keating and Howard set a different tone in their discussions about the moral and political responsibility of contemporary Australians for the genocide and ethnocide perpetuated for almost two centuries against Aborigines. Keating, in his Redfern speech, issued an official, public acknowledgment of the genocide against Aboriginal people. Largely in response to his policies on Aboriginal and immigrant rights, Howard and other conservatives in Australia posit that Keating's mistake in leadership was to force an elite "politically correct" agenda on "regular Australians." In contrast, Howard claimed to be building a "relaxed" Australia for "everyone." As part of this posture, Howard consistently played down the impact of policies on Aboriginal people and refused to offer an official apology following the report on the separation of Aboriginal and Torres Strait Islander children from their families (1996). He insisted that contemporary Australians bear no responsibility for policies of the past. Howard's position on Aboriginal political questions was perhaps best encapsulated in his caricature of their claims as a "black armband view of history." For Howard and the many Australians sympathetic to his position, Aboriginal claims unnecessarily stress the negative instead of celebrating the good in Australia and seek to secure unearned advantage for Aboriginal Australians over "regular Australians."

## ASIA

Its geographical proximity to Asia has also shaped Australia from its settlement as a colony. Consequently, any consideration of how Australia is imagined in relation to space must take into account how the idea of Asia has been a catalyst for defining the nation at various historical moments. David Walker traces Australians' perceptions of Asia from 1850 to 1939, highlighting the twin currents—fear and admiration. For instance, at the end of the nineteenth century Australians displayed fascination with India as the seat of Aryan civilization as well as the epitome of the success of British colonial rule over the natives. Similarly, in the mid-nineteenth century many Australians were enchanted by the aesthetic and ritualized character of Japanese culture (Walker 1999, 2–3). This positive disposition toward Asia generated some optimism that its proximity to Asia might allow Australia to serve as a cultural bridge between the mysterious East and the West.

However, at the same time, a fear of the rising power of Asian societies circulated. Walker writes, "Australia came to nationhood at a time when the growing power of the East was arousing increasing concern. This in turn came to influence how Australians saw themselves as an outpost of Europe facing Asia. Often at this time it seemed possible that Australia's survival as a nation might be at stake" (1999, 4). This perceived threat took on different forms and was projected onto different Asian states. Australians feared physical takeover, in military terms at times, but they also suffered from an anxiety of being overwhelmed by Asians through excessive immigration, illegal refugees, and domination of Australian financial markets. The environment also factored into the narration of an Asian threat. For instance, there was anxiety that Asians, like other brown-skinned people, were better adapted to surviving the Australian climate. Additionally, the industriousness displayed by particular Asian immigrant groups, such as Chinese miners in the mid-nineteenth century, raised the concern that Asians might be more entitled to the Australian continent because they could make more out of its resources than the European colonials who struggled just to populate the country.

What historian Geoffrey Blainey has phrased "the tyranny of distance" (Blainey 1982) shaped some of the initial legislation of Australia's first Parliament in 1901. In analyzing the 1901 immigration laws that made up the White Australia policy,[4] Fazal Rizvi explains how crucial they were to territorializing Australia as a white Western nation. He writes:

> The White Australia policy institutionalised racism in the practice of immigration control, and created a sense of an Australia as "an imagined community" . . . that was formed by myths of biological and cultural superiority of the European race. In this sense, the ideology of racism was central to the development of Australian nationalism, which was based on the assumption that only white people could be acceptable members of the Australian "nation" because it was only they who had the inclination and capacity for self-government by constitutional means. (1996, 176)

If we read the White Australia policy as one of the initial defining gestures of the nation-state, as Rizvi suggests, then Australia's inception was partly based on defining its geographical relation to Great Britain (Europe) and Asia. A fundamental means of defining the nation was locating it internationally. This was achieved, in part, by legally enforcing separateness from Asia, while simultaneously encouraging open flows of people between Great Britain and

Australia. As Rizvi notes, the White Australia policy assumed that whiteness was the basis of self-governance, but he also illustrates how whiteness and all the civilizing characteristics assumed to go with it were deeply dependent on geography.

Although the sense of Asia as a generalized threat against Australia's European culture and racial content was expressed differently in different eras, it has continued to remain an available discourse for defining Australia's culture and geography into the twenty-first century. Articulated as "the Yellow Peril" or the "Asian invasion," this discourse about geographical and cultural vulnerability was directed specifically toward Japan during World War II. The idea that geography rendered the whiteness of the nation at risk did not end with the close of the war. The post–World War II immigration campaign launched by Australia was largely justified as a security measure: If Australia had a larger European population it would be less vulnerable to Asian invasion. In the government's desire to protect itself from the racial threat of Asia, it stumbled into an ethnically diverse postwar migration, including Southern Europeans and Middle Easterners as well as Anglo-Celtic migrants.

Although Australia's economic relationship with Britain gave way to increased trading arrangements with the United States and Asian countries through the 1970s and 1980s, it was during Keating's leadership that significant political rhetoric was directed toward "recognizing" Australia's geography as part of Asia and a republican movement caught the public imagination. Earlier in his political career, Keating characterized Asia as "the place one flies over on their way to Europe," but as Prime Minister he campaigned for Australia to become more involved politically, economically, and culturally in Asia. He promoted the idea of Australia as a multicultural nation located in Asia by funding cultural and economic links between Australia and Asia, promulgating liberal immigration policies, and nurturing a better relationship with Indonesia. Under Keating's leadership Australia lobbied intensively to establish good trading terms with ASEAN (Association of Southeast Asian Nations) members, to participate in APEC (Asia-Pacific Economic Cooperation) meetings, and join AFTA (ASEAN Free Trade Area).

After seventy years of policies treating Asia as a threat, defining a closer relationship to Asian states has functioned to deterritorialize Australia's former imagined geography. However, the practical value of a more intimate economic relationship with Asian states did not automatically remove Australians' historical anxiety about Asia's threat to their nation. Thirty years later, in the 1980s, anxiety over being overwhelmed by Asia continued in the form of fear of Japanese and other wealthy Asian businesses "buying up" all of Australia. Moreover, fear of "Asian invasion" continues to be expressed in anxiety about the number of Asian immigrants, as displayed in the polemics of former Member of Parliament Pauline Hanson: "I and most Australians want our immigration policy radically reviewed and that of multiculturalism. I believe we are in danger of being swamped by Asians. They have their own culture and religion, form ghettos and do not assimilate" (September 10, 1996). Her comments echo the comments of Australian historian Geoffrey Blainey years earlier to a Rotarian group. He charged that "ordinary Australians" were alarmed at the "Asianisation of Australia" and criticized the Labor government for abandoning the traditional preference for British migrants (see Bottomley 1988, 173, for discussion of Blainey).

Australia's location and relation to Asia has often served as a means for discussing how things like race, civilization, and colonial structures shape relations between nation-states. Since the racial content and civilization of Australian identity were defined in part by its imagined distance from Asia, the need and desire to allow more immigration from Asia and to increase economic ties has functioned to deterritorialize the settler Australian nation. Imagining Australia as part of Asia was not merely a change in economic or immigration policy; it led Australians to reconceptualize ideas like race and civilization central to Australian identity.

## MULTICULTURALISM AND REPUBLICANISM

Historically, Australia has depended on immigration to populate the country. Before World War II, this immigration came from the United Kingdom and Ireland, except for a wave of Chinese immigrants during the Victorian gold rush in the second half of the nineteenth century. For much of the nineteenth and twentieth centuries, the cultural, religious, and class differences among Anglo-Celtics played a significant role in the political landscape. There was resentment among Irish in Australia of British policies in Ireland and of the disproportionate economic and political power of the English in Australia. The division between Catholic Irish and Protestant English was reinforced in the former's support of the Labor Party and Anglo support of the Liberal Party. Irish Australians also supported Australian involvement in World War I to a much lesser degree than Anglo-Australians. This division was largely neutralized after the 1960s when the racial, cultural, and religious differences presented by post–World War II immigrants appeared much greater in comparison. Nevertheless, although discussions of multiculturalism have tended to have non-Anglo-Celtic "ethnics" as their implicit subject, the division has not faded away completely. The significance of the hyphen was again evident in the differences between Keating and Howard. It was generally assumed that Keating's Irish background shaped his strong support of Republicanism and retrospective criticism of Britain's betrayal of Australia in World War II. Likewise, Howard's overt monarchism and appointment of Anglican clergyman Peter Hollingworth as Australia's Governor General was perceived to be in keeping with his Anglo ethnicity.

Despite the division between Anglo-Celtics and non-Anglo-Celtics for much of Australia's history, these differences were marked geographically to the extent that Republicanism aimed to weaken the imagined special relationship between Australia and Britain. It was the diversity of race and culture in 1950s immigration that prompted the more dramatic reconfiguration of nation by the 1970s. As Jeremy Beckett outlines (1995, 424), in their efforts to expand Australia's population base after World War II and inability to attract enough people from Britain, the Australian government first expanded its "Displaced Persons" to include those from Eastern and Central Europe. Failing to attract enough people from these regions, the government cast a larger net, to include "Europeans" from Italy, Greece, Yugoslavia, and then eventually in the 1960s stretching the definition of European and white to include Turkish and Lebanese immigrants. By the 1960s the political climate in Australia had changed, and the White Australia immigration policy was beginning to seem inappropriate. It was also during this time that governmental policies of assimilation toward migrants as well as Aboriginal people gave way to the concept of multiculturalism. Since 1978, over 10,000 Indo-Chinese were admitted to Australia on refugee status (Parkin and Hardcastle 1990). Many of these refugees were from the Vietnam War.

Initially, immigrants entered the Australian labor force as low-skilled workers enabling the social mobility of Australian-born workers and providing a larger domestic market for Australian manufacturing industries. Into the 1990s migrants from non-English-speaking backgrounds (Southern Europe, the Middle East, and Southeast Asia) continued to be overwhelmingly manual workers in manufacturing and construction. An exception occurred in the 1990s when, in anticipation of the return of Hong Kong from British to Chinese control, a number of wealthy Chinese migrants took up residence in Australia, remaining within the entrepreneurial class.

Post–World War II migration to Australia from South and East Europe and from the Middle East had significant implications for Australian culture and challenged the notion of Australian-ness as primarily Anglo-Celtic. This wave of immigrants disrupted the idea of Australians' collective "home" as England, even as it left the imagined association between Australia and European civilization intact.

Multiculturalism, a term used for the first time in Australia in 1973 by the Minister for Immigration, Al Grassby, became an official government policy during the Whitlam government. It was subsequently picked up and developed in the administration of every government after Whitlam. It was a fairly consistent narrative about national identity in Australia in the last quarter of the twentieth century, though defined differently by different administrations.

The social politics surrounding multiculturalism intersected with people's sense of Australia's geographical position within the issue of republicanism. The change of Australia's population from a dominant Anglo-Celtic ethnicity and culture to a multicultural and multiracial nation prompted the need to stop imagining Australia as part of the British Empire or Europe. This rationale complemented the nationalism that had grown steadily in Australia since the Whitlam government. The 1970s offered a new discourse about Australian-ness that became popular with sections of the population, especially among those on the political left. Under Gough Whitlam's (Labor) leadership, larger portions of the Australian public were open to the possibility of an Australian identity independent of the United States and Great Britain. The Whitlam government and sympathetic constituencies began to question Australia's subordinate position in relation to economics, cold war politics, and cultural status. Nevertheless, the Labor Party's critique of imperialism was cut short (though some say ultimately strengthened) in 1975 by the unprecedented move on the part of Governor-General Sir John Kerr (the Crown's representative in Australia) to dismiss the government elected by the Australian people. The dismissal of the Whitlam government was enmeshed with an unstable economy and with power struggles between the Labor and Liberal Parties discussed in great detail in Australian history texts. What is most important here is that the dismissal occurred within a growing discourse about Australian national identity independent of British imperialism and American hegemony. Whitlam's dismissal is also important because it fueled the call to redefine Australia as a republic and amplified the popular call to redefine Australia's "true identity."

Many have interpreted Whitlam's dismissal as a clear example of the imperialism Whitlam condemned and of the danger of having even symbolic ties with the Crown. Before his dismissal, Whitlam's reforms had sparked an interest in things Australian that led to the development of such things as the Australian film industry and the indigenous Australian garden movement. This historic moment seemed to influence the political agenda of former Prime Minister Keating (1991–96), who further developed the theme of Australian identity and independence from Britain during his leadership.

This reevaluation of Australia's relationship with Great Britain was entangled with a rearrangement of the international economic landscape that positioned former imperial powers, such as Britain, as more peripheral than new Asian economies like Japan and Singapore. These new political and economic realities have challenged former narrative constructions of a world geography that posited Western superiority over the East (and the "third world" more generally). As Lewis and Wigen note, changes in political and economic realities often prompt a redefinition of geographical categories so that geography can attest to the cultural and political ideological "truths" of the new era. They write, "It is no coincidence that sea changes in ideology are generally accompanied by a questioning of metageographical categories—or that those attempting consciously to formulate new visions of the globe often do so as part of a campaign to promote new patterns of belief" (1997, xi).

Republicanism as a political issue was contested outside official political discourse in Australia. For instance, in 1995 a contemporary sculpture of Queen Elizabeth and Prince Philip was placed outside the National Art Gallery in Canberra. The sculpture quickly drew controversy since the two figures were depicted sitting naked on a park bench (the Queen with a crown). The figures were the site of much contestation over republicanism and attracted vandalism and efforts to clothe them in plastic bags before being smashed beyond recognition. It is not entirely clear what political attitudes informed the impulse to clothe the Queen and Prince Philip (to protect their modesty or demystify the royals even more?) and to smash them (comment on republicanism or royalty?), but the statues clearly illustrate the debates around Australia's identity. The Republican movement deflated after a lost referendum in November 1999.

For some, characterizing Australia as multicultural has been a route to thinking of Australia as an entity unique to itself. Others have turned to Aboriginal culture as a unifier linking all Australians to the land and the past. Still others have conceptualized Australia as part of Asia, making multiculturalism a national narrative. Of course, many people did not connect multiculturalism to issues of land and territory. However, multiculturalism did reopen the question of what served as the unifying national culture and where the nation-state belongs geographically if its connection to British culture and history has shifted in the last half of the twentieth century.

Because John Howard has altered the direction of Australian politics, I end this section by describing some of the ways he has impacted these debates. While Howard continued to maintain the importance of fostering a relationship with Asia when he assumed leadership of the new coalition government in 1996, he cautioned that Australia must not make its geography take precedence over its history. This statement reflected his general identification with Britain and America. In 1999, Howard articulated his government's position as a departure from Keating's: "We have stopped worrying about whether we are Asian, in Asia, enmeshed in Asia or part of a mythical East Asian hemisphere." Instead, Howard defined Australia's geography as "a unique intersection—a Western nation next to Asia with strong links to the United States and Europe." His rhetoric has stressed the value of Australia's European past and its political ties to the United States.

*Figure 3. Contemporary sculpture of Queen Elizabeth and Prince Philip on display outside the National Art Gallery in Canberra in 1995.*

Howard has claimed support for the popular policies of multiculturalism and paid lip service to justice for Aboriginal Australians. However, multiculturalism under Howard was no longer either a program for social justice or the core of national identity as it had been for other administrations. He also altered immigration policy soon after taking office, limiting immigration on the basis of family reunification, which disproportionately affected Asian immigrants. He initiated greater stringency toward illegal refugees into Australia, a political debate that paid off for him after the September 11 attacks on the United States. Howard was also unflinchingly supportive of the United States' international campaign against terrorism and has used the deaths of Australians in the Bali attack to confirm his general apprehension about the security of Australia in the face of cultural, racial, and religious differences.

Simon Philpott notes how Howard's language of a confident identity for Australia reasserted a previous defensive posture toward Asia. He writes:

> John Howard asserts that because *we* know who *we* are, "a European, Western civilization with strong links to North America . . ." *we* no longer have to fret about whether *we* are part of Asia. We can, he argues, participate in region affairs " . . . on our own terms" . . . But arguably, this is not a discourse of confidence and assuredness but rather a reprise of "old white" fears. It is a discourse that reinstates a difference between white Australians (who value democracy and tolerance) and "Asians" who have other values. (2001, 374–75)

As Philpott argues, older racial fears of Asia have been rewritten as fear of Asian economic markets and "different" political values.

Despite important differences, Keating's and Howard's policies have not been as starkly different as Howard suggests. Running through both leaders' policies is the desire to subsume Aboriginal ("their") history and contribution to ("our") Australian nation, despite Keating's greater interest in reconciliation with Aboriginal people. Moreover, both have been committed to economic ties with Asia as part of a neoliberal economic vision. Both Keating and Howard underscored the importance of Asian markets for Australia, and, as Anthony Burke discusses (2001), supported authoritarian governments, such as Suharto in Indonesia, to enhance Australia's position in the global political economy. They have also shared a commitment to the process and logic of globalization that involved the privatization of government services in many cases and a faith in market forces.

## THEORY AND HISTORY OF NATIONAL SPACE

### National Geography as Power/Knowledge

Benedict Anderson's work provides a historical analysis of the processes by which nations manufacture a perceived organic connection between a people, their culture, and the geographical space to which they "belong" (1993).[5] He argues that the territorialization of peoples and national culture is a product of particular discourses about the nation that developed out of the colonial era. Further, nations are imagined in relation to territory whereby the mechanisms of census, map, and museum as well as various state policing apparatuses naturalize the link between people, culture, and territory.

Cartography as a kind of knowledge production underwrote the power of the nation-state as it developed as a hegemonic political entity in the eighteenth and nineteenth centuries. While certainly treaties and conquering armies were mechanisms for defining national space, more subtle forces were at play as well. Maps established the power of a state by writing the identity of the nation on the physical world. They helped create the impression of state boundaries as "natural" givens written in the landscape and reflected in cultural differences between groups of people. Numerous scholars have helped us understand how the development of maps (cartographic knowledge) allowed the nation to be thinkable and to define the jurisdiction of its power.

Anderson builds on Foucault's analysis of "tactics and strategies deployed through implantation, distributions, demarcations, control of territories and organization of domains" (Foucault 1980). Space came to be imagined or perceived as a territory known as the modern nation-state as a result of the knowledge gathered by seventeenth-century travelers, nineteenth-century mapmakers, military campaigns, record keepers, traders, and industrialists (Foucault 1980). The colonial expansion of the eighteenth and nineteenth centuries did much to fill in the depiction of space through maps. Armies and colonial mechanisms (such as the census) for gathering information about populations defended territories and solidified them as the domain of governments. Anderson draws on Thai historian

Thongchai Winichakul's argument that the "map anticipated spatial reality, not vice versa . . . a map was a model for, rather than a model of, what it purported to represent" (as cited in Anderson 1991, 173). Political power (with military backing) designated territorial jurisdiction, the boundaries of which then became the markers of geopolitical difference.

Geographer J. B. Harley further explicates the centrality of cartography to the nation's power:

> In modern Western society maps quickly became crucial to the maintenance of state power—to its boundaries, to its commerce, to its internal administration, to control of populations, and to its military strength. Mapping soon became the business of the state: cartography is early nationalized . . . maps are linked to what Foucault called the exercise of "juridical power." The map becomes a "juridical territory": it facilitates surveillance and control. (1996, 439)

Building on Foucault's insights concerning how knowledge is produced out of power relations and functions as a form of power, the passage above highlights the connection between mapping and power in the West.

Winichakul's work explores how maps constituted state control outside of the West. He also flags the importance of colonial bureaucratic systems in the development of national territory. In his study *Siam Mapped,* Winichakul discusses the development of new administrated regimes in the final two decades of the nineteenth century that depended on mapping and the registration of households as part of a new geographical consciousness. These administrative regimes connected political power more tightly to spatial demarcation and surveillance: "Mapping was both a cognitive paradigm and a practical means of the new administration" (1994, 120). Further, the mapping activities of French cartographer Auguste Pavie both represented and facilitated French imperial interests in Siam in the 1880s and 1890s well before any military presence in the region. Later, in various national contexts, anticolonial nationalists questioned imperialist control of space in their struggles for independence but did not change the terms in which space was imagined. Thus, even when colonial systems were dismantled, the fantasy of nations as bounded, primordial homelands remained the pervasive spatial imaginary.

Anderson also discusses the way the national community was imagined in spatial terms through the use of spatial iconography.

The European practice of coloring colonial maps with imperial dye helped embed the fiction of national territory in the popular imagination. Anderson writes:

> In this shape, the map entered an infinitely reproducible series, available for the transfer to posters, official seals, letterheads, magazine and textbook covers, tablecloths, and hotel walls. Instantly recognizable, everywhere visible, the logo-map penetrated deep into the popular imagination, forming a powerful emblem. (1991, 175)

The logo-map continues to be a means for naturalizing the connection between space and nations. The logo-map reproduces the nation-state territory, usually in silhouette form, and in isolation from neighboring countries. In doing so, it depicts the nation-state as a distinct, unified, and self-contained collective separate from other nation-states. Additionally, it makes the physical outline of the state a symbol of the nation. As such, geography functions as a primary signifier for the nation.

In linking technologies of census, map, and museums in the construction of national community, Anderson identifies three mechanisms that constitute distinct national territories developing out of the colonial era. With these mechanisms, he also identifies how people, culture, and territory become aligned and naturalized. In this partitioning of space, Anderson provides insight into why it eventually became impossible to imagine or tolerate people without a place or people out of place in what Liisa Malkki has called "the national order of things" (1992). The construction of history by museums allowed states to appropriate elements of the past as national precursors and connect them to a bounded, transhistorical national community.

> Map and census thus shaped the grammar that would in due course make possible "Burma" and "Burmese," "Indonesia" and "Indonesians." But the concretizations which have a powerful life today, long after the colonial state has disappeared—owed much to the colonial state's particular imagining of history and power . . . It created the series "ancient monuments" segmented within the classificatory, geographic-demographic box . . . the state itself could regard the series, up historical time, as an album of its ancestors. (Anderson 1991, 185)

In other words, the map, museum, and census created the "Thai people," "Thailand," and "Thai culture" by making these entities imaginable, inevitable, and aligned within a particular, bounded geography. The museum defined and encased national culture and rescripted history to identify the primordial roots and cultural precursors across time. People did not merely imagine a horizontal citizenship; the museum linked people across time and generations. It created "ancient monuments" that corresponded to and reaffirmed the spatial parameters of the nation-state. The census, map, and museum together constructed a narrative of consistent connection of a people to "their" territory or homeland.

Space also functions as a realm in which people create meaning and mitigate the fear of their own mortality. As geographer Yi-Fu Tuan explores, in the past, certain kinds of places were a conduit for people's spiritual connection to past and future generations. He writes:

> But the strongest bond to place is of a religious nature. The tie is one of kinship, reaching back in time from proximate ancestors to distant semi-divine heroes, to the gods of the family hearth and of the city shrines . . . This religious tie to place has almost completely disappeared from the modern world. Traces of it are left in the rhetoric of nationalism in which the state itself, rather than particular places, is addressed as "father land" or "mother land." (1996, 453)

Tuan's sociology of place shows how cosmologies are expressed in part through spatial practice and symbolic meaning associated with place. One goes to certain spaces to experience an imagined community across generations, be it religious or national in character. Tuan acknowledges how nation as a place has all but replaced religious cosmologies of place. However, he seems to draw a distinction between the *real* (authentic) space of the family hearth or city shrine and the more abstract "rhetoric" of national space.

Tuan's discussion supports Anderson's argument that the nation came to function so importantly in people's consciousness because it enabled them to imagine links with past and future generations at a time when the Enlightenment was undercutting religious cosmologies. Anderson asserts that the rational secularism of the Enlightenment was less able to provide people with a framework for understanding their own mortality. Below, Anderson describes the nation's ability to provide people with a cosmology for understanding their lives.

In Western Europe the eighteenth century marks not only the dawn of the age of nationalism but the dusk of religious modes of thought. The century of the Enlightenment, of rational secularism, brought with it its own darkness. With the ebbing of religious belief, the suffering which belief in part composed did not disappear. Disintegration of paradise: nothing makes fatality more arbitrary. Absurdity of salvation: nothing makes another style continuity more necessary. What then was required was a secular transformation of fatality into continuity, contingency into meaning. As we shall see, few things were (are) better suited to this end than an idea of nation. If nation-states are widely conceded to be "new" and "historical," the nations to which they give political expression always loom out of an immemorial past, and, still more important, glide into a limitless future. It is the magic of nationalism to turn chance into destiny. (1991, 11–12)

Tuan adds to Anderson's argument a stronger emphasis on the spatial dimension of imagined communities that links the past, present, and future. Physical places provided an important cosmology needed by people to explain their place in the cycle of life. Although Anderson notes that as early as the end of the thirteenth century "we can detect the seeds of a territorialization of faiths which foreshadows the language of many nationalists" (1991, 17), he does not theorize the importance of places or territories for experiencing continuity and community across generations. For Anderson, the imagined communities of the dynastic realm and later the nation are characterized by a territoriality as well as a connection to previous and subsequent generations. But he does not link territoriality to people's experience of a larger cosmology within an imagined community as does Tuan. For Tuan, people experience their connection to infinity (past and future generations) by visiting certain places. Places become symbolic containers of one's relationship with other generations.

Nevertheless, Tuan implies a distinction between the authenticity of the familial hearth and city shrine and the "rhetoric" (read: inauthenticity) of nationalism. While it is valid to distinguish between the level of abstraction in local communities and in the nation (see also James 1992 and 1994/95), his analysis of the religious function of some sites points to the fact that even the family hearth and city shrine are imagined geographies. Yes, one can more easily visit a family hearth and city shrine and therefore experience its physicality more immediately. But these sites, functioning as an intersection for the spirits of past, present, and future generations, illustrate how even the most intimate of places is nevertheless a form of imagined geography. In this sense, the nation is not so different from even the family hearth. It is a space in large part defined by the relationships it mediates.

But the nation and its territoriality are not exactly a "place" in the way, for instance, a city shrine is. The abstract quality of the nation means that we rarely bump into the nation as an identifiable place except when we stand in line in customs at the airport. The logo-map of which Anderson writes linked people and culture to territory in the popular imagination. This is also true of the weather channel, for instance, as it relays to us what the nation's weather will be for the next day. However, the symbolism of the logo-map does not let people enact or physically experience the nation in the way people in the past experienced imagined communities in the city shrine or family hearth.

Lauren Berlant explores the contribution of performative rituals (such as family and school pilgrimages to the nation's capital and its monuments) in constructing a national subjectivity. She writes:

> When Americans make the pilgrimage to Washington they are trying to grasp the nation in its totality. Yet the totality of the nation in its capital city is a jumble of historical modalities, a transitional space between local and national cultures, private and public property, archaic and living artifacts, the national history that marks the monumental landscape and the everyday life temporalities of federal and metropolitan cultures. That is to say, it is a place of national mediation . . . As a borderland central to the nation, Washington tests the capacities of all who visit it: this test is a test of citizenship competence. (1997, 25)

Berlant's analysis is suggestive about the function of particular spaces designated as "national" that prompt ritualistic pilgrimages. Capital cities, national gardens (such as the "native garden" in Canberra), and even museums are examples of space demarcated as "national." Additionally, national parks and environmental destinations imbued with nationalist meaning (Uluru/Ayers Rock in Australia) serve as spaces in which to experience the nation as a physical place. Following Berlant's lead, we could argue that the ritualized experience of pilgrimages to these national spaces functions, in effect, to mediate people's experience of the abstract idea of national territory. Since one's experience of the borders and territoriality of the nation is limited, except for entering and exiting the nation-state, spaces designated as national space represent (stand in for) the territoriality of the nation. They invite people to feel an ownership of the land claimed by the nation-state. National parks, for instance, do not just prompt people to admire nature at large. Typically, the park staff in their descriptions of the park and pedagogy for visitors constructs the experience of national parks as an experience of the magnitude and beauty of the *nation*.

Demarcated "national" spaces miniaturize the nation, so that it can be experienced as something tangible and concrete. This reduction of space, allowing it to be more easily consumed and incorporated into an individual's life, parallels Susan Stewart's observations about the function of the souvenir. Stewart writes, "Such a souvenir might mark the privatization of a public symbol (say, the Liberty Bell miniaturized), the juxtaposition of history with a personalized present" (1993, 138).

Monuments and other spaces demarcated as "national" and the souvenirs inevitably sold at such sites mediate the gap between national space as an imagined or abstract *idea* and an individual life. Monuments and parks allow the nation's territory to be consumed and intertwined with one's childhood; they allow the nation to be overdetermined by emotionally rich, intimate communities such as the family.

These "national" spaces are also places where people experience their connection with other generations of nationals. In this sense, pilgrimages to the capital or to national parks allow for a kind of structure of feeling (see Williams 1977; Steedman 1987) insofar as they reproduce the identity and imagined community not only materially, but also by passing on a sentiment or emotional disposition.

Equally important, Liisa Malkki's work on national consciousness explores contemporary practices by which nations, people, and culture are associated with a given territory and shows how this "rooting" is naturalized through language and through nondiscursive practices. She contends that too often scholars presume an unproblematic connection between people, culture, and place and reproduce the commonsense "national order of things," the alignment of people and their national land (1995). Malkki's analysis points out the use of metaphors of soil, land, and roots to denote and naturalize people's connection to their territory. These images assume that people are like plants that thrive best in their native soil and hence obey an almost biological imperative to be geographically rooted. She traces how these metaphors circulate in nonnarrative ways through such rituals as taking a piece of earth from one's homeland when leaving or through the popular desire that one should be returned to be buried in the soil of one's country.

Once in place, imagining space in terms of national territory needed to be enforced. It became a disciplinary framework. Today, national territory is not just a symbol, but a framework that lays claim to and legitimates control of resources and political power. Thus, the territorializiation of nation and culture empowers the state and its dominant groups. Khachig Tololyan observes:

> The [nation-state] always imagines and represents itself as a land, a territory, a place that functions as the site of homogeneity, equilibrium, integration; this is the domestic tranquility that hegemony-seeking national elites always desire and sometimes achieve. (1991, 6)

Anderson argues that those who spoke the vernacular language that became dominant enjoyed a greater legitimacy and access to the resources accompanying control of the national territory (Anderson 1993). Although Anderson does not connect this point to territory, the territorialization of nation is also a process by which people compete for power. It is the means by which people lay claim to land and resources and became positioned within or outside of the national imaginary.

The territorialized imaging of nations has consequences for groups like refugees, who are perceived to be uprooted, and for indigenous people imagined as ultrarooted. By examining such groups, we can see how the "national order of things" is a form of discipline for those who do not live within the framework of nation-states. Malkki's analysis of the pathologizing of refugees—of people who are out of place in the national order of things—reveals the way national difference is reinforced. If the arrangement of peoples into discrete cultures and territories provides the organizing framework for the "family of nations," then refugees are persons out of place.

They become liminal figures whose mere existence questions the naturalness and inevitability of the alignment of people, culture, and territory (Malkki 1995). Indigenous people, by contrast, are often celebrated for a presumed metaphysical connection to place. They are conscripted as evidence of the primordial quality of natural rootedness. Appadurai writes, "Natives are not only persons who are from certain places and belong to those places, but they are also those who are somehow *incarcerated*, or confined, in those places" (Appadurai 1988, 37). While refugees challenge the alignment between people and their places/homelands, indigenous people are required to testify to the naturalness of this organizing system. As a consequence, there is little tolerance for their displacement. They become deterritorialized and aberrant simply by moving out of their proper place—in nature—and into the city, for instance. And in places like Australia, the culture of indigenous people is used regularly by the state itself to construct a distinct national culture for the international tourist market and as a neutral identity for a multicultural population (see Povinelli 1998; Darian-Smith 1993; Lattas 1991, 1990).

The next section discusses how many of the social, political, and spatial changes of the second half of the twentieth century have undermined the imagined alignment between people, culture, and territory. Further, while Anderson in particular links state power to cultural practices in suggestive ways, like most scholars concerned with the territorialization of nation, his analysis concerns almost exclusively state practices. This literature invites us to build on its insights in order to understand the processes of territorialization in everyday, nonstate practices under the conditions of late capitalism.

## NATIONAL SPACE AND LATE CAPITALISM

In *The Condition of Postmodernity* (1990), David Harvey has contributed to our understanding of how economic changes have reconfigured the social organization of space. Although not positing a distinct break in history, Harvey marks the 1970s as a moment of significant change for the organization of capitalism and the imagining of space. Capitalism has evolved from a Fordist system into one of "flexible accumulation." This term is used to underscore capitalism's new flexibility in relation to labor processes, labor markets, products, and patterns of consumption (147). Innovations in transportation, technology, and telecommunications have enabled capitalist production to spread over a larger expanse of space, taking advantage of "better" labor conditions, markets, and production environments throughout the world. These technological developments have also shortened communication time. Harvey refers to the "annihilation of space through time" (241) and describes this "time-space compression" in the following passage:

> I use the word "compression" because a strong case can be made that the history of capitalism has been characterized by a speed-up of the pace of life, while so overcoming spatial barriers that the world sometimes seems to collapse inwards upon us . . . so we have to learn how to cope with an overwhelming sense of compression of our spatial and temporal worlds. The experience of time-space compression is challenging, exciting, stressful, and sometimes deeply troubling, capable of sparking, therefore, a diversity of social, cultural, and political responses.(240).

These developments in turn have meant that capitalist processes are less and less contained within the borders of a single nation-state.

Social theorists argue that the developments of flexible accumulation, combined with the dismantling of colonial systems, have led to a "deterritorialization" of people, place, and culture (see Appadurai 1996; Buell 1994; Gupta and Ferguson 1992; Hannerz 1996). For instance, better transportation and economic demands for transnational (cheap) labor has increased the traffic from the "periphery" or "third world" into first-world sites in immigrants, refugees, and guest workers. Changes in transportation mean that more tourists and business people cross nation-state borders more frequently. Developments in transportation and telecommunications have enabled diasporic populations, formerly cut off from their original country and forced to assimilate, to keep alive cultural, emotional, and business connections with their homeland as well as with other diasporic kin and friends (see Tololyan 1991; Rouse 1991; Ong 1998). Arjun Appadurai points to deterritorialization as a key condition of contemporary global politics:

> Deterritorialization, in general, is one of the central forces of the modern world because it brings laboring populations into the lower-class sectors and spaces of relatively wealthy societies, while sometimes creating exaggerated and intensified senses of criticism or attachment to politics in the home state . . . At the same time, deterritori-

alization creates new markets for film companies, art impresarios, and travel agencies, which thrive on the need of the deterritorialized population for contact with its homeland. (1999, 37)

Research programs have developed to address the impacts of diasporas on social, economic, and political structures as evidenced in journals such as *Public Culture* and *Diaspora* (see also Safran 1991; Gilroy 1993; Clifford 1997). Roger Rouse's analysis of Mexican migrant workers moving between Aguilla (Mexico) and Redwood, California, illustrates the restructuring of space and culture as people's zones of cultural contact are separated by thousands of miles. Rouse explains, "Indeed, through the continuous circulation of people, money, goods, and information, the various settlements have become so closely woven together that, in an important sense, they have come to constitute a single community spread across a variety of sites, something I refer to as a 'transnational migrant circuit.'" (1991, 14).

Aihwa Ong's work on Chinese cosmopolitans makes a similar point about the restructuring of national space. She discusses other forms of citizen subjectivity, such as flexible citizenship produced out of people's transnational movement and their political connections to imagined communities (Ong 1993; Ong and Nonini 1997). Space is reconfigured for the many people who cross borders regularly and for whom "imaginary homelands" are lived realities (Rushdie 1991).

A number of scholars have noted that deterritorialization is not reserved only for mobile groups alone. Even people who remain in place experience a deterritorialization as "foreign" images, products, and peoples show up in their local neighborhoods (see Gupta and Ferguson 1997a; Massey 1994; Appadurai 1980 and 1996). To the extent to which scholars have looked at the processes of deterritorialization for those who remain "in place," it has been to examine reactionary attempts to renarrate a cohesive national identity and not to understand processes of reterritorializing nation (see Gilroy 1987; Hall 1996; Hage 1998). The deterritorialization of the late twentieth century has generated new cultural forms not only for diasporas, but also for dominant groups who respond to the possibility of their own marginality in the national imaginary and their loss of control of land and resources.

Transnational circuits of people, products, capital, etc., have complicated the primacy of national territory in constructing social and cultural meaning. In this way, globalization challenges the authority and very territoriality of nation-states. However, Tololyan clarifies that these transnational flows have not undone the nation-state, noting:

> To affirm that diasporas are the exemplary communities of the transnational moment is not to write the premature obituary of the nation-state, which remains the privileged form of polity. Conflicts like the Gulf War revive and reaffirm the nation-state's legitimacy even as new forms of economic and political interaction, communication, and migration combine to erode its sharply defined borders, increasingly turning even the mightiest and most ocean-buffered polities, like the United States, into "penetrated" . . . and "plural" societies. (1991, 5)

Yet, because nations (and cultural identities) are contingent on social, political, and historical processes, new social and political arrangements require further research on the spatial construction of national and supranational communities. Anthropologist Robert Foster asks the important questions:

> How can the construction of national boundaries be sustained in a world now more than ever open to cultural flows? Can a collectivity imagine or be made to imagine itself as a bounded entity when its members are increasingly exposed to a "cosmopolitan cultural regime" through media, travel, and encounters with migrants and refugees? (1991, 237)

Appadurai asserts that "the task of ethnography now becomes the unraveling of a conundrum: what is the nature of locality as a lived experience in a globalized, deterritorialized world?" (1996, 52). The territorialization of nation and culture is complicated by the fact that, as scholars have noted, the international landscape is also in the process of being reconfigured (Ruggie 1998; de Bliji 1992; Lewis and Wigen 1997). These processes of globalization combine with other political factors, such as the dismantling of colonial empires and a shift in economic and political alliances away from cold war politics to a new focus on regional communities. Former narratives that naturalized the borders and political hegemony of Europe as an imagined supranational community were challenged by the economic success of Asian capital since World War II. Consequently, new international territorial alignments, such as the ASEAN community, the European Union, and the North American Free Trade Agreement have developed. These changes have required new ways of framing and legitimating divisions in the international landscape. For example, the development of "the Pacific" as a meaningful cultural and economic category helps economies on the United States West Coast and Australia justify their proposals for special economic links with certain Asian economies. Shifts in the international landscape have ramifications for the way in which individual nation-states define their national identity (especially in relation to ideas about race and civilization) and have implications for processes of territorialization within national borders.

Details about processes of territorializing the nation in Australia illustrate how people define the nation in relation to imagined supra-national communities and in response to the challenges of globalization. In this respect, the ethnographic analysis in this study illustrates that national space cannot be separated analytically from local and international space.

## THE LOCAL, THE GLOBAL, AND THE NATIONAL

Although much scholarly work since Anderson takes the nation as an imagined community constructed out of various material and discursive practices, a good deal of it continues to analyze the nation as if it were easily distinguishable from the local and international. Gupta argues that the intellectual move to treat the nation in isolation from the local and the international makes it difficult to remember that the nation is a "contingent form of organizing space in the world." He notes an unfortunate consequence of such scholarship: "National identity appears to be firmly spatialized and seemingly immutable, becoming almost a "natural" marker of cultural and social difference" (1992, 63).

Nevertheless, there is growing interest in the relationship of the supranational and transnational to national and local communities. These include studies of diasporic communities (see Leonard 1992, 1997; Appadurai 1996; Gilroy 1993; Clifford 1994) and studies of the processes by which supranational communities like the United Nations and the "family of nations" produce the nation-state (see Malkki 1994 and 1995). Others have traced how transnational processes and identities like modernity (Hannerz and Lofgren 1994) define individual national identities. Additionally, the works of Saskia Sassen (1991, 1996) and of Doreen Massey (1994) have looked at how economic change has brought the global into the local spaces of the city, and, as Sassen posits, generated the conceptualization of a new type of urban space called the "global city." These are all important studies that begin to articulate the relationship between the global and the local in the face of time-space compression and the regular flows of people, culture, and capital across nation-state borders. They also help us understand how cultures and political communities are imagined in relation to the globalized, "post-colonial" world.

Following these studies, I examine a nonlocal process in a local setting. Using ethnographic details about local, everyday practices of place making, I look at the way spaces overlap and mutually define each other, challenging the predominant depiction of the local as an authentic community in contrast to an inauthentic, polluting globalism. As Gupta and Ferguson observe, we would be mistaken to take the local as "the original, the centered, the natural, the authentic, and opposed to "the global" understood as new, external, artificially imposed and unauthentic" (Gupta and Ferguson 1997b). Rather, local identity is derivative of social processes and linkages that involve both local and supralocal social relations (see Featherstone 1993; Massey 1994; Pred 1990).

Australian scholars have considered the political and cultural significance of space, and of landscape in particular, in a number of ways. Australian literary scholars have examined the centrality of the landscape (the bush) to Australian national myth (see Carroll 1982; Schaffer 1988). They have considered the construction of Australian mythology and national identity through the bush legend in the work of Banjo Patterson, Henry Lawson, and others who form the national literary canon. The mythology of the landscape has also been traced in Australian film criticism (see Gibson 1992).

Such analysis has, along with scholarship on landscape painting in Australia, underscored the status of landscape as a key symbol in the emergence of a national narrative. This scholarship, much of which is from the 1980s and early 1990s in response to Anderson's work, was part of a flurry of literary studies exploring the means by which nations are imagined.

There has also been a series of studies that examine the ways

Australian space was culturally produced by explorers and early colonists so as to legitimate the British colonization of Australia. Paul Carter (1988) engages in a critique of "imperial histories" of Australia that treat space as a stage on which history unfolds, rather than as something that is created through the technologies of exploration (e.g., explorer journals, travel writing, and city planning). Simon Ryan, a literary critic, examines the tropes that spatially characterize Australia and legitimate the imperialist project. Like Carter however, Ryan takes linguistic activity as the prime mode by which Australia was spatially produced focusing on historical texts.

Several studies begin the work of understanding the spatial construction of Australia after colonial settlement. The collection *Myths of Place* (Foss 1988) undertakes a literary analysis of narrative constructions of place in Australia and offers new "myths" for defining the nation. As a cultural studies collection, it is concerned with narrative and representations and tells us little about the politics of belonging as enacted in everyday practices and landscapes. The essays examine historical practices and contemporary practices, but without considering how the former is echoed or reconfigured in the latter.

Jane Jacobs's *Edge of Empire* (1996) concerns the process by which imperial structures of power are reproduced and adapted within local contexts both in the imperial center (London) and within spaces formerly defined as on the edge of empire (Brisbane and Perth). By analyzing the negotiation of colonial and postcolonial relations in struggles over the definition of local places, Jacobs illustrates how the local, national, and international are overlapping spaces of political meaning and challenges the distinction between the heart of empire and postcolonial space. Like most scholars and in keeping with the traditions of geography, Jacobs limits her study to historical material and narrative as she traces the power struggles underlying the identity of place.[6] Nevertheless, her analysis provides a historical context and model for thinking about how the identities of places are informed by other places in the ongoing territorialization of nation.

Anthony King's (1995) social history of the bungalow in Australia and other colonial sites has also been a useful precursor to this study, although he is not directly concerned with the construction of nation. By examining the bungalow as a symbol of the circulation of people (e.g., colonial military personnel), ideas, and cultural forms between colonial sites and Britain, his study theorizes the transnational production of local spaces. His analysis sheds light on the nature of transnational processes as linked to local spatial forms, highlighting how domestic spaces are connected to transnational processes.

Thus far this chapter has been concerned with a general theoretical consideration of the ways in which geography has been important for imagining the nation-state and the political issues that have unsettled the legitimacy of the Australian settler state. The remaining sections look at how the identity of a political community is defined by its geography through notions of environmental determinism. Since Australia's identity has been so overdetermined by its geography, I examine this issue in the context of Australia's history. The historical information illustrates how Australia's geography has been used to define itself and the international landscape, well before it was settled as a colony. This historical discussion also lays a framework for the other aspects of Australia's history drawn out in later chapters as they bear on contemporary place-making practices in East Melbourne and Fitzroy.

## PUTTING AUSTRALIA ON THE MAP:
## A HISTORY OF GEOGRAPHICAL ANXIETY

Geographer William Cronon contends, "We can never know at first hand the world 'out there'—the 'nature' we seek to understand and protect—but instead must always encounter that world through the lens of our own ideas and imaginings" (1996, 25). "Australia" is no exception. Understanding the desires, fears, and projections that have informed the way the landmass known as Australia has been imagined tells us volumes about social, political, and intellectual history.

Geographers Lewis and Wigen discuss the "myth of continents" that justifies the political hierarchy between the Northern/first world and the Southern/third world (Lewis and Wigen 1997). They argue that the division between East and West, which today structures much thinking about world geography, developed out of a distinction originally made by the Greeks. The Greeks envisioned a "natural" distinction between Europe and Asia, marked by the waterways running from the Aegean Sea through the Dardanelles, the Sea of Marmara, the Bosporus, the Black Sea, and the Kerch Strait and connecting finally to the Sea of Azov. Greek mariners'

continental distinction did not place Europe and Asia in hierarchical relationship to one another; however, eventually political forces
began to attribute cultural values to the geographical divisions to explain Europe's "natural" superiority over Asia. Europe was defined
in relation to its superiority—progress, civilization, and reason—
over the less-evolved Asia. And geography was used to mark political and racial difference. As Lewis and Wigen argue, "With the
triumph of European imperialism . . . the contemporary European
view of the divisions of the world came to enjoy near-universal acceptance" (1997, 33).

Geography was a dimension of the Orientalism that Edward Said
identified as central to the identity of the West. In defining the essential motifs of "European imaginative geography," Said writes,
"A line is drawn between two continents. Europe is powerful and
articulate; Asia is defeated and distant" (1996, 419). These distinctions have been central to Europe's modern identity as civilized and
progressive. Central to international hierarchies was what geographer J. M. Blaut calls *eurocentric diffusionism,* the little-challenged
belief that there has been a unidirectional flow of culture, innovation, and overall human causality from a European center to a
non-European outside (1993). While there have been contexts in
which Asia is praised and used to critique qualities associated with
Europe, the assumption that these qualities correspond to natural
geographical differences has remained mostly unchallenged. As
Lewis and Wigen note, "In practice, the continental system continues to be applied in such a way as to suggest that continents are
at once physically and culturally constituted—i.e., that natural and
human features somehow correspond in space" (1997, 42).

This geographical binary has informed and haunted the construction of Australia. Before the capitalist success of Asian states in the
late twentieth century, this hierarchical geography left Australians
in an awkward position. Australians aspired to be associated with
European civilization but were vulnerable to exclusion based on
their country's location outside the geography of Europe.[7] Caught
in a geographical no-man's-land, not physically in Europe and dan-
gerously close to Asia, geography came to be a symbolic site of anxiety for many Australians. Because of its geographical liminality in
relation to the symbolic binary of Europe and Asia (at other times
articulated as the West and the rest), geography came to function as

an important signifier of Australia's identity and the racial content of that identity in particular, as discussed in later chapters.

Australia was defined in terms of its distance and difference from Europe long before it was "discovered." Robert Hughes (1988) writes that Australia was imagined and assigned an identity as Europe's "geographical unconscious." As early as 50 AD, geographers argued in favor of a southern landmass that they believed exists to balance the weight of the northern continents and prevent the world from spinning off its axis. The work of Renaissance geographer Ptolemy later corroborated Pomponius Mela's original argument as did Marco Polo's sighting of a southern landmass (which turned out to be modern Vietnam). The mythical southern landmass was finally legitimated by the maps of sixteenth-century cartographer Mercator (Hughes 1988, 44). Hughes notes that Australia functioned as the geographic unconscious of a Europe that projected its desires for a land of angelic beings and great sums of gold and jewels as well as its fears that the farther south one moved, the more grotesque and dangerous the world became (Hughes 1988, 44).

In their genealogy of the geographic divisions of the contemporary international landscape, Lewis and Wigen note these early speculations about the antipodes:

> The existence of another such "island" in the antipodes of the Southern Hemisphere—an *Orbis Alterius*—had often been hypothesized, but it was assumed that it would constitute a world apart, inhabited, if at all, by sapient creatures of an entirely different species. Americans, by contrast, appeared to be of the same order as other humans, suggesting that their homeland must be a forth part of the human world rather than a true alter-world. (1997, 26)

Such historical insight into European perceptions of the southern hemisphere before colonial explorations show that the antipodes were constructed as an "alter-world" in the European imagination. The "other-worldliness" that was imagined in both positive and negative forms (land of gold and land of deformities) illustrates how Australia's geography was used to constitute its identity in often contradictory terms.

Geography was no less central in defining Australia when speculation gave way to exploration in the eighteenth century. Cook's official charge in the voyage of the Endeavor (1768–71) was to contribute to an international effort to observe the transit of Venus not repeated again until 1874. By observing Venus' passage from different locations, Cook's mission would help astronomers better calculate the distance between the earth and the sun. Furthermore, the confirmation of a landmass in the antipodes offered the possibility of a strategic military location for Britain near the spice routes of Asia. There was much interest among natural scientists in the Royal Society and at Court for Cook's exploration of the South Pacific in order to confirm finally the much speculated upon *terra australia incognita*. The scientific community was interested in further information about the geography and the environment in this unexplored area of the map (Gregory 1994). For this reason, botanist Joseph Banks was able to persuade Cook to allow him and two naturalists to join the expedition.

While traveling along the east coast of Australia and especially in Botany Bay, botanists and crew members discovered new species of animals and plants such as the kangaroo, the black swan, the platypus, the flying fox, and 1,600 specimens of plant life previously unknown to European science. Cook's exploration of Australia in 1770 dispelled more far-fetched speculations about the southern continent, but also reinscribed its status as a land of aberrations. Michael Crozier makes the point, "Cook's charting of the east coast of New Holland—what would become known as Australia—did not so much diminish the power of the antipodean myths as it availed them to fresh opportunities for articulation. His mapping offered new imaginative and empirical resources for European antipodal dreaming" (1999, 843).

Initially, Australia seemed to offer little to commercial and political constituencies, compared to other sites that Cook explored, such as Tahiti and New Zealand. Australia's indigenous population was seemingly incapable of engaging in trade. The continent seemed to have few obvious resources to exploit, and its location was not convenient for traders on the spice route. Initially, some were interested in the Aborigines as a curious example of Rousseau's noble savage; however, the more the Aborigines resisted colonization, the less appealing or practical they were as a basis for theories about human nature. The scientific community was excited by the notion of Australia as a land of oddities and inversions (White 1981, 6).[8] Consequently, the scientific insights procured by the voyage colored perceptions of Australia more than other aspects of the continent did and helped reinforce Australia as Britain's imaginary Other.

Although Australia has typically been perceived as remote from the center of Empire, the scientific exploration of Australia and its colonial settlements was at the heart of the new scientific paradigms of European Enlightenment. The environmental "aberrations" of Australia and the effort to master its strange environment were important in developing scientific taxonomies that further dismantled Christianity as the primary epistemology for European civilization. Dorinda Outram writes:

> The imagination of the Enlightenment is as incomplete without the new plants and animals, minerals, fossils, and geographies recorded and brought back by explorers. At an even deeper level, what explorers reported about the new human societies they encountered made the whole issue of human difference itself a central problem in the Enlightenment. (1999, 282)

Cook's expedition also fostered the discipline of geography as a modern science based on principles of objectivity, realist description, systematic classification, and the comparative method of explanation (Gregory 1994; see also Stoddart 1986). Cook's subsequent voyages, which included botanists Johann and George Forster, further extended modern scientific methods to the study of (indigenous) people and their cultures (ibid.). Thus Pacific and Antarctic explorations of this period were fundamental to the growing importance of scientific knowledge and the Enlightenment faith in the human ability to understand the world through careful observation and categorization (Dunlap 1999).

Australia was central to the Enlightenment not only as a result of the official explorations and collections of Joseph Banks, but also in large part as a consequence of seemingly inconsequential botanical cataloging of colonial settlers. William Lines highlights the role in developing the Enlightenment achieved by the amateur botanical collecting of Australian settlers like Georgiana Molloy in the early nineteenth century. In the following passage, he describes the importance of the circulation of clippings and seeds between Molloy in the Western Australian colony and botanist Charles Mangles in England.

> The exposition of Charles Darwin's theory of evolution, or, descent with modification, in *The Origin of the Species* (1859), lay two decades beyond Mangles's reception of Molloy's boxes of southwest

specimens. By then, the southwest was known, and Darwin cited the species endemism and floristic richness of the southwestern corner of Australia several times in the course of his argument in support of the theory of natural selection. Darwin argued that the characteristics that naturalists—including botanists—considered as showing true affinity between species were those that had been inherited from a common parent; all true classification was genea-logical. Community of descent, not some unknown plan of creation or great chain of being, was the bond that naturalists had been un-consciously seeking. (1994, 261)

In this way, Australian explorers and colonialists trying to develop a sense of mastery over the unfamiliar landscape were players in the philosophical shifting of the Enlightenment.

Australia attracted more interest after the American colonies re-fused to accept more convicts to relieve Britain of its overcrowded prisons. Additionally, by the mid-eighteenth century British politi-cians and traders were interested in developing a military site closer to the Asian spice trade.[9] Hence, when British authorities were searching for a site to relocate its convicts, Australia was yet again defined by its geography and imagined distance (moral and physical) from Europe. Australia served as a penal colony for Britain from 1788 until 1868. Its distance from Britain made it an appealing location for Britain's deviant citizens. And its reputation for aberrations in nature gave it symbolic appeal.[10]

Perhaps not surprisingly, the discourse surrounding convict trans-portation produced Australia as a dystopia. "Transportation" aimed to rid the social body of its enemies and to deter others from com-mitting crime. Consequently, the middle and upper classes in Britain were invested in highlighting the horror of Australia. Earlier images of Australia as a land of natural inversions became conflated with ideas about moral deviancy and lower class vulgarity.

Australia served as a means by which the upper classes disci-plined the lower classes. Australia functioned as both a threat of punishment and a lens through which to scorn lower- and working-class tastes, lifestyles, and hopes for class mobility. The upper classes projected all their criticisms and anxieties about their social inferiors onto the image of "vulgar" Australia.

Characters like Magwich in Dickens's *Great Expectations* illus-trate the way the English characterized Australians. Magwich, a char-acter Pip meets early in his life when Pip is orphaned and destitute, is transported to Australia as a convict. Late in the novel the reader learns that Magwich has made his fortune in Australia and is the unknown benefactor responsible for transforming Pip into a gentleman. Magwich is symbolic both of the opportunity Australia offered the destitute and, as evidenced by Pip's ambivalence toward the aspiring and uncivilized Magwich, also of the English discomfort with the prospect of social mobility for convicts and the lower classes. While Magwich might transcend poverty or criminality, he has no hope of appreciating high culture or the finer things in life. For Magwich, and Australian colonials in general, money may buy revenge, but it cannot buy taste and true social standing. Dickens may well be offering a critique of the snobbery of Britishness in the form of Pip but he also captured and reproduced the association of Australian colonials with the lower class.

Consequently, at a time when criminality served to define the identity of a class, it became a way to define the identity of a nation. In *Inventing Australia,* Richard White describes the way criminality was projected onto Australia during the colonial era.

> The lowest element of British society was to be cast out among the lowest form of human life; unnatural vice was to be exiled as far from home as possible, where nature itself was inverted and nakedness knew no shame; thieves were to be condemned to a land where there was nothing of value. The macabre analogies meant that Australia remained, for a time, a mine of extravagant conceits for the cultured elite. Sydney Smith labeled it the "land of convicts and kangaroos" and Charles Lamb, in a precious bit of clowning, explained how kangaroos were "like a lesson framed by nature to the pick-pocket . . ." The idea of an antipodean inversion was extended to describe a land where "vice is virtue, virtue vice." Minor poets such as William Bowles and Erasmus Darwin, Charles Darwin's grandfather, mused about how the new civilization would turn out, with such inauspicious beginnings. (1981, 16)

Culturally, Australia symbolized criminality and vice. Jokes about pickpocket kangaroos set Australia up as "naturally" suited for moral and legal deviants. Just as its natural environment was full of perversities like the kangaroo and black swan, so it was the ideal site for the socially aberrant like the convict. Such assertions illustrate a kind of environmental essentialism used to articulate the identity of many places, but it functioned centrally in defining Australia in particular. The environment was seen as naturally generating a certain social form. For cynics, the "oddness" of the Australian landscape (unfamiliar species, different climate, etc.) served as proof of the inferiority of Australia. As a society and as a physical location, Australia was imbued with the shame and degeneracy the English middle class projected onto the criminal class. By exiling criminals to Australia, the English could define Britishness in terms of lawfulness and in opposition to Australian-ness.

A popular movement of Abolitionists who aimed to end the transportation of convicts to the Australian colonies began as early as 1822. Among those who wanted to see an end to transportation, Australian middle-class reformers argued that without the continual infusion of deviant people (convicts), Australia could be a sober and respectable society. And so, while not challenging the dominant conception of crime as a mark of inherent, unredeemable deviancy, abolitionists and free settlers challenged the symbolism assigned to the Australian environment. Like many British critics who took the natural environment to be a reflection of a society, Australian abolitionists continued to treat the natural environment as reflecting a kind of truth about Australian society. However, they asserted a utopian vision of the Australian environment and stressed its power to produce healthy, strong members of society. The goals of reformers dovetailed with others who benefited from attracting more free settlers to the colonies, such as agents who booked passages and employers in Australia who were desperate for laborers. Therefore, while there was a strong representation of Australia as an environmentally generated dystopia, it was also produced as an environmentally generated utopia for free settlers.

Australia was produced as a workingman's utopia through the promise of jobs and flattering representations of its landscape. Promoters of Australia described it as a pristine park that offered salvation to free settlers in contrast to the problems of industrial England. Borrowing from Judeo-Christian themes, Britain was paralleled with Paradise Lost when compared to the redemptive possibilities of the less-developed Australian landscape. Nineteenth-century literary figures also contributed to the construction of Australia as an Arcadian space.[11] Dickens, in particular, painted Australia as a glamorous alternative to England.[12] He was among several to herald the discovery of gold in Australia in 1855. In his writings, Dickens transformed the dry, dusty interior of the Australian continent into one of ample riches. He wrote, "It was found, it is said, that the country from the Mountain Range to an indefinite extent in the interior, is one immense goldfield" (Dickens 1855, quoted in Proudfoot 1985).

In the image of Australia as immense goldfield, the Australian landscape itself came to embody opportunity and class mobility. And in other instances, Australia as an Arcadia was frequently compared with an English park. Richard White notes:

> Arthur Bowes, surgeon in the first fleet, reported that the country around Port Jackson excelled in beauty "any nobleman's grounds in England" and Elizabeth Macarthur that "the greater part of the country is like an English park." In 1802 Port Phillip was thought to fall "nothing short, in beauty and appearance, of Greenwich Park," while in 1828, country further east was seen as resembling "the park of a country seat in England, the trees standing in picturesque groups to ornament the landscape." Thomas Mitchell, exploring "Australia Felix" in 1836, thought the country "had so much the appearance of a well kept park" that he was loath to drive his carts across it. (1981, 30)

The park-like and bucolic imagery offered promise of relief to the working classes who hoped for better living and working conditions than in England. Moreover, because in England green spaces and parks were reserved for the wealthy, the imagery also held strong appeal to those who longed for class mobility. The equation of Australia with an English park demonstrated again the idea that Australia's identity is defined by and reflected in its geography. Geographical and environmental determinism at the international level sets up a hierarchy between civilizations that serves to define Australia in both negative and later positive terms.

Almost two centuries later, in July 1995, Australian Foreign Minister Gareth Evans (Labor) arrived at the Asian foreign ministers' meeting with a map in tow depicting the "East Asian hemisphere" with Australia located centrally therein. This Australian map was one of many efforts by the Keating government (Labor) to redefine Australia as an objective member of the geographical region of Asia. Several years and one federal government later, Liberal Prime Minister Howard asserted that Australia need not choose between its history and its geography, signaling his intention to temper increased intimacy with Asia by a revalidation of Australia's links with Great Britain and the United States. Although these two recent prime ministers appealed to geography to highlight their political vision, Australia's geography has long been an instrument in political contestations. Its geographical and moral distance from an imagined center has been an issue in which Australian-ness has been defined and debated at different historical moments. Australia's location and landscape have been concepts through which people have long struggled over definitions of social and, later, national identity.

These details about Australia provide important insight for our understanding of how the nation is produced in relation to geographical categories. It is also useful to examine geography's function in defining Australia in historical context in order to see how Anglo-Celtic Australian nationalism has been conceptualized in territorial terms. As argued above, all nations are territorialized through imagined links between people, culture, and territory. Certainly, the presence of diasporic communities in the local landscape and the circulation of people, commodities, and capital across state borders have complicated the territoriality of national communities in many places other than Australia. But the idiosyncrasies of Australian colonialism and its development as a nation imagined as "down under" have meant that geography and spatial practice have been particularly important in Australian nation-making. They are compounded by other issues, such as Australia's reorientation away from an imagined British homeland to a definition of the nation as a cosmopolitan member of an "Asian" region. These factors, as well as challenges of indigenous land rights, have unsettled the Australian settler nation in especially poignant ways. The overview in this chapter has been provided as a necessary background for understanding how the spatial practices and use of geography to imagine nation in the two ethnographic sites of this study draw upon and continue a longer tradition of invented geographies in Australia.

## RESEARCH PRINCIPLES AND STRATEGIES

My study, based on twelve months of ethnographic fieldwork in Melbourne, Australia, is concerned to understand how everyday, local place making is connected to, and indeed produces, the nation and the international order. It asks how an imagined community is linked to physical place—not simply through governmental acts like mapmaking or treaties, but by planting gardens and by overpolicing Aboriginal spaces of sociability, for example. Ethnographic analysis helps us understand the importance of local and international geography in the production of nation and space as an important plane of state power and ingredient of political community. This study draws heavily on theoretical and secondary sources in many disciplines beyond political science. It engages with social geography, anthropology, history, and contemporary social/political theory in order to better understand political community, power, and the reimagining of the connection between people, culture, and territory in an era of increased globalization.

Most empirical political science is concerned with the behaviors of elites in formal political institutions or with nonelite behavior directed toward influencing government. But there has been too little attention paid to the relationship between everyday activities and political phenomena. Political theorists have dealt with noninstitutional forms of politics as they theorize power, gender, and political identity. However, political theory displays a strong tendency to focus only on textual analysis and the history of ideas. While normative political theory has expanded to include an analysis of film, literature, and law, political theory has on the whole remained centered on texts.

As in a growing area of social and political theory (and many "constructivist" studies in comparative politics and international relations), I trace the discursive practices (of which printed texts are one form) that constitute regimes of knowledge and frameworks of power. However, unlike most political theory as largely practiced since the 1950s, I am concerned with the content and effects of knowledge produced by people with little access to publication or institutional power. How do their practices and discourses reflect, reproduce, and contest power and knowledge? In this respect, this is a study of power and political process as it circulates outside of traditional political sites and within, for example, the private sphere or policing practices.

To this end, I have borrowed from anthropological methods of ethnography. As Gupta and Ferguson note, anthropology, despite the criticism that it has participated in colonial discourses, has nevertheless functioned as one of the few disciplinary sites in the academy concerned with marginality and the subaltern (1997b). Ethnographic methods have been particularly useful since my study is concerned with power, subjectivity, and political community as they are constructed in the everyday world. Further, given this study's attention to spatial production, ethnographic methods also permit access to observation of nonnarrative activity. Other fields and studies have given primacy to the social construction of space and place. But these have generally been oriented toward theorizing space more abstractly, or analyzing the social relations defining a particular place, as did Jon Bird's study of the London Docklands (1993; see also Dunn and Leeson 1993) or Jane Jacobs's analysis of the Swan Brewery in Perth (1996).

My study takes a different approach by examining the nature of spatial practices and their political effects. Other studies also rely almost exclusively on narrative and individuals' commentary about the struggle to define place and political policy. In contrast, ethnographic methods allow us insight into how spatial practices, both narrative and nonnarrative, configure local, national, and international space and constitute a political engagement with current political debates.

Traditional ethnographic methods offer a powerful way to understand the connection of local practices to larger structures (e.g., gender, economics, colonialism). More recently, ethnography has explored processes in the relationship between places (see Gupta and Ferguson 1997b). Innovative ethnography has been done on transnational processes such as homelessness (see Malkki 1995), diaspora (see Gilroy 1993; Leonard 1992) and marginality (see Tsing 1993). More and more, anthropology has shifted from looking at locality as a bounded site to examining the nature of community and locality as connected to other locales and global processes. In doing so, anthropology offers us a method for studying the construction of political communities and new political spaces in an era of globalization.

Because this study tries to think critically and to challenge the presumption of the physical and cultural boundedness of political community, I have used a multisited ethnographic approach[13] in order to understand how activities produce spatial, social, and political identity. The communities I studied, a police station and an amateur garden club, were defined by their activities but are not closed cultural systems. Instead, I have tried to make clear the ways in which these communities of practice are very much connected to other communities and spaces.

I selected a police station[14] and an amateur garden club[15] as my two field sites because each was actively engaged in constructing the local landscape in ways that suggest links to political hegemony. The gardeners did this through weeding, planting, and making decisions about plant varieties in the context of discussions about Australia's past, present, and future. The police engaged in place making through the surveillance and ordering of the cityscape and through their definitions of criminality and "Australian-ness." Although engaged in quite different activities, the police and gardeners did not occupy completely distinct worlds. Police members constructed the natural environment and gardeners defined antisocial behavior. I engaged in participant observation and formal interviews in the Fitzroy Police Station, where observing spatial practices helped me understand the links between disciplined territory and the production of national and supranational political community. This site also helped me see the importance of space for the operation of power in the modern state. At the same time, the spatial practices among members of the East Melbourne Garden Club illustrated the importance of disciplined natural landscapes for the construction of the settler state in both colonial and contemporary Australia. I have used pseudonyms for the people in both research sites to protect their privacy.

In what follows, I include ethnographic detail to the extent necessary for supporting my theoretical argument about the spatial construction of community and power and the reproduction of modernity in these sites. Such detail is necessary in that power is circulated and subjectivity produced in everyday life. If nonanthropologist readers are puzzled as to why they should weed through the names of the species planted in a native Australian garden or the specific interactions of police officers with people on the local streets of Fitzroy, they should recall that this is a study of the production of national and international political identities through mundane spatial practices. And they should keep in mind that phenomena such as modernity and deterritorialization do not mean much as abstract concepts if they are not embedded in everyday acts. Understanding these phenomena demands that we understand them as manifested in idiosyncratic ways in specific social locations.

Yet my ethnographic description does not fully describe the cultural milieu and the ongoing set of characters because urban communities of practice are not as tightly bounded as other kinds of communities. In the case of the gardeners in East Melbourne, their community of practice must be understood in terms of their historical links to colonial gardeners in Australia. Instead of elaborate description of these communities in relation to the cultural whole, I engage in thick description of spatial practices within the cultural debates that have unsettled settler Australians and the historical practices to which East Melbourne place making corresponds.

Interdisciplinary studies no doubt challenge the way in which expertise, authority, and funding have been compartmentalized in the twentieth-century academy. While I am not particularly invested in protecting the idea of disciplinary distinction, I do not believe that interdisciplinarity should lead to homogenous research methods. Although I employ ethnography, geography, and historical analysis, my study asks certain questions that I believe distinguish it as a study of politics. It inquires into the way people reestablish an imagined link between people, culture, and territory necessary to the legitimacy of the nation-state. It examines the processes by which people (re)legitimate their political community in relation to historical practices and to contemporary political issues challenging the settler state's imagined authority over land in Australia. My study attempts to speak to the nature of political hegemony and the imagination of political community.

Ethnographic research allowed a more subtle understanding of the Fitzroy Police and the members of the East Melbourne Garden Club. Undertaking a historical genealogy is a useful way to complicate what society and even scholars take for granted, as Foucault's work illustrates. But there is an additional usefulness in studying people in specific contexts rather than as historical categories—the police, middle class, psychiatrists, etc. Thinking about the meaning of the social practices of people we have met and with whom we have formed relationships compels us to be more attuned to nuances and complicated subject positions. In this respect, ethnographic methods help us represent the material world in all its complexity and, in turn, to produce more complex theory.

# A Picturesque Nation for a "Barren" Continent

The reterritorialization of the settler Australian state through the taming of natural landscapes that this chapter examines took place within the neighborhood of East Melbourne. Although the East Melbourne Garden Club was located on the border of the city's central business district, members nevertheless defined nation and class in the shifting landscape of republican politics and multiculturalism in Australia.

The suburb was divided from the heart of the city's financial and government district by the Fitzroy Gardens, whose original path design in the late nineteenth century, it was rumored, was arranged to form the shape of the Union Jack. In addition to being isolated by the city's finest park, East Melbourne conveyed the sense of being centrally isolated by the fact that the suburb[1] was separated from its two neighboring communities, ethnically diverse Fitzroy and Richmond, by the highly congested Hoddle Street and Victoria Parade and by the beloved MCG (Melbourne Cricket Ground). As a consequence, East Melbourne, with its relatively homogenous upper-middle-class population, two internal parks, cluster of small shops, café, and local library, allowed residents to remain surprisingly sheltered from the hustle and bustle of the larger city.

Thus, judging from the people on the streets in East Melbourne, walking their dogs in the park or gardening in the front of their homes, one would never guess that several blocks away (across Hoddle Street) in Richmond was the busiest district of Vietnamese restaurants and shops in Australia. But because East Melbourne was one of the few inner suburbs with no housing commission high-rise apartments like its neighboring suburbs, its gentrification had been the most thorough, and its population remained economically and racially homogenous.[2]

Since the 1980s, the majority of East Melbourne residents have been of Anglo-Celtic ethnicity. The residences consisted almost entirely of fully restored Victorian terrace houses. The terrace houses were strung together in rows of three or four and were painted traditional Victorian colors (deep brown and green) in keeping with the community guidelines laid out by the voluntary association, the East Melbourne Group.[3] Few alterations to the original Victorian architectural design were visible from the street because the East Melbourne Group carefully regulated changes in historical structures. This neighborhood association aimed to protect the historical authenticity of the neighborhood. Those architectural changes visible from the street usually predated the 1980s, made before the time when the gentrification of the suburb set in and the community began to manage its identity more carefully.

The vegetation in East Melbourne was a feature that distinguished this inner suburb from many others in Melbourne. A number of the streets that crossed Simpson Street in East Melbourne still had large trees, many of which were Dutch elms. However, the elaborate residential gardens offered an air of tranquility even on streets that had been more severely blighted by Dutch elm disease. The restored heritage houses that characterized East Melbourne had, at a minimum, small lawns and decorative bushes. However, most residents had been more ambitious and developed flowerbeds, if not complete English cottage gardens. The picturesque cottage gardens complemented the British colonial design of most of the houses and created a "heritage" feel for the neighborhood. The cottage gardens usually sat behind small iron fences along which were often clusters of flowering bushes like daisies, roses, or camellias. True to tradition, East Melbourne cottage gardens contained many English and European species such as violets, tulips, lavender, fuchsia, and begonia, arranged in an asymmetrical form reminiscent of eighteenth-century English peasant cottage gardens. However, most gardeners had also incorporated flowering native Australian species into their traditional English cottage gardens.

*Figure 4. Elm-lined George Street in East Melbourne.*

*Figure 5. English-style park in East Melbourne.*

The manicured gardens and carefully restored Victorian houses of East Melbourne created a pleasant experience for people walking through the neighborhood. They were also part of the construction of place that defined East Melbourne and Australia in the complex political and cultural landscape of multicultural Australia. This chapter examines the processes by which political cosmologies are enacted through the production of English cottage gardens, house renovation, and modes of sociability in East Melbourne. It considers these spatial practices as they relate to the historical production of picturesque landscapes and to the contemporary challenges of ethnic and cultural diversity ("multiculturalism") with which white settler Australians have been confronted in the last part of the twentieth century.

Aesthetic taste, usually presumed to be a reflection of individual preference, can also be read as a code that reflects and reproduces larger social cosmologies. As this chapter discusses in more detail, the picturesque sensibility reflected in the careful gardens of East Melbourne was originally imported to Australia as part of the larger colonial effort to appropriate the Australian continent for Anglo-Europeans. The picturesque English cottage garden was a technology for taking authority—literally and symbolically—over the land in Australia. At the end of the twentieth century, while Australians sought to radically rewrite Australia's political relationship with Britain through the erasure of British cultural forms from the Australian landscape, members of the East Melbourne Garden Club tended, cultivated, and reconfigured Australia's links to Britain with their elaborate cottage gardens.

The picturesque ascended as an aesthetic form in the late eighteenth and the nineteenth centuries. As Ann Bermingham argues in her work on art and ideology, this sensibility must be understood not merely in terms of the formal qualities that characterized it, but also in terms of the politics that circulated through the "picturesque" (see Bermingham 1986). As an aesthetic "sensibility," the picturesque helped mediate dramatic social and political transformations in both Britain and the Australian colonies.

In this respect, the work of Pierre Bourdieu is useful for understanding how taste and social practices, which he calls "habitus," grow out of one's position in social structures; they function to reproduce social divisions (hierarchies) and stabilize political arrangements. While Bourdieu had in mind the political structure of capitalism, this chapter explores how political orders such as colonialism or national identity might be maintained and stabilized through a particular aesthetic sensibility and through the enactment of "taste."

In *Distinction* (1984), Bourdieu details how social divisions or categories are marked by income and education levels, but also, and importantly, by "taste." He defines the habitus in the following terms:

> The habitus is both the generative principle of objective classifiable judgments and the system of classification (principium divisionis) of the practices. It is in the relationship between the two capacities which define the habitus, the capacity to produce classifiable practices and works, and the capacity to differentiate and appreciate these practices and products (taste), that the represented social world, i.e. the space of life-styles, is constituted. (170)

The habitus is the act of creating meaningful social distinctions using signs that circulate under the banner of taste or lifestyle (e.g., the class standing signaled by a velvet Elvis painting versus an original abstract art piece). Furthermore, social distinctions are marked on our bodies in the form of adornment but also more subtly by our posture and body form. The habitus depends on and cultivates people's ability to read social codes and to associate them (typically in an unself-conscious way) with the material social divisions of class or other social categories that they signify, reproduce, and naturalize. Bourdieu draws the link between taste and class explicitly when he writes:

> Taste is the practical operators of the transmutation of things into distinct and distinctive signs, of continuous distributions into discontinuous oppositions; it raises the differences inscribed in the physical world of bodies to the symbolic order of significant distinctions. It transforms objectively classified practices, in which a class condition signifies itself (through taste), into classifying practices, that is, into a symbolic expression of class position. (1984, 174–75)

As this passage reflects, Bourdieu has helped us appreciate the important way class is reinscribed on the body. However, as the ethnographic material in this chapter suggests, social identity is also inscribed, and thereby reproduced, in the physical landscape and in the way bodies move through space. Social identities, for instance, are constituted through the clothes we wear, the food we eat, the gardens we produce, and also through patterns of sociability. This chapter examines the processes by which social identity and belonging were produced in East Melbourne, Australia, through the construction of the suburb as a quasi-English village. This identity was created through landscape design and, in some instances, through the enactment of village life.

And while Bourdieu emphasizes class, multiple social structures and identities are produced through habitus. Individuals and groups use codes of taste to define nation and race as well as class. For instance, in East Melbourne, gardens and architectural renovations undertaken by East Melbourne garden club members operate as "practical metaphors" for class identity, but also for a particular political vision of the nation at the end of the twentieth century.

Bourdieu treats aesthetic dispositions as stable blocks that people reproduce within class categories. What is clear in examining the production of English cottage gardens (chapter 1) and of native "bush gardens" in contemporary Australia (chapter 2) is that a variety of political debates take place within the realm of taste. In this sense, they are vocabularies through which political or social contestation takes place. Further, the spatial practices of this study demonstrate that the class-based habitus that Bourdieu illuminated are inflected by racial and gender identities and that class positions are anything but singular. The ethnographic analysis that follows extends Bourdieu's original framework by examining the political contestations that are also enacted through the articulation of taste. Taken together, this chapter and the one that follows illustrate two competing visions of nation that are both located within the middle class. Both are concerned with how the tastes cultivated in East Melbourne reflect and maintain political positions in relation to debates over Australian national identity as well as how "taste" consolidates other social identities such as class, race, and gender.

The next two sections summarize some of the political content of the picturesque in Britain and then look more closely at its uses in the colonization of Australia. This history is important to understanding the spatial practices of members of the East Melbourne Garden Club at the end of the twentieth century, since the landscapes they produced both reflected the earlier English cottage gardens of colonial Australians and marked their difference from their colonial precursors. As this chapter and chapter 2 illustrate, in both historical eras the picturesque allowed people to territorialize the white Australian nation in a literal sense as well as configure a structure of feeling that allowed them to psychologically inhabit the continent. This chapter is concerned primarily with the picturesque English cottage garden because it was instrumental in defining British nationalism at the turn of the eighteenth century and was later a means of inscribing Britishness in the Australian colonies. The next chapter discusses the "natural style," another landscape aesthetic developed in the eighteenth century alongside the picturesque, because it provided the aesthetic and ideological basis for the Australian native garden movement in the 1970s.

## THE PICTURESQUE AND BRITISH NATIONALITY

At the end of the eighteenth century, the English countryside reflected the significant social and economic changes Britain was undergoing. Imagining landscapes and physically shaping them were a means by which people sought to shape those conditions. The Napoleonic Wars, which ended with England's victory at Waterloo in 1815, set into motion dramatic changes within Britain. Agricultural demand during the wars led the English Parliament to pass more than 1,800 land enclosure bills between 1796 and 1815 in an effort to expand the agricultural industry (Lines 1996). When crop prices fell at the end of the wars with France, many overextended farmers and landowners who had taken mortgages during the prosperous war years were bankrupted. Consequently, large numbers of laborers, jobless and without land, subsequently migrated into the cities to fill out the ranks of the new industrial armies of the nineteenth century.

Land enclosure bills first altered the countryside during this period by taking common land and converting it to agricultural land. As cities and towns enlarged after the Napoleonic Wars to accommodate a growing industrial population, the countryside around them became suburban (Bermingham 1986). The elite class became more socially and spatially distant from the poor, who suffered under abysmal conditions in the rapidly industrializing cities and endured the social tensions created by a "surplus" population in England. The landscape inhabited by the poor became increasingly regulated by a stringent legal system. The middle or bourgeois class, consisting of farmers who had prospered during the Napoleonic Wars and an emergent industrialist class, also swelled during the Industrial Revolution. Their numbers and instrumental role in the industrial economy gave the bourgeois a new historical importance. It also prompted them to craft a social identity to distinguish them from both the lower class and the "morally bankrupt" upper class; the picturesque aesthetic was instrumental in helping the bourgeois to define their social and national identity and to navigate their ambivalence toward many of the social changes that surrounded them.

Developing at the end of the eighteenth century, the picturesque linked art with nature and gave the English countryside an aesthetic quality (Bermingham 1986, 1994). Derived from the Latin and French meanings of painting or suggesting a picture, *picturesque* generally describes a wild or natural beauty or mountain scenery. It is also used to describe something that is pleasantly unfamiliar, strange, or quaint. Picturesque also can mean to call up a mental picture, such as in a picturesque description. As a general artistic expression it was developed through landscape paintings that expressed the beauty and melancholy of unaltered landscapes and vistas. Later, the picturesque was applied to the cultivation of the landscape through garden and landscape design and in relation to architectural design and village planning. As I discuss at greater length in the next chapter, the picturesque emphasized preserving older landscapes without dramatic or excessive alteration of their original form. The landscape design and picturesque gardens attempted to express nature's original beauty, enhancing irregularity and asymmetry instead of creating sculptured, overly cultured spaces.

The aesthetic was based on a philosophical premise that rejected rationalizing the natural world in favor of the expression of the sublime, personal, and "irrational" experience of beauty in the natural world. The work of Edmund Burke's 1757 essay, *Philosophical Enquiry into the Origin of our Ideas of the Sublime and the Beautiful*, was one of the earliest statements of this aesthetic movement. Burke's work was followed by William Gilpin's essay entitled *Observations, Relative Chiefly to Picturesque Beauty Made in the Year 1772* and then by many other writers in subsequent years who used the picturesque to interpret the British landscape.

Landscape historian Christopher Thacker describes the picturesque ideal generated by Burke and Gilpin's work in the following passage:

> In his treatise Burke codified the division of beauty into two kinds: the beautiful, for things which were smooth, regular, delicate and harmonious, and the sublime, for things which also moved us to aesthetic approval, but were rough, gloomy violent and gigantic . . . Gilpin, for his part, while accepting Burke's division, felt that a further refinement was needed to sort out the qualities necessary to make a landscape suitable for painting. In Gilpin's work the picturesque qualities of landscape are descended from the hilly countryside views of Claudian painting, but are translated into British landscape, generally of a wild, rugged and gloomy kind, and most often with the buildings, if they appeared, of a ruined and Gothic character. (1979, 212)

The picturesque both responded to the political climate of the era and gave an aesthetic quality to some of the social and political transformations taking place in Britain (Bermingham 1986). On the one hand, the picturesque served as a critique of the legislated land enclosures and of the industrialization of the landscape; it did so by nostalgically depicting the rapidly disappearing countryside through painting, amateur sketches, and landscape design. On the other hand, however, landscape painting in particular depoliticized the effects of the displacement of the peasants from the countryside by creating beautiful, melancholy landscapes with old barns, cottages, and mills but absent of beggars and gypsies who increasingly populated such landscapes in the nineteenth century.[4] Picturesque landscape painting converted poverty and industrialization into art and thus kept it at a manageable distance from the bourgeois and the upper class. This nostalgia was further fed by popular guidebooks such as those by William Gilpin, which made even the unfamiliar landscape of Wales, Scotland, and the Lake District unthreatening, "safe," and accessible (see Thacker 1979).

Although picturesque gardens reflected a larger fashion that the middle class shared with the upper classes, the middle-class picturesque cottage gardens that developed at this time took their inspiration from humble peasant gardens. While the upper class cultivated picturesque landscape design on their estates, the financial constraints of the bourgeois led them to apply the picturesque to garden design.

Like the picturesque more generally, the English cottage garden style celebrated unbound nature and romanticized working-class cottage life. Its aesthetic appealed to members of the bourgeois who found charm in the perceived simplicity of country life. Before this period, the cottage garden was merely the working and domestic space of peasants who grew native English wildflowers within the confines of their yards, interspersed with their vegetables and livestock. These original peasant gardens would have contained decorative flowers such as columbine, carnations, wild roses, snapdragon, sweet william, double marigolds, lilies, peonies, nigella, and hollyhocks (Scott-James 1981).

The popularity among the bourgeois of the picturesque cottage home and the cottage garden was in part a product of the transformation of the countryside into suburbs. Industrialization produced more housing around town centers and substituted private garden plots for undeveloped public countryside. Picturesque cottage living allowed people to express their nostalgia for country life, which, because it was disappearing from the lower class, could live all the more vividly in the imagination of the middle class. Many in the middle class, captivated by the charms of cottage life, either bought and greatly elaborated existing cottages or moved into newly constructed cottages. In the newer constructions, town planners reproduced the idea of a village green to appeal to the nostalgia for village life, and architects designed "workers cottages" for their bourgeois clientele, complete with irregular plots and porches that could be decorated with climbing jasmine and framed by a well-placed acacia, pine, or cedar tree in front (Scott-James 1981). The use of native English wildflowers in peasant gardens and their irregular, haphazard arrangements appealed to picturesque sensibilities.

As the middle class embraced the glorification of simple country existence in their more suburban village cottages, the cottage garden became more elaborate. The original hardy plants remained, but were joined by climbers (fruit trees, jasmine, climbing roses, or ivy) and bedding plants (geranium, dahlias, wallflowers, and China aster).

With the industrial revolution, bourgeois capitalism restructured space into more rigidly differentiated public and private spheres. Middle-class men distinguished themselves from the upper class, for whom the aristocratic estate combined the domestic and economic, and from the lower classes, who also had historically intertwined the economic with the domestic by growing their food and manufacturing products in their houses. As Anne McClintock writes in *Imperial Leather*:

> By the nineteenth century, a major transformation was underway as the middle-class men laboriously refashioned architectural and urban spaces to separate, as if by nature, domesticity from industry, market from family. Manufacturers slowly but steadily moved their houses away from the factories, shopkeepers stopped living above their shops, bankers set up separate banking houses and the suburbs were born. (1995, 167)

The picturesque English cottage and cottage garden helped the bourgeois define its identity by more clearly reflecting the separation of work from family in a new, gendered division of the public and private. The "idleness" and leisure of Victorian women was used to signify patriarchal and bourgeois social prestige and bourgeois ideology about the family (McClintock 1995).[5] The cottage garden highlighted the border between public and private, and as a border site was a useful site for the middle class to display the empty, leisure hours of women in its development and upkeep.[6]

The cottage garden wildflowers' "native" status was also attractive to a British public who wanted to celebrate British political and cultural forms after their victory over the French in the Napoleonic wars. As Simon During explains, cultivated picturesque landscapes and the English garden symbolized the ideal of improvement in nineteenth-century British nationalism. During writes about the territorialization of the British nation during this historical era:

> But of course, the nation earthed itself by other means than visual or discursive representation: it built too. Not least, it created expressive environments for itself in the rich man's cult of landscape gardening . . . The English Garden which Brown championed was much more than a fashion: as nature artificially and laboriously transformed into an ideal version of itself, it was the aesthetic expression of 'improvement'—of the technologisation and capitalisation of agricultural property. But the English Garden also provided the environment which was supposed best to nurture English national character. (1998, 41)

Picturesque landscapes, be they in the form of the estate landscape design of the wealthy or the cottage gardens of the middle class, provided a symbol for the values of industry and improvement that came to the fore in nineteenth-century Britain. The cultivated picturesque landscapes were a vehicle for imagining these qualities as natural to Britain and thereby inherent to British people.

Philanthropists in England applied this ideal of "improvement" through industry to the lower class. For example, Thomas Bernard argued in a pamphlet entitled *Account of a Cottage and Garden Near Tadcaster* (1797) for a national scheme aimed at assisting laborers to own a cottage plot through tax exemptions and loans (cited in Scott-James 1981, 26–27). Another government report from 1860 illustrates the use of the idea of the cottage and cottage garden as an instrument in civilizing the lower classes within Britain. The document of 1860 states:

> On entering an improved cottage, with a neat and civilized garden, in which the leisure hours of the husband are pleasantly and profitably employed, it will be found that he has no desire to frequent the beershop, or spend his evenings away from home, the children are reared to labour, to habits and feelings of independence, and taught to connect happiness with industry, and to shrink from idleness and

immorality; the girls make good servants, obtain the confidence of the employers, and are promoted to the best situations. (cited in Scott-James 1981, 58–59)

This government document promises that the garden creates respectability and morality, at the same time as it preserves class relations. The "neat and civilized" gardens generate neat, civilized, and chaste girls who make excellent servants for the upper class.[7] As British colonial expansion got underway in Australia in the second half of the eighteenth and the nineteenth centuries, the picturesque was a tool for inscribing British nationalism on colonial space, and it was a mechanism for safeguarding the physical and moral character of British colonial subjects.

## PICTURESQUE AUSTRALIAN COLONIES AND RACIAL ANXIETIES

In Australia, the picturesque guided the production of English cottage gardens both in the cities and in the more arid regions of the countryside (the "outback"). This aesthetic sensibility was also enacted through landscape painting, architecture design, and the pastoral economy in Australia. Christopher Lee observes, "Picturesque landscape granted the settler possession and control through the transformation of the land into a pedagogical discourse organised as the settler subject's Power/Knowledge" (1996, 53).

As in the British Isles, middle- and upper-class Britons produced picturesque travel accounts and sketches of the Australian countryside as part of colonial expansion on the continent. Paul Carter (1987) and Simon Ryan (1996) both analyze the political import of the popular use of the picturesque in explorers' descriptions of Australia. The picturesque descriptions and sketches of the landscape in Australia, which the colonial travelers experienced and presented as a spontaneous response to the objective qualities of the Australian landscape, were actually an application of British aesthetic fashion to the colonial context.

Humphry Repton, a noted advocate of the picturesque in Britain, claimed that the cultivation of picturesque landscapes distinguished "the pleasures of civilized society from the pursuits of savage and barbarous nations" (cited in Ryan 1996, 73). Repton understood picturesque landscapes to reflect the natural division between civilizations. The picturesque as developed in Australia actually illustrates how this aesthetic sensibility functioned as a mechanism that *produced* the barbarism of Aborigines and the civilization of Europeans. For instance, travel writing and sketches regularly excluded any sign of Aborigines from the landscape, helping to perpetuate the fiction of *terra nullius*. Ryan also notes, "Aesthetic descriptions which show pleasure in the way nature has 'arranged itself' move easily into speculations about the suitability of these arrangements for the colonising enterprise. Often, the Australian landscape is seen as ready-made for the occupation of a European power and its agriculture" (1996, 73). The imaging of the landscape in such a way had a significant ideological force for justifying its European colonial appropriation.

The production of the Australian landscape as picturesque had a profound role in emotionally inhabiting what was often experienced and described as a hostile environment. As Ryan's analysis indicated, it suggested that the continent was perfectly compatible for European occupation, but it also helped the isolated settlers anticipate the society that would follow from their presence. Carter makes this point about travel writing: "This picturesque interplay between space and time, between present loneliness and future sociability, between visible Nature and invisible Culture, was equally the appeal of picturesque views after Salvator Rosa. It looked forward to a cultivated society" (1988, 244–45). And of course, at some level it begins the work of appropriating the land by imagining the landscape in terms of a British cultural form.

The aesthetic production of the landscape was a useful method for mystifying the colonial appropriation of land underway in Australia. Turning the Australian continent into an English countryside and farmland helped erase the physical evidence of Aboriginal presence and influence on the land. Michael Shapiro notes how in the North American context indigenous spatial meaning and propriety was negated through the erasure of indigenous names. Such erasures were a means of negating the historical significance and vantage point that was involved in Apache practices of "speaking with names," for instance (Shapiro 1997, 27). Reshaping the land by renaming places and by physically restructuring it into a picturesque landscape were ways of appropriating the land symbolically while imperial forces took possession of the land on a more literal level through wars, through forced removal of indigenous people, and by wiping out the indigenous population through the spread of diseases.

In Australia, the aesthetic production of the landscape negated Aboriginal hunting zones, sacred sites, homes, and other physical manifestations of a propriety the Aborigines had exercised over the Australian landscape until their displacement by colonial forces. In the cultivation of a picturesque landscape in the colonizing project in Australia, many native Australian species were perceived and treated as "weeds." In her history of the colonization of the American West, Frieda Knobloch comments on the politics of importing botanical species (exotics) and the designation of native species as weeds. She writes, "Likewise, exotic plants were fundamentally part of the social phenomenon of invasion in the American West (and elsewhere). Weeds become objectionable not because their growth is rapid and unchecked, but because they take some territory and profit from agriculture in some way" (1996, 114).

Knobloch's study of the American West highlights how altering the biosphere was an important component of the colonizing process in colonial spaces like North America and Australia (see also Dunlap 1999). The designation of certain plants as "weeds" was not an objective aesthetic categorization but, as Knobloch argues, was a designation based on how useful various species were to colonial expansion. Elsewhere she posits, "Colonization is an agricultural act" (1996, 1). In the Australian context, designating many species as weeds supported the representation of the Australian continent as empty and uncultivated. "Weeds" and "shaggy" eucalyptus trees suggest no cultivation of the land, despite the fact that Aborigines engaged in a form of land management through systematic burnings and through the Dreaming.[8] In short, the designation of many species as "weeds" helped legitimate the appropriation of the land under the terms of *terra nullius*. More generally, the classification of native Australian botanical species as weeds and as part of an environment "hostile" to European civilization may also have reflected an anxiety about being so far away from the material resources of Great Britain. And it expressed the colonial settlers' sense of vulnerability to the violent response Aborigines often had to their dispossession by the British.

Additionally, picturesque spatial practices distinguished colonial subjectivity from the perceived degenerate nature and race of Aborigines and Asians. Such spatial practices helped Australian colonials bridge the geographical separation with Britain by shaping the Australian landscape to look as much like the British landscape as possible, which no doubt resulted in a lot of unhappy rosebushes. That is, the production of landscapes was an important means by which political and social identity was constructed in colonial Australia. The manipulation of landscape and climate in Australia was a way in which Australian geography was defined within European civilization.

Australian colonials also used the picturesque to protect their status as European, given their distance from Britain. They reproduced landscape as picturesque in the face of the perceived threat of miscegenation by the environment (heat, sun, humidity) and by Aboriginal people.

During colonization, the British used the climate as a marker of the superiority of Europeans. This self-serving environmental determinism held that "temperate climates alone produced vigorous minds, hardy bodies, and progressive societies, while tropical heat (and its association with botanical abundance) produced races marked by languor and stupefaction" (Lewis and Wigen 1997, 42; see also Bhabha 1990, 319–20; for a discussion of the uses of English weather to define nation in opposition to third-world spaces).[9]

Christopher Lee (1996) writes that people were concerned, as they were in other parts of the British Empire, that hot climates could have an undesirable effect on Europeans. The hot and humid climate partially explained for settlers the presumed inferiority of Aboriginal people. As a consequence, people were concerned that the European "race" would begin to deteriorate after several generations in the landscape and climate of the Australian colonies. Climate was one important way in which Australians produced their national and racial identity historically through spatial practices. Christopher Lee writes:

> The deployment of the Social Darwinist discourses on climate in Australia led to serious concerns over the future of the Anglo-Saxon stock. From the initial moment of this continent's European invasion the invader settlers were concerned by anomalies between their skin colour and its associated genetic genealogy and the humid tropical and sub-tropical climate. The fear was that if inferior (black and yellow) races were products of their "hot" environments then the European presence in Australia might be expected to result in stock degeneration (1996, 54; see also Tiffin 1987).

If environment could produce character, then British colonials and their subsequent generations living in Australia were at risk of degenerating to the level of Aboriginal and Asian civilizations. While perhaps miscegenation could be avoided by strict policing of sexual relations between racial groups, European narratives about civilization and environment positioned Australian colonials as at risk of becoming less than fully white and fully civilized because of the potential effects of the landscape and climate. The Darling Downs region of Queensland was discursively constructed as a picturesque landscape that offered a cooler climate and civilizing vistas that could protect the European race from the miscegenation resulting from the Australian environment. It was a sanctuary of civilization within Australia in that its altitude provided a more temperate, "European" climate and permitted the maintenance of a European identity for its Australian inhabitants. Lee notes:

> Cultural hierarchies of the high and low provide both the political and rhetorical context for the imperially enabling pedagogical claim that the health-giving climate of the Darling Downs offered an ideal environment in which to "raise a splendid race of stalwart sons and daughters who, when the old people sleep with their fathers, will continue to add to the prosperity of the colony, following in their father's footsteps and steadily building up the Australian nation." (1996, 55)[10]

Lee's analysis suggests how the picturesque aesthetic was a means by which British and white identity was imagined and produced in colonial Australia. It was not simply that the picturesque was a visual form that would make Australia look like Britain; it allowed for the physical reproduction of British subjectivity in the form of healthy bodies located in a particular "European" landscape. In this way, the picturesque was used to ward off anxiety within the colonial experience. Delineating such "European" spaces outside of Europe allowed colonial Australians to continue to claim an identity that was coterminous with Britishness.

While the Australian landscape was colonized through the clearing of land for an agricultural economy and the fetishing of temperate "European" zones, it also was colonized through the production of picturesque British cottage gardens. In particular, gardens were an instrument for taking emotional possession of the continent, for imagining it as a British homeland. This process is documented in the letters of Georgiana Molloy (1805–43), one of the early colonial settlers in Western Australia's Flinders Bay region (Hardy Inlet on the Blackwood River). Molloy's correspondence with her family in Scotland illustrates how the landscape was overlaid with a feeling of ambivalence for many early settlers to Australia. She experienced her homesickness for Scotland and family through a longing for her family's garden at Rosneath, among other things. She wrote to her mother, "Oh my dear and lovely Rosneath—my heart bleeds when I think of all the happy, celestial days I spent there and all the violets and primroses are fresh in my memory."[11]

In his biography of Georgiana Molloy's life, William Lines describes her use of the seeds and clippings in Australia that were given to Molloy by her mother upon her emigration from Scotland. There was a steady circulation of plant clippings and garden literature between Britain and the colonies. Sometimes emigrating settlers brought seeds and plant stock from their families' gardens with them. Others received seeds on the regular transports carrying supplies and news between the imperial center and the colonies. In her first act of place making in Western Australia, Molloy used the seed clippings to plant a cottage garden. Lines comments, "As a refugee from industrialising England, Molloy carried the prevailing passion for flowers with her to Australia . . . This cultivated, domestic space provided reassurance and a sense of rootedness" (1994, 137). Molloy's experience illustrates how the picturesque garden, in fashion in nineteenth-century England as a response to the industrial revolution, was transplanted to Australia to address emotional and political exegeses particular to the Australian context. Planting a garden with vegetation reminiscent of her home in Scotland was a means of shaping the unfamiliar Australian environment into something recognizable and emotionally safe. Lines describes Molloy's process of settlement in the following passage:

> From her house she looked out over Hardy Inlet to the undifferentiated blue-green forest that appeared unbounded, without limits, unimaginable, unknowable, and therefore suspect. She shared John Bussell's ambivalence towards her surroundings. Augusta was beautiful and picturesque but also wild, savage, and uncompromising. The land needed taming, reshaping into recognisable and familiar forms . . . A flower garden, however, could start the process of recla-

mation, of redemption. Domesticated flowers were emblematic, comforting, and soothing. A well-ordered, regulated, and colourful garden set amidst the disorderly and monochromatic bush would provide an imaginative escape. Happily for Molloy, the seeds and cuttings she planted in June throve in the damp Augusta soil and, by the time of her first Australian spring, were in flower. (1994, 128–29)

Although she eventually became one of the earliest advocates of native Australian vegetation, Molloy's initial strategy for creating a sense of rootedness became widespread as the colonization of Australia continued. Colonial subjects took economic and emotional possession of the territory of Australia through the masculine pursuit of clearing and farming and through women's activities of cultivating domestic gardens. In this regard, Georgiana Molloy exemplifies the agency women exercised in territorializing the British Empire in Australia; like many women in an unfamiliar environment, she planted a garden.[12] Molloy and other colonials' placemaking efforts illustrate the Australian cultural form labeled the "homesick" garden. As contemporary Australian landscape designer Graeme Law describes these gardens, "There was a great sense of loss, and a love of what was left behind, experienced by our earlier settlers, many of course being reluctant migrants. These 'homesick' gardens still prevail within our communities" (1999, xi).

The remainder of the chapter analyzes a community of people in East Melbourne who continue to draw on British cultural forms in imagining the Australian settler state at the end of the twentieth century. Although plenty of people criticized English cottage gardens and the continued elevation of British identity in contemporary Australia as clinging to the past, my analysis highlights the enactment of British-style landscapes is an active gesture to reterritorialize settler Australians' links to place and nation in thoroughly contemporary terms.

## "IT'S JUST A LITTLE COTTAGE":
## REMEMBERING BRITAIN IN EAST MELBOURNE

In mid-nineteenth-century Australia, the suburb of East Melbourne was brought into being as a consequence of the cadastral survey that, characteristic of British colonial rule in many parts of the world, divided the land into a grid formation. The grid rendered the territory easiest and most profitable to govern. Louise Johnson argues that the reproduction of British suburban forms in colonial Australia from the 1860s expressed the cultural norms and social expectations of the British bourgeois in the colonies. Australian suburbs reproduced a bourgeois moral order and family ideology as a consequence of the labor of the women who maintained the house and garden. Johnson writes:

> Housing was a means to generate, but also representative of, colonial affluence. Its suburban form—modeled on the English country cottage—was a statement of cultural difference and deference. This was registered in a built environment resembling a cross between an agricultural village and a town house. (1992, 41)

The neighborhood of East Melbourne began as a fairly middle-class suburb; however, by the mid-twentieth century, like many of the inner suburbs of Melbourne, it had evolved into a lower-class neighborhood characterized by boarding houses, first generation immigrants, and prostitution. The first signs of middle-class renovations were visible in East Melbourne in the late 1970s and peaked in the 1980s and 1990s. Initially, these houses sold for very reasonable prices because they had not undergone serious renovations

*Figure 6. Renovated Victorian worker's cottage and English cottage garden in East Melbourne.*

since the end of the nineteenth century. Most had makeshift kitchens and many still had outdoor toilets. However, by the mid-1990s, it was a solidly upper-middle-class neighborhood located close to public transportation, public parks, and several of Melbourne's best urban shopping areas.

The renovating efforts of people in East Melbourne were very much oriented toward "restoring" the historical style of their homes. The East Melbourne Group had passed community recommendations for the use of Victorian colors (especially on the exterior of houses), and the city council restricted changes to the facades of historical homes. As in many parts of the world, people happily invested great amounts of money and time in commissioning builders to restore moldings, remove alterations done to the houses from the 1950s to the 1970s, and paint and wallpaper with Victorian colors and designs. People also spent untold hours searching for appropriate antique furniture and decorations to complement the historical character of the houses.

On receiving any praise of her carefully and tastefully restored Victorian terrace house, one East Melbourne resident and garden club member, Vivian, insisted, "It's just a little cottage, but it's right

*Figure 7. Interior of renovated Victorian worker's cottage in East Melbourne.*

for us now." And in such modesty, Vivian was not unique. Residents of East Melbourne were very quick to point out that theirs were simple worker's cottages built during the great economic boom in Melbourne at the end of the nineteenth century. They were happy to walk interested guests through the stages of their renovations and could usually narrate parts of the social history of the house, sometimes pointing with amusement to a thumbprint left in a brick made by convict labor. The tour usually began with the formal parlor area, typically the first room off a corridor that ran the length of the Victorian house. This was also the room that served as a showcase for the best antiques and furniture and for expensively framed photos (typically black and white) of previous generations of family. Often, as in the case of James and Vivian's house in East Melbourne, the formal parlor would have large, almost full-story windows that provided glimpses into the cottage garden at the front of the house.

Usually following the parlor was a series of bedrooms (two to three), typically small but with a Victorian coal fireplace as a central feature. The homes that were professionally renovated in the 1990s, as Dora's house across the street had been, often had a bathroom off of the master bedroom that extended one of the chief luxuries of the modern suburban home to residents of the renovated Victorian cottages. At the center of many of the renovated Victorian cottages in East Melbourne was the dining room, followed or adjoined by a more informal living room. The informal living room, although tastefully decorated, was typically the room where people made the most concessions to modern standards. Usually this room contained more comfortable furniture than the formal living room, as well as a television set. At the back of the house was the kitchen, in keeping with its placement in the original Victorian design. However, the most significant difference was that in contemporary East Melbourne cottages the kitchen was not separate from the house, which was always the case in original Victorian cottages.

Many people in East Melbourne attempted to construct a garden to complement their renovated historical house. The East Melbourne Group officially recommended the English cottage garden in order to keep the community's landscaping consistent with the historical nature of the architecture. Not everyone in East Melbourne had a fully developed cottage garden, but at minimum people tended to have some arrangement of exotic flowering plants, even if only in limited quantity. People also reproduced the asymmetry of the cottage garden rather than the formal design of some of the gardens of Mediterranean immigrants in the suburbs of Carlton or Brunswick, for instance. While some gardens had birdbaths and fruit trees, as an Italian garden was likely to have, East Melbourne gardens on the whole avoided concrete slabs, nonflowering bushes, and straight rows of flowers.

Given their eclectic mix of botanical species from around the world, the gardens in East Melbourne had more in common with the nineteenth-century bourgeois gardenesque version of the English cottage garden than with the original eighteenth-century peasant cottage gardens. It was not uncommon for East Melbourne gardeners to include native Australian species or bonsai plants in their gardens, but one would never confuse their gardens with a native Australian bush garden (discussed in the next chapter) or a Zen garden. People chose botanical varieties for their ability to create the effect of the English cottage garden. They chose plants that would add color, flowers, and interesting shape to the garden.

For most, the front garden had a small plot of soil for growing and a small front veranda (porch) on which people placed potted plants. Many also trained climbing vines to scale the decorative ironwork on the front of their Victorian terrace houses. Usually the back garden contained little to no uncovered ground. Most were covered with red brick that had lovely texture and an inviting softness resulting from age. The smallness of the back area, its access to a service alley, and the brick ground covering were telltale signs that the back of the house, when designed at the end of the nineteenth century, had served the utilitarian purposes of washing and cooking. In contrast, contemporary residents crafted beautiful patio gardens by using potted plants and by making the most of what little exposed soil remained. Although the bricked backyards were rarely torn up to allow residents access to the soil underneath, those residents who renovated houses in which the back had been covered in concrete usually did spend as much money as necessary to have the concrete torn out.

Lawns were rare. Instead residents used their small areas to cultivate urban-style gardens that used shared walls separating properties to grow climbing vines. Climbers like jasmine and wisteria

*Figure 8. English cottage garden outside Victorian worker's cottage in East Melbourne.*

softened the human-made surface and brought color up to eye level. The gardens were also shaped to create intimate sitting or eating areas and irregular paths that might lead to a storage shed or garage at the back of the yard. The back gardens in East Melbourne were particularly charming, lush oases for their urban dwellers and anyone lucky enough to be entertained in them.

Class was as complex in East Melbourne and the other rapidly gentrifying urban neighborhoods at the end of the twentieth century as it had been in England at the end of the eighteenth century, when the English countryside was being transformed into suburbs. As Anglo-Celtic Australians became interested in living closer to the city in the 1970s and rediscovered the charm of inner suburban historical houses, the spatial organization of class in Melbourne began to shift. Like many cities worldwide, the process of renovation in Melbourne required displacing the working-class residents. Some were Italian and Greek families who gladly moved to larger suburban houses in the outer suburbs, others were Koori families and working-class Anglo-Australian renters who moved into public housing, to inner suburbs yet to be gentrified, or to the outer suburbs.

The residents of East Melbourne incorporated into their description of their community stories of the histories of the people now displaced from East Melbourne. The traces of people who lived in East Melbourne before them added "color" to the history of their suburb. Peter, an East Melbourne resident and avid gardener, recounted with amusement how his house had been one of the many boardinghouses in East Melbourne whose tenants were considered to be morally suspect by respectable people in Melbourne. Dora, like a good archeologist, led a team of renovators who peeled away layers of imitation brick (often added by post–World War II immigrants from Italy and Greece) and room dividers to discover beautiful, turn-of-the-century moldings and cozy fireplaces. Susan, younger and bolder than the average garden club member, laughed with self-deprecating humor at the shady past of the house she had come to own. She narrated stories about the prostitutes and "two-bit actresses" among the boarders who had lived in the house she renovated and those across the street. Susan speculated about the prostitute who formerly lived across the street and was amused in remembering how she had been taken for a prostitute when she first moved to East Melbourne. She recounted, "She [the prostitute] probably disappeared into the dark streets of St. Kilda because she was far gone. And then when Ray and I went for membership at the Hilton Pool, they 'sussed' us out thoroughly. They thought we were two prostitutes coming in to work the hotel!"

People in this suburb enjoyed the layers of social and architectural history embedded in their community. They all had interesting stories of the genealogy of social history that they uncovered in the process of "restoring" the house to its colonial Victorian origins. To aid in this process, the local library also served as an archive for information about the original owners of the workers' cottages in East Melbourne. East Melbourne had become, through the residents' individual real estate speculations and renovations, a fashionable and affluent suburb in which to live. But the residents played down their good fortune with modesty by emphasizing the humble origin of their houses.

Despite a nostalgic narration of the former presence of other classes and cultures in East Melbourne, renovating these houses to recreate the workers' cottages always entailed the removal of most of the physical signs of the people who had lived in the houses since the beginning of the twentieth century. Doors and locks on individual rooms for boarders and prostitutes were eliminated, and signs of any ethnicity besides the Anglo-Celtic tradition were usually sacrificed in the effort to restore the house to what was perceived as a more authentic Victorian condition. The imitation brick and the carpeting were discarded and latticework was reinstalled on the outside. The cement paving in the backyard was dug up; flower gardens replaced the vegetable beds. Council ordinances were passed to prevent cultural practices that would lower property values or would offend others. For instance, in Carlton, another gentrified suburb that had historically attracted first-generation Italian immigrants, an ordinance was passed to prevent residents from keeping chickens. In East Melbourne, regulations restricted people from modifying their houses in a way that departed too radically from Victorian or Edwardian design.

A number of positive things resulted from gentrification. The inner suburbs in Melbourne tended to be safer from violent crime (although prime targets for house and car burglaries), and many historic buildings were well maintained. Geographer Sharon Zukin (1991) has pointed out that people involved in gentrification have

*Figure 9. Back garden of Victorian terrace house in East Melbourne.*

created a set of priorities—one that privileges historical context and special characteristics of place—that has successfully competed with a purely economic approach to urban development. Although Zukin's analysis comes out of a consideration of American cities, her argument has relevance for Australian cities in their development after World War II. She writes, "Since that time [1960s], however, gentrifiers have become so pervasive in all older cities of the highly industrialized world that their cultural preferences have been incorporated into official norms of neighborhood renewal and city planning" (192). In many instances, middle-class interest in urban neighborhoods like East Melbourne prevented them from being leveled for new office buildings or other types of development.

However, there is some irony in the fact that in the effort to recapture or restore the colonial "workers'" history in East Melbourne, most signs of working-class cultural forms were lost. The functional backyards of the Victorian workers were turned into gardens, and the signs of mid-twentieth-century working-class immigrants and boarding house residents were removed. Lower-class taste was effectively erased from the buildings and gardens. So although the Victorian workers were immortalized in the discourse of the present residents, the houses themselves, with their elaborate fireplaces and furnishings, bore almost no trace of them.

Again, Zukin describes this process of preserving older histories over more recent working-class cultural histories. She argues that such a class erasure is typical in a gentrification process fueled by the energies (and private budgets) of more highly educated people oriented toward the consumption of high culture and "trendier" styles. For this demographic, historical aesthetics (Edwardian, Federation, Victorian, etc.) hold a highly class-oriented appeal that working-class culture does not. In describing the classed nature of the taste of people who gentrified urban neighborhoods she writes, "Most of them anyway tend not to mourn the transformation of local working-class taprooms into 'ye olde' bars and 'French' bistros. By means of the building stock, they identify with an earlier group of builders rather than with the existing lower-class population, with the 'Ladies' Mile' of early-twentieth-century department stores instead of the discount stores that have replaced them" (1991, 193–94).

In East Melbourne, traces of the twentieth-century working-class and non-Anglo-Celtic residents were erased from the houses and gardens in favor of Victorian histories. And even though the modesty and humble origins of the houses were emphasized, only those elements of the original workers that would signify upper-class taste were preserved. So the "workers'" cottages ended up reproducing British colonialism and contemporary class privilege despite the fact that residents emphasized the neighborhood's previous diversity.

Tony Bennet comments on a similar move made by the Australian National Estate in its incorporation of Aboriginal identity into a unified representation of the nation: "Its raison d'être is to enfold diverse histories into one, often with the consequence that the histories of specific social groups are depoliticized as their relics come to serve as symbols of the essential unity of the nation, or to highlight its recently achieved unity, by standing for a divisiveness which is past" (1995, 149).

Similarly, the cultural and class differences that have existed in East Melbourne and Australia were enfolded into a single national history through the stories residents told about their houses and neighborhood. In many respects, the residents of East Melbourne constructed an unofficial national history with their renovated Victorian workers' cottages and cottage gardens. By "renovating" the past, they were reproducing an origin story about the Australian nation. The many renovations, neighborhood guidelines, and historical preservation restrictions functioned to reproduce Australia's history as British history; whereas in contrast, Chinese cultural forms that may have existed since the turn of the century, or working-class Greek and Italian aesthetic forms like fake brickwork on interior walls, were not targeted for historical preservation. It was only the Anglo-Celtic colonial working class that was identified as authentic history and worthy of preservation.

Most middle-class neighborhoods are encoded in ways that distance them from the cultural norms of the lower classes. As Stuart Hall has discussed in his work (1996), identity is constituted through the play of difference, a difference that, as Derridian deconstruction has shown, is not fixed but entails an endless construction of categories of meaning. For middle-class identity, the lower class is usually an important point of difference. In this respect, residents in East Melbourne were not unusual. East Melbourne residents signified upper-class taste with the many objects they incorporated into their homes and gardens. The incorporation of antique leaded glass and stained glass windows, heirlooms and expensive, labor-intensive plants were just some of the ways in which people reproduced the structure of symbolic space that signaled gentility and wealth. As Judith Kapferer notes about Australian housing, "The more closely a dwelling approximates to the traditional colonial homestead, the more desirable and prestigious it is conceived to be, even if (and perhaps particularly if) that dwelling happens to be in the city" (1996, 105).

Additionally, the working-class cottages in East Melbourne permitted the middle-class residents to participate in the national mythology that celebrated the "average bloke" or worker. By creating imagined links between themselves and the original workers ("battlers") of these Victorian cottages, residents were engaging in a similar romanticism of working-class poverty that English cottage gardeners did in post-Napoleonic England. Yet, they were also participating in a distinctly Australian ideal in which the working-class male embodied the nation. The working-class origins of the Victorian houses in which garden club members lived allowed residents to downplay their wealth in a country that prides itself on "pulling down tall poppies."[13]

In contemporary Australia, where people were debating national identity, those who defined Australia in terms of British-ness often defended their perspective by recourse to the "objective fact" that Australia's history and origins are Anglo-Celtic. And indeed, looking around at much of the architecture and "history" in Australia, there was much to support their argument. However, the practice of restoration in East Melbourne illustrates that British heritage is continually constructed in the present.[14] While other identities were recognized as part of Australia's present, Anglo-Celtic identity in particular was often privileged as the primary history within Australia's (multiracial, multicultural) history.

Although renovations are usually taken as a process of resurrecting some authentic beginning, it is more appropriate to see the Victorian era as a history that has been continually reproduced in contemporary Australia. It has continued to be added to the city and nation's landscape—added over layers of Aboriginal, Mediterranean, Chinese history in Australia—much like a fresh coat of paint. And yet the construction of historical neighborhoods and landscapes was often interpreted as neutral preservation, by both

British sympathizers and Republicans. Tony Bennet reminds us that contemporary interests and priorities inevitably shape our presentation of the past. He writes, "Similarly, the past, as embodied in historical sites and museums, while existing in a frame which separates it from the present, is entirely the product of the present practices which organize and maintain that frame" (1995, 130). While Bennet focuses his analysis on "official" sites of history such as museums and the National Estate, the spatial practices of the East Melbourne renovators clearly illustrate how national history is also produced by people in their everyday choices about which history or cultural form is assumed to be worthy of preservation.

National identity is usually taken to be static; however, to the extent to which it is popularly conceived to be produced, the nation is believed to be man-made through activities such as the construction of constitutions, literary or popular ballads, soldiers, etc., all of which are associated with the public sphere. Yet, if we understand nations, as Hobsbawm and Ranger (1983) do, as being largely legitimated through claims to heritage and the "invention of tradition," then the invisible labor of women in the definition and territorialization of the nation is important. Anne McClintock's description of the domestic woman under liberal rational ideology is very useful for us in considering the renovated Victorian workers' cottages and gardens in contemporary Melbourne. Women, positioned as safeguarders of tradition, are often the ones directing the design of homes and gardens. Within the domestic sphere, women direct the preservation of national history and thus actively assemble narrative and nonnarrative discourses about national identity. Since women's labor in the private sphere is generally trivialized and historical preservation is viewed as a passive project, women's spatial production of the nation generally goes unnoticed (outside of birthing new citizens and sewing during wars).

As contemporary spatial constructions, these nostalgic landscapes figured as an important political stake in reterritorializing Australia at the end of the twentieth century. For example, defining heritage in terms of British settlement provided a pro-British counterpoint to the critique of British imperialism by Republican supporters in Australia and by Aboriginal land rights activists. It was also a way in which the importance of Anglo-Celtic identity was reasserted in opposition to a strong republican movement that sought to redefine and limit Australia's ties to Great Britain. And as I explore in more depth in the final section of this chapter, it was also a means by which racial separateness was delineated in a multicultural social landscape. Not only did their restoration efforts and corresponding gardening practices function as a political vote in the ongoing cultural battle to define the nation, for some they also served as a response to the complexities and challenges that accompanied a multicultural environment. Far from being dated remnants, the tastes embedded in the English landscapes created in East Melbourne at the end of the twentieth century represented a dynamic relationship with contemporary questions about Australian identity and multiculturalism, and further, being misinterpreted as apolitical nostalgia, rather than as an active construction of Australian identity, helped empower this political perspective all the more.

## PERFORMING THE VILLAGE

In addition to garden design, life in the English rural village was recalled in contemporary East Melbourne through the social exchanges of residents. The patterns of sociability recalled the eighteenth-century picturesque English village that has been immortalized and updated in British situation comedies viewed on Australian television. The social gestures of East Melbourne Garden Club members and their own characterization of their community constructed their landscape as a British village in the heart of the urban Melbourne. Producing East Melbourne as a form of British landscape served to do more than reestablish an imagined correspondence between Australia and Britain at a time of republican political debate. It was also a means by which people responded to the challenges of an expanding multiracial, multicultural population.

The older residents, in particular, fostered the idea of a parallel between East Melbourne and village life. Through their everyday practices East Melbourne residents reproduced the rural village community popularly associated with England. Although many within this group were critical of aspects of England—Churchill's neglect of Australia's security during the World War II, Prince Charles' relationship problems—they appropriated the English country home as the best of Britain and community for their own era. A significant mechanism for doing this was to celebrate the interconnectedness of the residents, by speaking with pleasure about how friendly everyone was and by laughing at the misfits and "characters" of the kind that show up in any good British situation comedy or novel about village life. For instance, although she herself was a member of the garden club, Edith habitually referred to it as "the village glee club" as a way of poking fun at and celebrating the banality of their mission.

The retired people in East Melbourne frequently socialized over their small fences and through organizations like the garden club and the East Melbourne Group or at lunches organized on the first Sunday of every month. The younger families in East Melbourne knew many of their neighbors as well. They shared the burden of taking their children to private schools, socialized in the evenings, and attended occasional garden club meetings to stay connected to the older residents.

Since there was limited ethnic diversity in East Melbourne, the major social divide within the suburb was between homeowners and apartment dwellers. Apartment dwellers were excluded from many of the activities through which East Melbourne residents met. A few did attend the garden club meetings, and others formed friendships with residents through casual street conversations. However, in the main their social interactions were limited by the fact that they had no yards or other private spaces that allowed for interaction with the larger community. Their smaller units also inhibited apartment dwellers from having dogs or children, excluding them from two modes of meeting and talking with strangers in the small parks within East Melbourne. Additionally, apartment buildings had also been the harbinger of a denser residential population in the suburb, bringing many more cars and people per square acre and taxing the communal services and the patience of area homeowners. Although there had been apartment buildings in East Melbourne for more than fifty years, the continued threat of new developments kept intact a chasm between the two groups.

Many disparate, unrelated everyday behaviors contributed to the production of East Melbourne as the epitome of traditional community. A particularly overt way in which East Melbourne gardeners and other residents recreated rural England was through use of the term "village" to refer to their suburb. Calling it "the village" transformed it from an inner-city neighborhood into a stereotypical English village where neighbors walk the streets and everyone is familiar with one other. Judith walked her dog, Midge, several times a day and developed many relationships in the community, thus keeping abreast of the news and opinions of other residents. The staff of the George Street Café ordered a newspaper for Marion every day and delivered it, along with any requested pastries, to her house next door on particularly rainy days to keep her from slipping. People in the garden club organized "working bees" to create the monthly meeting notices. The carefully crafted meeting announcements were then hand delivered to several hundred houses in East Melbourne and parts of Richmond by a small brigade led by Judith and dog Midge.

Furthermore, in East Melbourne it was standard practice to strike up conversation or even request a plant clipping from another resident who was outside gardening. In fact, James and Vivian had taken to scheduling their gardening during off-peak walking hours since they spent so much time talking with friendly pedestrians that they had difficulty completing their tasks. Edith and Judith would occasionally meet and chat over a glass of sherry at the end of the day and exchange opinions about such political topics as the limits of tolerance for cultural diversity; Judith supported the fact that the government had designated English as the official language in Australia. While she sympathized with older immigrants who were not willing or able to learn a new language late in life, in general she argued for the importance of immigrants learning English. Often inclined to interject a humorous dimension to a topic, during the discussion of whether the community rubbish collection notices should be printed in several languages, Judith remarked ironically, "They should at least be able to take the trash out in English!" Judith and Edith would also chat about growing up in Victoria and compare impressions about books, music, and other things that might be on their minds at the close of the day.

Several of the women in East Melbourne recounted with humor encounters they had with fellow East Melbourne residents. In the following excerpt, a garden club member, Iris, spoke with amusement about an elderly woman who habitually scolded her for neglecting her plants.

> There's a dear old lady, an English lady, who comes along, and quite a long time ago I put a few—you know, remember we had the man on the cactus talking about cactus—and I put some out on the window

sill there. Do you know that she knocks on the door and said, "You haven't been watering your plants again." I said, "I've just watered them this morning." She said, "Well, it must be weeks." She said, "I wondered whether I should knock on the door and tell you" . . . Oh, I laughed, you know. I thought, "Isn't that funny." But every time she goes to the shop, every day practically, she peers in at every little plant, you know.

Iris was delighted, rather than offended, by this woman's remarks about her gardening. And indeed, the encounter had the sort of irony one might find in a British situation comedy about village life. But neither Iris's experience, nor her amused response, seemed to be an isolated event. On a different occasion, Judith narrated an encounter with a similar theme as she showed me around her garden.

I have a funny story about that, stop me if I have told you. But I was out pulling a couple of weeds in my so-called front garden one day, and a lady came along and said, "You're the secretary of the garden club, aren't you?" And I said, "Oh yes." And she said, "Hmm. I would have thought you would have had a better garden than this." And I said, "No, I am too busy being the secretary of the garden club to do any gardening!" [laughter]

The humor in these two situations is interesting and perplexing. Both women were recounting stories in which women, previously unacquainted with them, approached them to criticize their gardens. The humor depends on an inherent irony. One way to read the irony is that a stranger was violating middle-class norms of privacy: not only was each woman giving her opinion where it had not been solicited, but also she was giving a negative opinion. Both were bluntly chastising the narrators for falling below accepted community standards.

One might wonder why neither Iris nor Judith took offense. However, their response celebrates what is popularly imagined to be village life, where nosy old ladies police the morality of younger ones. If that is the case, perhaps we might read Iris and Judith, both of whom were past sixty years of age, as flattered to have someone scold them like schoolgirls. It was also ironic that someone should scold them for neglect or poor gardening, given their active involvement in the garden club and the community more generally. Rather than creating feelings of alienation, nosy neighbors allowed these older women to feel embedded in and physically safe within community, despite the fact that they lived in modern, urban Australia.

Ironic stories of nosy neighbors and odd characters functioned to construct a romantic social and physical landscape in which old-fashioned community survived in the heart of one of the most urban areas of Australia. This was possible in large part because, despite substantial cultural diversity in the abutting suburbs of Richmond and Fitzroy, East Melbourne was ethnically and economically homogeneous. That is to say, its status as a village was possible, in large part, because of its cultural homogeneity. The pleasant, spontaneous conversations that provided a sense of belonging were possible because everyone spoke the same language; unsolicited advice of strangers about one's garden was humorous because everyone agreed on what a garden should look like. And if there was any doubt, council ordinances forbidding people from keeping chickens, and local historical codes regulating house facades ensured consensus. Such structural factors as these discouraged diversity, even if other ethnic groups could have afforded the housing prices in East Melbourne. They silently and invisibly protected the borders of the suburb.

While the residents of East Melbourne were not troubled by the disappearing countryside in the way in which eighteenth-century Britons may have been, they too experienced ambivalence about the changing physical and social landscape in which they lived. The homogeneity underpinning the sense of village community East Melbourne residents produced at once allowed them a sense of safety and, as well, stood in tension with the democratic values people had about the importance of diversity and inclusion.

Paul Gilroy has written about the way in which the potential threats of the urban and of blacks to white social order has been expressed through the image of the defenseless white woman and the black youth (usually male and young). In *Ain't No Black in the Union Jack* he discusses a particularly effective image used by anti-immigrant groups in Britain that depicted a frail elderly woman living in fear in her neighborhood and within her own home. This narrative of national decay produced the black immigrant as lawless and a threat to the national community and, at the same time, used elderly frail white women to represent the vulnerability of the nation.[15]

Images of urban decay in Melbourne's inner suburbs have existed historically, but they circulated in slightly different ways in

Melbourne than they did in Gilroy's description of contemporary England. The inner suburbs of Melbourne had been represented as a locus of moral degradation and slums for much of the century (see Birch 1994 and Kapferer 1996). Yet because there had been gradual, and by the end of the twentieth century extensive, gentrification of the inner suburbs, there was a general sense of safety and optimism about living close to the city center in Melbourne's inner suburbs (neighborhoods). Further, given that in Melbourne there was a relatively small number of blacks (few Aboriginal Australians compared with other cities and small population of immigrants from Africa), discourses about urban crime rarely fixed on blacks in the way that scholars writing about the British, South African, or United States context have identified. Nonetheless, like many people in Melbourne, residents in East Melbourne with whom I interacted were aware of and concerned about urban crime as it related to certain immigrant groups. Most tended to keep their doors closed and locked when they were inside, and some showed concern about the safety of my bicycle even when I had locked it to a fixed object on the footpath (sidewalk). And all were aware of news stories that appeared with regularity about the violence associated with "Asian triads" in Melbourne. While these notions of crime in the Melbourne context did not focus specifically on blacks, they were often racialized and articulated a sense of threat from Asian immigrants who had criminal links with their countries of origin, as I discuss at more length in chapter 4. Given this context, the spatial production of East Melbourne as a British-style village offered participating individuals a sense of community and safety that countered the urban legends about violence and decay that circulated in the city.

As I have mentioned, East Melbourne was one of the most urban communities in Australia. It was a kind of island in that it existed as a relatively homogenous community bordered by either parks or busy streets that buffered it from two of the city's most racially and economically diverse communities. As one garden club member, Thomas, observes:

> It's interesting in terms of ethnicity, we haven't had a very big Asian population in East Melbourne. I don't know why that should be. There will be—I mean I happen to know families of partial Chinese

descent, for instance. But they are the descendants of long term—they're not recent arrivals. But I don't know—but the school here has a good preponderance of children from Vietnam. And very nice they are too. They use the library here. I think their parents, very few of them actually live in East Melbourne. I ran into them and thought what very nice youngsters they are. Really well behaved and very happy.

We're at the borderline of a very big Vietnamese community, a very big Greek community but I don't, off hand, know of anyone of Greek extraction in East Melbourne. There's no reason why it shouldn't be so—it just hasn't been so.

To a certain extent, the high price of real estate in East Melbourne might explain why few immigrants from Vietnam lived in the suburb since most came to Australia as refugees with few financial resources. However, economics alone would not explain why other ethnic groups who had entered the middle and upper middle class in higher numbers (such as the Chinese, Greeks, or Italians) were not part of the East Melbourne community. During this conversation, Thomas was anxious that this lack of ethnic diversity (despite the Vietnamese community next to East Melbourne) not appear to be a consequence of hostility from him or anyone else in the community.

And indeed, there were few signs that individual hostility kept East Melbourne homogenous. In fact, East Melbourne was not so unusual from other middle-class communities in multicultural contexts (cf. Caldeira 1996 and 2000; Ellin 1997; and Low 1997) that fortress or enclave as a means of protecting residents from the dangers (real or imagined) that racial diversity historically has held for whites.

In East Melbourne, people were buffered from some of the challenges of diversity not in such direct ways as putting up gates around their community, but through their construction of themselves as a British-style community. Their spatial practices promoted a vision of the country in a way that implied continued links to Britain at a moment when republicanism was being debated in formal political circles and informally in everyday conversations. And it allowed people to appreciate multiculturalism from a distance. For instance, many wandered over to Richmond with great regularity to eat at Vietnamese restaurants or enjoy the open markets of the Vietnamese vendors; but the construction of identity that residents created through their imagined village and through design regulations helped minimize the anxieties that cultural contact often creates.

The spatial segregation Thomas described facilitated the sense of British community with which this chapter has been concerned. People all spoke the same language and shared similar norms about the appropriate balance in being involved in each other's business (offer unsolicited opinions about flowers, but not, for instance, about how to raise their children or other more private or controversial issues). They shared the same "tastes" insofar as they shared similar norms about what is clean, visually appealing, and in general, desirable. In more diverse neighborhoods, the pleasure of community is sometimes hindered by battles over noise and smells, by disagreements about whether it is acceptable to grow corn or raise chickens in one's front yard, and by the fact that residents cannot speak the same language. In an atmosphere of change in the city, the rural imaginings of English village life reconstituted urban Melbourne as a much more manageable landscape. The more manageable kinds of differences and misunderstandings that are found in village life—nosy neighbors, petty crime—took prominence over the very significant issues of difference such as language, race, and cultural mores that confronted Melbourne as a whole. The re-creation of a community in the shape of the English country village also fostered an environment that felt safe and friendly for the many elderly residents of East Melbourne.

Of course, it is quite possible that people with different tastes or social norms (be they a result of cultural or class difference, or simply individual idiosyncrasies) might move into East Melbourne. However, the appreciation of historical preservation and other aspects of the collective aesthetic in East Melbourne, in fact, had been institutionalized. They were protected or enforced (depending on your perspective) by building regulations that sought to preserve the historic style and details of the houses and community and through "recommendations" issued to the rest of the community by the East Melbourne Group.

And of course, these regulations enforced taste along class lines, as well as along cultural/racial lines. Marion, president of the garden club, described her attempts to clarify for the rest of the group the distinction between a backyard and a back garden. She explained,

"I gave a lecture to the garden club once on the stupidity of calling the back garden the 'backyard.' I can't *bear* it. To me, a backyard is a place in the slums, where it is mostly paved. Broken paving of course. A broom hanging somewhere and a dustbin, and nothing else. Perhaps a dead fern."

Marion delineated with refreshing bluntness the way in which landscape is a means of encoding class status. As she is one of the only first-generation Britons in the Garden Club, her garden club lecture about terminology has a humorous ring of the authentic Brit teaching the colonials how to be civilized. In this example, Marion gave a linguistic lesson in how to produce desirable landscapes. This exercise, much like the more official community regulations, helped demarcate class and cultural distinctions.

Marion's frankness in advocating distinctions between gardeners in East Melbourne and other social groups was more pronounced than in many other cases in East Melbourne. What is clear from Thomas's description in this section, a description that paralleled the impression I formed in interacting with others in East Melbourne, was that on an individual level people supported diversity and did not advocate segregation of any kind. In one of our discussions Thomas contrasted the Australians' openness to diversity with the racism he had witnessed in Chicago years earlier. Thomas, like many in the community, wanted Australia to be a tolerant society. To underscore this goodwill, he eagerly affirmed his approval of the Vietnamese children who used the East Melbourne library and made it clear that he perceived them to be well-behaved citizens. However, in Thomas's discussion of his plans to move into a community in the northwestern suburbs and his wife's ultimate refusal, we get a hint at some of the anxiety people nevertheless felt at the prospect of living in a community that had great racial and cultural diversity. Thomas describes:

> My daughter lives over in Flemington and that's an old suburb. There would have been changes; I think they call it gentrification, don't they? Some areas, and that's been an area also, of course, where they have very big housing commission developments and that has been again a large Vietnamese population over there and changes and that kind of thing.
>
> But as far as I know it hasn't been negative. It's just change. But I can't think of anybody who has a sense of there's been a problem arising from it. Although I myself bought a house over there with a

view of moving. But when it came to the point, my wife didn't want to leave East Melbourne, although she agreed with the decision to buy the house. I thought it would be nice to live near my daughter. That was an expensive mistake.

Thomas's discussion of his plans to move to a more ethnically diverse neighborhood to be closer to his daughter further illustrates the conflict with which people seemed to struggle between gaining a sense of security from homogeneity and enforcing it through a more contemporary form of spatial segregation. Segregation that was enforced through the regulation of taste and history (and obviously a strategy available to middle- and upper-middle-class whites much more so than working-class whites), was devoid of all language about race. However the effect on some level was to manage racial and cultural diversity. Contemporary forms of spatial segregation created through *policy* and *taste* meant that people could manage difference without overt action on their part. They enabled Anglo-Celtic Australians in particular to support multiculturalism in principle as an expression of democracy. Nevertheless, at moments people ended up with an ambivalence similar to that expressed by Thomas. They had a sense of unease that they, in fact, do not participate in the diversity of multicultural Australia that they promoted (outside of eating in ethnic restaurants) and simultaneously gain comfort from the fact that they had done nothing individually to maintain the social and spatial distance that allowed them to enjoy the political simplicity of a more homogenous community.

Thus, manipulating the landscape in particular was a strategy by which residents held on to democratic principles but tempered some of the complications of multiculturalism. Cultivating a picturesque (national) landscape was a means by which people responded to the way multicultural population had deterritorialized Australia; that is, multiculturalism has thrown into question what Australia's history should be, opened up to question whether Australians should celebrate Captain Cook or the First Fleet, raised the dilemma of whether English should be required of everyone or whether public notices should be printed in many different languages. And the list of difficult political questions goes on.

This chapter illustrates how aesthetic sensibilities, such as the picturesque, inform people's spatial practice. These sensibilities and

practices are very much intertwined with political, cultural, and social issues. That the picturesque in Australia marks a link to Britain
is often assumed in Australia. Many people offered me an interpretation of East Melbourne residents as people hanging on to a former
vision of Australia. This interpretation viewed the cultivation of
British cultural forms as a form of unfashionable false consciousness and as a static identity.

However, the use of an aesthetic sensibility to territorialize
Australia was anything but static. Comparing the picturesque in
nineteenth-century Britain, in colonial Australia, and in Australia
at the end of the twentieth century underscores how the picturesque
has been a tool for expressing a cosmology through the manipulation of the landscape. This manipulation can be done through a picturesque "sensibility," that is, through how one looks at a landscape
and in the way the elements of a landscape organize themselves in
the mind and produce pleasure. And the picturesque can involve
physically manipulating space by carefully training a rose vine to
climb a trellis or by performing a form of village community life.
The national landscapes of East Melbourne gardeners were active, political assertions of Australian identity and location in the
world. And they demonstrate that Australia's history is and always
has been intricately connected to its geography, often through nonnarrative forms and often within intimate spaces.

### "YOU REALIZE, I HOPE, THAT THE LADIES IN EAST MELBOURNE AREN'T EXACTLY TYPICAL . . ."

This study as a whole explores the gardeners' construction of intimate natural landscapes in the domestic sphere, in contrast with the
public landscapes of the Fitzroy Police. In many ways, the differences between these two ethnographic sites confirm the traditional
gendered binary opposition between culture and nature, public and
private, and public and intimate. Given that men and women are
very much channeled into separate public and private spheres in
Western society and that this study examines how people produce
the nation in their everyday spaces, we are not surprised to find such
contrasts in place-making activities between the police and the East
Melbourne gardeners. It is perhaps not surprising that a group of
fairly traditional women and retired men would shape the nation
by domesticating natural landscapes and that their activities would

be less overtly connected to social and state power. And it is not surprising that men's activities on the whole would take place in the public realm and entail rationalizing space.

But the ethnographic material in this study undermines these binary categories at the very moment it reinscribes them. One of the lessons of which we are reminded in an analysis of the history of space and nation in Australia is that nature is inevitably already a cultural category. Nature exists as a physical reality independent of our imagination, yet its meaning for us is always circumscribed by our cultural constructions of it. Thus, the disciplined landscapes of the East Melbourne gardeners are very much cultural spaces. Further, while women's gardening activity in Australia has been located in the private sphere, it has always been part of a larger project of defining identity in Australia; their gardening and designing activities have therefore always been a political (and therefore "public" or social) activity. As the historical material about cottage gardens in Australia and the contemporary landscapes of East Melbourne gardeners suggest, the cottage garden has been one realm of agency in a larger conversation about nation and social distinctions (be they racial or class). The many fine analyses of the construction of national identity through literature or other cultural practices, such as beauty contests (see Bhabha 1990; Benet-Weiser 1999), have taught us that political identity and hegemony are produced through cultural activities that take place outside the formal corridors of political institutions. However, these studies have still concentrated on *public* activities. The spatial practices of the East Melbourne gardeners are especially interesting in part because they produce nation in intimate, domestic spaces. Their spatial practices are part of a longer tradition of significant social and political work that has been accomplished in these intimate spaces—whether reproducing white civilization through hygiene regiments (see Cooper and Stoler 1998) or marking Western bourgeois identity through the display of leisure (see McClintock 1995; Suleri 1992).

The East Melbourne Garden Club "ladies" fell into categories that are very often dismissed socially and politically: they were economically well-off, white, elderly women and some had never worked outside of the house. In short, they fit the profile of a person to whom society accords very little importance. And, given current academic trends, at first blush they seem far too privileged to interest social theorists. The hierarchy of social importance was encapsulated nicely in the concern expressed by the son-in-law of one East Melbourne gardener upon hearing that I was conducting most of my research on the production of political identity in Australia within the East Melbourne Garden Club. He was silent for a moment as the implications of my statement sank in, then responded with the embarrassed air one might have when telling a near stranger that she has spinach stuck to her front tooth. He replied gingerly, "You realize, I hope, that the ladies in East Melbourne aren't exactly typical?"

The son-in-law then recommended that I interview people in migrant communities who could give me a much better sense of Australian national identity since Australia is a "multicultural nation, after all." Perhaps part of the son-in-law's concern came from a sense that research means *survey research,* and therefore must be representative. However, the son-in-law's anxiety also echoed a larger perspective among people in Australia who were excited by former Prime Minister Keating's vision of Australia as multicultural and as post-British. The son-in-law himself took much pride in the Australian native garden he cultivated at his beach house outside of Melbourne. In light of this political perspective, it would be disturbing to him to think that a group of older, Anglo-Celtic women busily planting cottage gardens and drinking sherry in the evenings would be chosen to define the nation.

The "ridiculousness" of the wealth, education, and desire to reproduce British cultural forms is captured in the writing of cultural theorist Stephen Knight as he describes Australian cottage gardeners:

> It was flowers, mostly, that led the cottage garden, fragile ones, white, pink or delicately red. They matched the blooms on the curtains and chair covers inside, and the Peter Pan collars and floral hair clips of the superior peasants who . . . worked on their gardens with expensive gloves, elegant tools, kneeling pads and, above all, books. (Knight 1990, 31)

Knight's description is particularly economical as he manages to mock the activities of Australian cottage gardeners in terms that also remind us of the unimportance of all things feminine—blooms on the curtains, Peter Pan collars, floral hair clips, etc. By disqualifying this social group on account of their expensive reproductions of peasant cultural forms, Knight also caricatures cultural forms associated with the middle-class, suburban women.

Needless to say, the general social unimportance of the older women in East Melbourne was rendered even more questionable by the fact that they reproduced British cultural forms in Australia. They did so despite the popular "recognition" that Australia was not a continuation of Britain, but instead is located in Asia and is capable of formulating its own indigenous cultural forms. In this respect, the East Melbourne gardeners approximated a little too well Dame Edna Everage, the fictional suburbanite from the Melbourne suburb Moonee Ponds, who worships the British Royals. Barry Humphries, who plays Edna Everage by dressing in drag, has made a very successful career of satirizing the Australian suburbanite whose idolization of British royalty and "class" marks her own Australian banality.

Moreover, younger people outside of East Melbourne often explained the reorientation of Australian national identity in terms of a generational change; it was presented as a shift contemporary Australians were making away from the "colonialist mentality" of previous generations. As such, elderly white Australians were at times used symbolically to represent older forms of a national false consciousness that the nation was in the process of shedding.

Thus, the representation of women like the East Melbourne gardeners allowed other groups within Australia to mark their political positions and cultural forms as "new," "progressive," and distinct from the "colonial mentality" of the European settlers who abused the Australian landscape as part of its imperial project.

The next section examines the way in which members of the East Melbourne gardening community also marked their difference from the colonial practices of settlers in Australia and as such complicates the idea of the East Melbourne "ladies" as anachronistic. Although they cultivated an Anglo-Celtic history in Australia, their cultural landscape was modified to also include the symbolic use of native Australian vegetation to mark their loyalty to Australia and express their critique of colonial practices. This political, spatial practice has some significant similarities with proponents of the Australian native garden movement whom I discuss in the next chapter. They express a common critique of the denigration of Australia during colonialism in aesthetic terms and in terms of ecological destruction. However, in East Melbourne, where most people reproduced an aesthetic of British village life, this colonial critique is launched through the placement of Heidelberg-style scenes of the "natural" Australian landscape inside their homes.

## AUSTRALIAN LANDSCAPE PAINTING: SEEING AUSTRALIA "AS IT REALLY IS" IN EAST MELBOURNE LIVING ROOMS

Many people within and outside of the East Melbourne Garden Club remarked on a profound change in attitudes about the aesthetic value of the Australian landscape. They suggested that being able to recognize that Australia was a beautiful land marked a change in people's pride and commitment to the country. Many in the East Melbourne Garden Club differentiated between their parents' generation and their own in their appreciation of the look of Australia's natural landscape. Although most did not identify it as a process of colonization, people regularly noted that the homesickness of earlier generations of Anglo-Celtic settlers led them to recreate England in Australia. They pointed to landscape art as a particularly telling example of this misrecognition of Australia's worth by colonials. Instead of seeing the "truth" about the colors and quality of the Australian bush, early landscape painters depicted Australia so that it resembled the British countryside with its colors, vegetation, and soft light.

Eva, a member of the East Melbourne Garden Club, remembered her mother's futile attempts to grow fragile European plants typically found in the English cottage garden, such as camellias and roses, in the arid landscape of South Australia. Margaret, another East Melbourne gardener, emphasized her appreciation for Australia in opposition to earlier generations of Australians who expressed their longing for Britain through their reshaping the landscape, as Eva's mother had done, as well as in their misrepresentation of the Australian landscape. Margaret contrasted her awareness of the beauty of the Australian landscape with both colonial landscape painters and her parents' generation when she explained:

> When they first were out here, they painted everything as if it were European, the European trees and such. They didn't like the colors that were here, the blue-greens. And then gradually, the next generation did. They started to see the beautiful blue-gray in the gums [eucalyptus trees]. And I think other things have followed; art usually leads. And so people started seeing that, yes, there is a kind of beauty here. I think they saw it as a very harsh country . . . when we were

children, we heard nothing. It was really just to tell us about the explorers and they were really going quite slowly with camels and everything. But as children, we got such a picture of it being such a ghastly country with shimmering stones. And really, it's quite beautiful.

Margaret recounts a change in national consciousness within Australia symbolized by people's changing perspective of the landscape and appreciation of the eucalyptus tree. Although Margaret suggests that after the first generation of settlers, people began to recognize and appreciate Australia's worth, her memories of the way in which Australia was represented to her as a child in the first half of the twentieth century indicate that the process of change spanned more than a single generation.

Art historian John Brack throws light on Margaret's description when he writes, "The Australian artist's attitude, then, has been governed largely by the Romantic sensibility. Yet both artists and the public have always supposed that what the painter was trying to do was concern himself with the 'truth' about this 'strange' country" (Brack 1968, 5).

As noted in the previous chapter, much interest in Australia as a bucolic escape from England was a response to rapid industrialization and urbanization. People also responded to these dramatic social and economic changes with a heightened and nostalgic appreciation of nature. Since the first settlements in Australia coincided with the Romantic Revolution, it is not surprising that a romantic preoccupation with the landscape dominated aesthetic concerns in Australia.

Margaret indicated a break in artistic and popular sensibilities from a kind of false consciousness that originally dominated depictions of the landscape in Australia. The Heidelberg School, a dominant tradition in Australia from the late nineteenth century through the first half of the twentieth century, has been credited with finally creating a "realistic" depiction of the Australian bush; it has received credit for being the first to accurately render the vegetation, quality of light, and the distinctive colors of the Australian landscape.

As a style of painting, it had not merely gained public support but had generated enough imitators that Heidelberg School–inspired landscapes hung on the walls of more than half the garden club members with whom I spoke in East Melbourne. The Heidelberg

School is actually situated in the Impressionist tradition, but it was overlaid with additional moral and patriotic privilege by much of the Australian public. In their oral histories, people identified the "foreignness" of the original landscape paintings insofar as the early painters represented the Australian landscape as if it were European. In contrast, the Heidelberg tradition was perceived as authentically Australian and as inspired solely by elements from within Australia. The nationalist use of Heidelberg landscapes does not acknowledge the way this tradition also borrowed from European impressionism. Instead Heidelberg landscape paintings were spoken of as reflecting an unmediated relationship between people and place and treated as testimony of the rootedness of the people who identified with the Heidelberg tradition. Typically, this connection was asserted tacitly by noting how the aesthetic of British colonials reflected their displacement.

Art historian Anne-Marie Willis unpacks some of the moral significance associated with the Heidelberg School and links it to the issue of national identity more broadly.

> Why so much significance is given to the idea of artists discovering "the real Australia" is that this is a metaphor for national liberation—throwing off the shackles of a European vision, installing the distinctively local pride of place in both high and popular culture (the art of the Heidelberg School belongs to both), taking possession of a new land, feeling at home in it. The production and circulation of visual imagery then is closely bound up with the psychological occupation of the land. (Willis 1993, 64)

Margaret's narrative seems to bear out Willis' thesis that the Heidelberg School symbolized a cultural emancipation from Europe for many Australians and a psychological occupation not only for the artists, but also for all of those who now "see Australia as it really is" in their appreciation of the Heidelberg School style.

Not only did many people in East Melbourne have paintings of the Australian landscape in their homes, these paintings were typically given a highly privileged position in the home. They were treated as high culture and hung in formal living rooms, dining rooms, and entranceways where they would be highly visible to guests. They were always set off in formal, expensive frames.

Susan Stewart's analysis of collecting and miniatures in *On Longing* helps us understand how these landscapes allow individuals to incorporate the national past into the personal present. Her insights into souvenirs are suggestive in thinking about the display of landscape paintings in East Melbourne:

> The souvenir reduces the public, the monumental, and the three-dimensional into the miniature, that which can be enveloped by the body, or into the two-dimensional representation, that which can be appropriated within the privatized view of the individual subject . . . Temporally, the souvenir moves history into private time. Hence the absolute appropriateness of the souvenir as *calendar*. Such a souvenir might mark the privatization of a public symbol (say, the Liberty Bell miniaturized), the juxtaposition of history with a personalized present. (1993, 137–38)

Once it had become a significant national symbol, the miniaturizing of the Australian landscape allowed people to incorporate it into their own personal aesthetic and subjectivity. The national imaginary (native landscape) as miniature allows it to be incorporated symbolically into the personal. Further, by displaying their appreciation of the Australian landscape (painted as it "really is"), people were actively inserting themselves into a collective national subjectivity that had a "healthy" appreciation of its territorial position.

Given the proliferation of English cottage gardens in East Melbourne, one might be surprised by garden club members' homage to Australian landscape painting within their carefully restored Victorian terrace houses. However, in discussing their thoughts about the Australian landscape, even people with impeccable English cottage gardens often pointed to their paintings as illustration of their deep emotional connection to Australia and love of its "unique beauty." Thus, despite their reproduction of the English cottage garden style in their city homes, many members of this community demonstrated their recognition of Australia's beauty by elevating it to high art on their living room walls. Not unlike the native garden "fanatics," other members of the garden club used the Australian landscape to display that they were loyal Australians, distinct from earlier colonial generations who slavishly imitated Britain in Australia. Although others might categorize their English cottage gardens as an unreflective reproduction of a "former" national identity in Australia premised on Britishness, the honor with which they treated the Australian landscape by elevating it to high art enabled them to escape the charge of having a false consciousness about their national identity that fails to see the true worth of Australia. Their aesthetic constituted a spatial practice insofar as they were reproducing Australia as a certain kind of place (a non-European place) and they were asserting a connection (loyalty, love, undistorted recognition) between themselves and the (natural/national) landscape.

In his research Andrew Lattas argues that Australians collectively represent themselves as alienated from the Australian environment; although this alienation is presented as a kind of absence of national identity, it is actually a means of defining national subjectivity: "This conceptual space of alienation mediates national selfhood. It produces nationalism by continuously calling on people to reflect on their collective sense of self. The separation and distancing of Australians from their environment creates a conceptual space for the nation's identity, it posits a space of subjectivity that we are invited to occupy" (1990, 51).

Moreover, Lattas argues that with the discursive construction of themselves as alienated from an authentic self and from the landscape, white settler Australians manage to reimagine their claim to the land and thereby recuperate Aboriginal dissent. He writes, "Their suffering becomes white settler society's right of ownership to the land, the means by which they are reconciled and enter into communion with it and its original inhabitants" (1990, 56).

The ethnographic material from the garden club supports Lattas's observation of how contemporary Australians employ a sense of alienation from the landscape in producing a national subjectivity. However, the spatial practices and overall self-positioning of white Australians in East Melbourne illustrate how this process is conceptualized as a failing of earlier generations in Australia and presented in *contrast* to contemporary Australians. People marked earlier generations of Australians as alienated, more so than they used alienation from the landscape as a description of their own subjectivity. Repositioned as capable of seeing the truth about the beauty of Australia, even people who continued to imagine Australia in relation to a historical connection to Britain could distance themselves from some of the violence of colonialism. Coding Britishness as Australia's history and the natural Australian landscape as their contemporary national consciousness, people in East Melbourne reterritorialized the nation among many complicated political and moral considerations.

# 2

## Going Native

*The flora, fauna and landscape of a nation contribute to the identification of a national soul.*

— GORDON FORD, AUSTRALIAN LANDSCAPE DESIGNER

Although most members of the East Melbourne Garden Club were firm loyalists to "exotic" plants (imported species) and had a penchant for the English cottage garden form for their own urban gardens, some members were very interested in the ecological push to plant "native" (indigenous) plants. Similar to that of many people who promote native gardening in other parts of Australia and worldwide,[1] the aesthetic of native garden proponents was articulated in terms of a larger philosophical agenda about environmental protection. In Australia and among members of the East Melbourne Garden Club, however, native Australian gardening was also very heavily intertwined with ideas about nation and colonialism. It was a means by which people crafted a vision for Australia and contested other political agendas. The spatial practices of East Melbourne Garden Club members and people within the larger community in Melbourne allow us to see how the native garden aesthetic functioned as a means through which people defined their national identity, responded to British imperialism, and redefined their relationship to Aboriginal people.

## THE (BRITISH) ROOTS OF THE AUSTRALIAN
## NATIVE GARDEN MOVEMENT

What was referred to as the "native garden movement" was not a movement in the traditional sense. There were no official spokespersons, political rallies, or political pins. It was a discourse and set of practices about nature, aesthetics and, at times, about Australian identity. People took different positions in relation to native Australian vegetation (usually called "natives"). Some members of the gardening club perceived indigenous planting as an important political and ecological corrective and contributed their energy to this cause either in their domestic gardens or by working with community groups who undertook planting in the "bush."[2] Others did not donate their labor or money to support the cause but agreed with it in principle; still others were critical of the moral overtones often associated with native vegetation because they found them naive or because they were offended by the way native vegetation was used as a reason for denigrating Australia's cultural ties to Britain. But everyone was familiar with the general argument behind planting native species, since this perspective carried a lot of social authority in the larger society. The argument for the importance of protecting native Australian vegetation was more than just an aesthetic perspective. It also constituted a moralizing discourse about nation and ecology.

The native Australian gardening aesthetic was part of a broader "natural style" garden design that rejected formal, classical landscape design in favor of asymmetry. The natural style promotes *genus loci* (the special characteristics of a place), rather than approaching the garden as a collector's space unrelated to the larger surroundings. This style has its roots in eighteenth-century Britain; it can be traced back to the serpentine paths of William Kent and the efforts of Lancelot "Capability" Brown and Humphry Repton to blur the distinction between garden and English wilderness on the estates of aristocratic clients.[3] The efforts of these men were important contributions in Great Britain to a more general rejection of Napoleonic rationalism in design (Jellicoe and Jellicoe 1995). The naturalist style represented not only a different set of aesthetic choices about vegetation and form but also a different approach to nature. In the mid-eighteenth century, Capability Brown referred to his landscape design as "improving" nature, which reflected his philosophy of preserving the integrity of the natural landscape and simply regenerating it by replanting thousands of trees in the English countryside. Geoffrey and Susan Jellicoe describe this shift in their history of landscape design: "Nature was no longer subservient to man, but a friendly and equal partner that could provide inexhaustible interest, refreshment and moral uplift" (1995, 233).

The work of Capability Brown and others was connected to the picturesque cottage garden style discussed at length in the previous chapter in that, like the picturesque, the "natural style" was part of the larger picturesque aesthetic known as the English landscape school. Both branches of this school (picturesque cottage garden and the natural style) celebrated British species through asymmetry and informality in design. They differed insofar as the picturesque style was typically articulated as a poetic, romantic response to the environment, whereas the natural style was a pragmatic emphasis on "improvement" and on blurring the distinction between garden and natural countryside. Eventually, the naturalism underpinning both branches of the English landscape school was usurped by the gardenesque style as the dominant landscape trend in nineteenth-century England. The cottage garden style proved more malleable and was adapted to gardenesque principles, which replaced the natural and asymmetrical approach with more formal planning and labor-intensive exotic species. Gardenesque landscape design, embraced by the rising bourgeoisies, drew on the many exotic species made available in England in the nineteenth century by British imperial expansion. It is interesting to note that during the gardenesque heyday of the nineteenth century, there was fascination in botanical circles with unfamiliar species shipped back to England from Australian colonials such as Georgiana Molloy. It was the gardenesque version of the cottage garden that was reproduced in colonial and contemporary Australian suburbs.

Later letters (1830–43) written by Georgiana Molloy from the Western Australian colonial settlements of Augusta and Vasse to relatives and acquaintances document her growing sense of home in the Australian colonies, marked by her collection and cultivation of native Australian vegetation. She is an early example of the emerging curiosity, love, and respect for the Australian bush and the growing understanding of the value of native species. Her cultivation of

Australian species in her domestic garden and her botanical collecting and categorizing were indicative of her recognition of Australia as culturally significant. This was reflected in the letter to Captain James Mangles of the Royal Navy when she described one of the Australian species she was collecting for him:

> I beheld a Tree of great beauty . . . The flowers are of the purest white and fall in long tresses from the stem. Some of its pendulous blossoms are from three to five fingers in length and these wave in the breeze like the snow wreaths; they are of such a downy white feathery appearance, and emit a most delicious perfume resembling the bitter almond; and like all human, or rather mortal, delicacies, how quick these lovely flowers fall from the stalk on being collected. (March 14, 1840, quoted in Lines 1994, 283)

Despite her initial cultivation of the "homesick garden,"[4] collecting Australian botanical species enabled Molloy to develop a sense of home and identity. As William Lines notes about her later years in the colonies, "Whereas her neighbors had seen a wilderness in need of taming, she had uncovered a natural beauty beyond compare" (1994, 267).

Molloy is also an interesting figure because, as William Lines's biography of her makes clear, the collection of Australian botany that she carefully organized and shipped to Britain circulated as part of a larger interest in exotic species and the gardenesque movement in England in the nineteenth century. While many people were planting "homesick gardens" in Australia that aspired to reproduce Britain in the Australian colonies, Molloy was beginning what would become a more general structure of feeling (see Williams 1977) by developing a sense of home and social identity in Australia through the cultivation of "native" landscapes. And, ironically enough, at the same time she was feeding the growing gardenesque movement in England with her shipments of native Australian botanical species to amateur naturalist Captain Mangles. Although Georgiana Molloy is best remembered for her early advocacy of Australian native species, she was not a particularly important figure for people who promoted the Australian native garden. This is probably because the native garden movement in Australia was often articulated as a critique of European settlers, of which Molloy was obviously one. Moreover, the Australian native garden movement was also more than an appreciation of native vegetation species. It contained a distinct philosophy about landscape that originated with the British Landscape School tradition but also provided Australians a vocabulary for critiquing Britain's imperial relationship with Australia.

In the 1950s Australian native plants began to be used in conjunction with the "natural style," as developed by Capability Brown. In his account of the rise of an Australian expression of the natural style, Melbourne landscape designer Gordon Ford situated his own career of more than 2000 projects within a larger shift from cultural dependence on Britain to the development of a sense of place unique to Australia (Ford 1999). The 1950s saw the beginning of experimentation in design and building around new conceptions of place and identity in Australia; Ford was part of a community of people in the semirural suburb of Eltham, northeast of Melbourne center, who used Henry David Thoreau's notion of living simply with nature to develop a sense of place in what they promoted as a beautiful natural Australian environment. They experimented by designing with natural Australian resources like mud-brick for houses and indigenous vegetation for landscape design. During this same time, other artists were defining a unique Australian sensibility in painting, music, and literature with the publication of an *Antipodean Manifesto*. For instance, in Melbourne, architects Peter McIntyre, Neil Clerehan, Guildford Bell, and Kevin Borland used indigenous vegetation in the landscape design surrounding their modernist architectural design. Additionally, Ellis Stones's landscape design and rock formation further contributed to the increased stature of native Australian vegetation.

Edna Walling is one of the most noted early advocates of a landscape design that drew upon native species. Beginning in the late 1940s, she advocated indigenous planting along roadsides and the use of indigenous species for cottage garden–style gardens; she promoted the artistic possibilities of Australian plants throughout the second half of the twentieth century.[5] Her work inspired Ellis Stones and a generation of landscape designers (including Gordon Ford and Glen Wilson). In the 1960s this generation of designers cultivated a specific style called the "bush garden" that reflected a more general, growing interest in defining a new relationship with the Australian natural environment (Ford 1999). The bush garden expressed a new appreciation for the Australian bush, using the British natural style from the eighteenth century. Despite the ways in which it built on the British natural style, the bush garden has been endorsed as a "uniquely Australian" style of gardening.

Treating the bush garden as "idealised bush, an aromatic and visual artifice evoking a love of the real bush," designers of the bush garden aimed to reproduce the multilayered quality of Australian bush areas (Ford 1999). In its reproduction and idealization of the bush, the bush garden would typically include an upper story of eucalyptus trees and she-oaks (*Allocasuarina* spp.). The bush garden specifically challenged the notion of the garden as a completely controlled cultural space by using the asymmetry of the "shaggy" gum tree; it rejected the controlled "British" symmetry of the gardenesque landscape and instead tried to encapsulate some of the "wild spirit" of the native Australian landscape in a personal landscape. The middle layer of the bush garden often included smaller trees such as the textured bracelet honey myrtle *(Melaleuca armillaris)*, which flowers in the spring and summer; the small, drought-tolerant willow-leafed hakea *(Hakea salicifolia)*; lemon-scented tea tree *(Leptospermum petersonii)*, which produces a creamy white flower in the summer; or the sticky wattle *(Acacia howittii)*, a species particularly fragrant after a rain. Finally, the bush garden usually included a lower story that might feature a combination of shrubs (e.g., *Callistemon, Banksia,* or *Grevillea* spp.), ground cover (e.g., *Brachyscome* spp., *Viola hederacea,* or *Myoporum parvifolia*), and native grasses or reeds (*Lomandra longifolia, Anigozanthos* spp. [kangaroo paw], or *Orthrosanthus multiflorus*).

Many of the activities in which people engaged to redeem native vegetation (bush gardens, community planting, admiring native species) allowed people a forum to articulate and actively delineate what belongs in Australia and what does not. In such discourse and spatial practices, an international environmental narrative was localized and used to think about specific issues facing the nation. This perspective in Australia held that the continent of Australia has a logic that allows the environment to function productively and support its inhabitants. Yet, the logic of the Australian environment had been greatly violated by colonialism. The environment had been jeopardized and its balance disrupted by previous generations of Australians who, in their ignorance of the land's needs and

*Figure 10. Australian native botanical garden in Canberra.*

in their desire to be someplace other than Australia, imported plants and animals that continue to endanger the biosphere. This critique was similar to the critique that many East Melbourne cottage gardeners made about the representation of Australia in landscape art. However, the Australian native gardening proponents connected their critique to environmental practices and often activism, beyond a critique of representation.

Some members of the East Melbourne gardening club did articulate environmental critiques. In the following passage, Eva, a garden club member, comments on the environmental destruction of her mother's generation. Eva critiqued her mother's futile attempts to create a cottage garden in semiarid conditions in rural South Australia. She highlighted the impossibility and tenacity of her mother's efforts to create "something out of nothing." "I'm interested in gardening; my mother was a keen gardener. And back when I was little, we lived on the west coast of South Australia, right out in the bush. And so she would bring home things like camellia bushes and they would die. She was a really committed person to try to make something out of nothing. I was never really interested in gardening. To me, it seemed like trying to grow weeds."

The image of Eva's mother "growing weeds" contrasts sharply with her aspirations for her own garden. In fact, in her gardening philosophy Eva consciously modeled herself in opposition to her mother's generation, who did not consider the mandates of the soil and climate but tried to plant camellias in the desert. Eva strove to redress damage done to the soil and environment by planting vegetation that would help to hold down the soil and by consciously trying to attract native bird life back to her community.

Eva's criticism echoes a more widespread position held by many in Australia. It posits that early generations of settlers who introduced plants and animals to the country with little regard for their effect on the biosphere damaged the Australian environment. This damage occurred out of ignorance of environmental issues but also out of a colonialist mentality. More specifically, people had not come to terms with being in Australia and expressed their yearning for "home" by reproducing Great Britain culturally and aesthetically in the southern hemisphere.

The discourse borrowed from an international environmental discourse that holds that the earth has a proper balance or logic;

the environment has needs that must be respected and fulfilled if humans are going to have a sustainable life on earth. Indeed, according to the logic of such environmentalism, the ways people are threatened by the environment, such as the increasing threat of skin cancer, droughts, and fires, are testimony to and consequence of a popular mistreatment of the environment. This idea was reflected in a newspaper article written during a period of devastating bush fires in Sydney in 1994. The article began with the modernist tension of man pitted against nature and man enduring a devastating punishment for environmental hubris: "For the past five terrifying days, nature has taken its revenge in Australia. The firestorms that have raged for 600 miles along the seaboard of New South Wales have brought urban Australians face to face with a terrible truth about the fragility of the relationship with their ancient, rugged land."[6] Nature not only has a will that must be respected, but it also has a moral imperative that catches humans up short if they transgress it. In Australia, many believed that colonialism's moral bankruptcy was reflected in the way it violated the natural logic of the Australian environment.[7]

A defining element in the discourse about Australian natives, shared even by those who did not plant them, was that natives helped Australia's ecological balance. They were "meant" to be in Australia; they grew best without much attention because they were compatible with the soil type, climate, etc., in Australia. What is more, natives helped *correct* imbalances that had been created through the introduction of foreign plants during the European colonization of Australia. Native vegetation attracted native birds that, in turn, kept insects in check without the use of pesticides. They required less water, thus placing less stress on the continent's natural resources. Additionally, native species drew butterflies and indigenous animal species to places where they had been displaced by development and by nonnative vegetation. Most of the responsibility for exotics was placed on early Anglo-Celtic settlers, although "foreign" plants that continue to be introduced to Australia from other countries were also believed to pose an ongoing threat to the nation's ecology.

The native garden aesthetic that had been developing since the 1950s became much more popular in the 1970s, when many Australians were searching for alternative ways to define the nation. Native gardening made sense and took on political importance at a time when members of the society were actively negotiating Australia's historical and future relationship to Great Britain. The "nativism" of the bush garden aesthetic was useful for people wishing to criticize British imperialism in Australia and looking for a way to define an Australian "spirit." Planting indigenous species offered a method to undo the ecological damage and the "cultural cringe" of the colonial settlers who planted "homesick gardens" in an effort to make Australia into an English homeland. Thus, a number of people used native Australian vegetation as a means to design and inhabit their ideas for the future and to (re)conceptualize the past.

## "I LOVE A SUNBURNT COUNTRY": REDEEMING THE BUSH AND REJECTING THE "HOMESICK GARDEN"

One strategy in reimagining Australia through its landscape was to "unearth" the symbols through which the British claimed Australia.[8] People literally uprooted Britishness in Australia by weeding out willow trees and rose gardens, replacing them with new symbols of a non-British homeland. Morag Fraser observes, "Our Australian gardening and landscape history—even our current practice—has much to do with fear, nostalgia and imposition: bluebells in dry clay, box parterre in Wagga Wagga" (1999, ix).

As noted already, Australian history has taught that the British made the unfamiliar land of Australia their property and their "home" by shaping it into a more familiar landscape. They grew crops, fenced in the bush, cultivated picturesque gardens, and extracted the land's natural resources. Simon Ryan highlights the way the cultivation of a picturesque landscape served the colonial mission: "By framing the Australian landscape, the explorers combat its threatening vastness and unfamiliarity; moreover, the fact that they may still employ picturesque aesthetics in a foreign land is proof of the transportability and universal validity of European visual taste" (1996, 283). Consequently, Australian native vegetation served as an important signification of Australian autonomy. While the Republican debates and even much of the commentary around the native garden movement verbally rejected the continued definition of Australia as part of the British Empire, these nonnarrative place-making practices changed the physical reality of what Australia is and reshaped (inverted) the codes of colonialism in Australia.

In addition to planting native Australian gardens, people worked to redeem Australia from the mistakes of earlier generations through the clearing and replanting of bush areas. This activity was particularly popular in communities farther out from the city center (fifteen to twenty miles) that had larger expanses of uncultivated bush area and more agricultural land.[9] In Melbourne, the popularity of the native landscape and garden was helped by the transformation of inexpensive land to the east into suburban developments. These communities retained more of the original native bush vegetation than the urban communities, such as East Melbourne, that were developed at the turn of the nineteenth century. The aesthetic in the Eltham community in the 1950s foreshadowed the feel of many communities developed in the 1960s and 1970s, such as Lilydale, Mount Dandenong, Emerald, and Doncaster, among others. People who desired a semirural setting that afforded them more personal land and a greater connection to nature gravitated to such communities. The native Australian landscape style offered an aesthetic that was economical for developers initially and was low maintenance for people who bought houses with a large area of land to manage.

Decisions of the state government at this time also enhanced and reflected the gradual change in status of indigenous vegetation in Australia. In 1967, the Victorian government funded a university development (Monash University) located along the eastern corridor of the city, which relied almost exclusively on native vegetation in its landscape design. Further, in the early 1970s, the Victorian state premier, Sir Rupert Hamer, created a major metropolitan park system that converted bush areas around the rivers and creeks into parks and created new public gardens in the developing outer suburbs. A number of these parks and gardens, Jells Park (Waverley), Cranbourne Botanic Gardens, and the Maranoa Gardens (Balwyn), helped train people to see native species as a cultural form rather than view "natives" with the hostility held by many earlier generations. In her social geography, Libby Robin describes the change in sensibility between the 1960s and 1970s in Australia: "Some Australians were beginning to locate their nationhood in National Parks, in biodiversity and in a legislatively protected frontier. For one generation, bush-bashing meant heroism, for the next generation, it meant vandalism" (1998, 123).

Additionally, beginning in the 1970s, the state government funded state nurseries throughout Victoria that provided native plants and grants for community organizations to weed out "exotic" plants that threatened the Australian environment and replant indigenous botanical species in their place. State nurseries also propagated rare and threatened indigenous species. One resident of Victoria outlined the aims of these nurseries in a letter to the *Age* newspaper: "The nurseries were originally established to rectify years of environmental destruction in our state. They have quietly educated us about the value of native plants and made them available to us."[10]

Like many individual gardeners who chose to plant indigenous species, community groups understood their activity in terms of a commitment to restore an ecological balance to Australia. Community groups were composed of residents in the outer suburbs who were committed to the environmental benefits of replanting in bush areas, people living closer to the city who shared this goal, and others who just enjoyed community landscaping projects as a pleasant way to spend a day in nature with others. Volunteers spent up to one weekend a month on average clearing bush areas of species whose unchecked spread threatened the well-being of native species. They also planted indigenous species, often provided by state government bureaus. They also undertook special projects, such as the building of boardwalks that would encourage bush walkers and direct their wanderings in a way that would protect the wildlife.

Such community groups were literally reshaping Australia. Not unlike colonial Australians who constructed an identity for Australia by planting European plants like roses and Dutch elm trees, the community activists also set out to define the character of the nation-state by manipulating its physical environment. They systematically uprooted plants determined to be invasive, such as the blackberries and other ground cover that existed in many bush areas in the state of Victoria.

They aimed to return bush areas such as the Mount Dandenong area to their proper ecological state as well as to create ways in which people could enjoy the natural Australian landscape. Most people who engaged in such community efforts, like the community groups in Eltham in the 1950s, were motivated by a love of the indigenous landscape in Australia. In a community group working in the Dandenong Ranges, many people gestured with pride at the various forms of eucalyptus trees, commonly referred to as gum trees. Gum trees, such as the lemon-scented (*Eucalyptus citriodora*), mahogany *(Eucalyptus botryoides)*, manna *(Eucalyptus viminalis)*, red box *(Eucalyptus polyanthemos)*, spotted *(Eucalyptus maculata)*, or yellow box *(Eucalyptus melliodora)* varieties, were a predominant feature of the landscape in Victoria; they were fast growing, hardy and drought-resistant. The bark of most eucalyptus species sheds regularly, giving them an appearance that had been denigrated by earlier generations of Australians as "shaggy" and inelegant. However, contemporary admirers of the gum tree in the Dandenong volunteer group reinterpreted this bark feature as providing different "moods" for the landscape and contributing a fascinating array of shades and textures to the bush.

Since the ecological groups saw part of their function as pedagogical, people were very enthusiastic about introducing outsiders to the positive qualities of native vegetation. One volunteer, David, instructed that the small leaves of the eucalyptus remain on the tree all year long and turn sideways to the sun, instead of lying flat and absorbing the bulk of the rays on the leaf. Jan, a public school teacher in her thirties, pointed out that this peculiarity of eucalyptus trees is what gives Australia its unique quality of light. Repeatedly, people both inside and outside of community groups explained that earlier generations of Australians criticized the gum tree for not providing the extensive shade cover that trees in England provide and consequently characterized the Australian landscape and "Australian sun" as hostile to Europeans. Part of the mission of community groups engaged in the task of clearing paths for recreational use in the Dandenong Range was to reeducate the Australian public and redeem the reputation of the eucalyptus tree. They did so by planting trees instead of clearing them and by directing others to admire the trees' impressive height and the blue-gray color of its leaves.

The soft colors of the eucalyptus trees complemented other colors in the suburban bush areas targeted for protection. They were joined by the golden yellow tones of the wattle, a small tree that blooms in the late winter, and complemented the muted red bloom of the bottlebrush tree *(Callistemon* spp.). Again and again, people in community groups and "lay people" were quick to point out and defend the fact that the colors of the natural Australian bush areas were not the bright reds, greens, and violets of the English countryside or English cottage garden. Because earlier generations of Australians had been so critical of Australia, advocates for Australian bush passionately celebrated the less intense silver, gray, blue-green, gold, and maroon of native trees, grasses, and flowers. The asymmetry and "wildness" that people associated with indigenous Australian vegetation were perceived to provide a unique and distinctly Australian sense of place that some claimed corresponded to "the easy-going Australian temperament" (Ford 1999, 32).

For many, the work they did with community groups was part of a larger commitment to living in harmony with nature. For instance, Cathy chose to live out in the Eltham area in a house that rested in a heavily wooded patch of eucalyptus trees and that boasted an original landscape painting by artist and Australian of the Year (1995) Arthur Boyd in its entrance. Living so intimately with the Australian bush was part of a larger lifestyle choice that included sending her children to Steiner schools, being vegetarian, and teaching her children respect for the environment. Similarly, Anne and David, who lived on Mount Dandenong even though it meant a longer commute to work for them, took pride in the house they built in 1978. Like many houses in the eastern suburbs, their house had many windows along the back and a large veranda that allowed them to enjoy the still-dense bush area surrounding their house. Staying with them for the weekend on Mount Dandenong, one is treated to cockatoos on their porch rail, wallabies in their yard, and a pet possum. They were very proud of their relationship to the natural environment. Many of the houses in the Eastern (outer) suburbs were designed to highlight the surrounding bush. Houses in more densely suburban communities than Anne and David's, which did not have views of the mountain range or bush, often expressed the natural environment by incorporating windows that opened into a central courtyard with lush vegetation or did so by creating vistas onto the section of the "back garden" that had the most greenery.

In some cases, communities used policy to create more of a "bush feeling" for the community as well as to provide a habitat for native birds, such as white-naped honeyeaters, wattle birds, and spine-billed honeyeaters. For example, Eltham passed "recommendations" for the type of plants and gardens that residents should grow on their property. Additionally, the council town planners and local Tree Preservation Society in Blackburn, in response to pressure from the community, used indigenous trees and shrubs to disguise necessary public utility units wherever possible.

Given that Anglo-Celtic settlers made the Australian landscape symbolic of their anxiety and disappointment in their colonial appropriation of Australia, it is not surprising that cultivating that same maligned landscape would be used to redefine place and nation in Australia. People's engagement with native Australian vegetation was a strategy for erasing the codes by which British settlers tried to transform Australia into a British homeland and for defining an Australian homeland that was not dependent on a British referent. In her promotion of the bush garden form that Australian landscape designer Gordon Ford perpetuated, Morag Fraser declares fervently, "It is tempting to say that Gordon Ford's gardens make you feel as though you have come home. Certainly they help one to understand what 'home' might mean in this complex land of dwellers, immigrants and settlers" (1999, ix). Fraser's words suggest that the "native" Australian landscape aesthetic allowed people a way of imagining their relationship horizontally across cultural divides of "dweller" and immigrant, and across time, connecting contemporary Australians to previous generations. Environmental planner Graeme Law captures the use of the bush garden as a vehicle for defining nation when he asserts, "The richness of the multi-layered natural garden in urban environs plays a significant role in not just the ecological well-being of our country, but also in its development as a nation proud of its unique standing in the world" (1999, xii).

The spatial practices and insights of another East Melbourne Garden Club member, Margaret, help us begin to understand how redeeming the native Australian bush was a means of positing a critique of British colonialism in Australia and of envisioning a new identity for contemporary Australians. Although Margaret herself had a garden that contained mostly exotic, potted plants that she inherited when she bought her house from another member of the East Melbourne Garden Club, she was very concerned with issues of social justice. Discussing the need to redress past ecological destruction in Australia was one means by which she articulated the problems resulting from colonization in Australia.

Margaret was a nurse by training and spent many years working in the field of Aboriginal health. Her work with Aboriginal people fueled her concern for the inequality experienced by most Aboriginal people and gave her an understanding of the British colonial settlement of Australia that was sensitive to the violent and systematic dispossession of Aboriginal people. Her work in Aboriginal health also took her to the Northern Territory to work temporarily with Aboriginal people in the outback region. She cited her trip to the Northern Territory as marking a profound change of perspective for her toward the native Australian landscape and of Australia's worth more generally. She realized that it was very beautiful, in contrast with the depiction of the natural Australian landscape as harsh and ugly that she had read in history books as a child.

In the following passage Margaret describes the activities and goals of her daughter's community group with whom she sometimes worked. Margaret's discussion of her work with her daughter's group in Emerald gives insight into the way replanting natives allowed people to reshape their identity as Australians and to criticize Britain's colonial domination of Australia.

> I mean, before, people just didn't question it at all . . . There has been a real rape of the land; no doubt about that. And mistakes made. And of course they never listened to the Aboriginal people who could have told them so much . . . And to think that people would have agreed to farm soft-footed animals instead of the hard-footed ones who break up the land. I think a couple of generations ago it wouldn't even have been mentioned; but now I think people are beginning to think about it.
>
> My daughter has a lot to do with a group, she lives up in the hills of Emerald, and they've joined together and they're getting rid of all the foreign trees. Of course, they usually go mad. Sycamores—some had put in sycamores and there's a forest of sycamores and they'll go on forever. They're very bad for the ferns and the other trees that should be there. This has been going on for some years now, and bit-by-bit they're getting rid of those and they're planting the natives that should be there. And of course they're doing beautifully because they should be there. They're in the right spot. And pulling out the weeds along the creek and all. And there are now council nurseries where they provide those trees and so they, every so often the council nurseries will send them, they'll send them 2000 of these little trees. And then they plant them and all the time they try to get rid of the little blackberries and creepers that have absolutely taken over . . .
>
> But there are a lot of groups like that now. Planting trees everywhere; and, of course, they are native trees . . . Like last year they

had a big day where they had a lot of publicity about it and they got
school groups to go and help them. They will have a special work
day, because it's a big job. And then they'll put in and they've got
grants to make boardwalks and steps and such. And the men quite
enjoy that. And then they've got the farmers involved. Which is a
big thing that they wanted to do, was get the farmers interested and
enthusiastic because a lot of their properties go down to the creek.
And then they say, well I heard one farmer's wife say, "Well, I still
miss the willows." [laughs] Which is understandable but apparently
they do terrible damage to the creeks and such. And to the other
plants too and of course it's also not what the native birds want
either—and so it all links up.

Margaret's comments highlight the way the spatial practices of
community groups were conceptualized as a curative for the mistakes of earlier generations in Australia who acted in ignorance of
the particular needs of the environment. They treated Australia as
if it were England by farming sheep whose hard hooves broke up
the ground cover of the soil and by planting crops that stripped the
soil's nutrients, both resulting in a dry land that would blow away
in a windstorm. For Margaret, the earlier settlers stood in contrast
to the sensitivity Aboriginal people have historically had in relation
to Australia's environment.

Margaret's language is also informative of the way that advocating native plants over "exotics" was expressed in terms of "listening to the environment." Given the political work that shaping the
landscape with exotic plants achieved in colonizing Australia, replacing exotics with native plants was, of course, also a highly political activity. However, rather than being expressed as a political
position, these activities were posed in terms of restoring what was
*meant to be*. As Margaret summed up in her last sentence: it's what
the other plants and birds want. Such language literally naturalizes
the social vision spatially enacted by community groups and individual bush gardeners by representing it as an apolitical fulfillment
of nature's mandate.

Furthermore, the victimization of native plants by "mad" exotics also functions as a powerful metaphor for colonial relations
between Australia and Britain. Native plants that were "doing beau-
tifully because they should be there" were envisioned as victimized,
as strangled by the roots of "little blackberries and creepers that

have absolutely taken over" and willows that "do terrible damage to the creeks and such." Such language set up a natural order of things that belong and things that dominate and violate.

The distinction of natives as the righteous, potential victims of European and British plants becomes an especially potent image at a time when the society is actively debating the notion of becoming a republic, independent of England. British plants (and exotics more generally) function as a metaphor for the imposition of British imperialism on white Australians. The damage done to the Australian environment by colonial environmental practices, which meant that later generations inherited a land vulnerable to drought and fire, helped position white Australians as victims of British imperialism. The vulnerability of the native plants to the imposition of imported "exotics" stands in metaphorically for the victimization of settler (Anglo-Celtic) Australians by the British. Such an interpretation of history echoes the political critique of Britain seen in the story of the Battle of Gallipoli, which positions Australians as underdogs to British power.

Garden club members Margaret and Eva were of the same generation. They were the children of soldiers returning from World War I. When analyzing how the landscape served as a means of defining Australia, both pointed to the returned World War I soldiers as those who perpetuated many of the problems and attitudes that many contemporary Australians now reject. The World War I "Diggers" were infused with interesting symbolism in these spatial and narrative constructions of Australia. The following comments made by Margaret outline what seemed to be a "typical" story of misfortune for World War I soldiers upon return to Australia. They were given marginal land by the government and as a consequence ended up victims of the depression.

MARGARET: All the soldiers were volunteers in the First World War and they went home to help England. Then a lot of them became very embittered; the fact that they, many of them, were killed, first of all. But apart from that, they came back and then there was a big depression. So they found it very hard, if they ever got on their feet. I mean, my parents had an orange grove because my father was told to go into the dry country because he was invalided off of Gallipoli, and had a bad chest and a bad heart and all that sort of thing. So he went there and they had beautiful oranges, before the salt came up into the earth and killed them . . . the roots of the orange trees hit the salt, partly because they were irrigating them, and they didn't know this and so the trees died. After that, the next lot of people planted grapes, and they have such shorter roots and they don't go to the salt level . . . And they sent them [the oranges] all down to market and they said, "Sorry, the depression's on. There's no sale." They sent them all back on the train and they [the farmers] had to pay the freight. So you see, they had no hope. They just had to struggle, struggle . . .

AC:         Did he end up having to sell his farm?

MARGARET:   Oh, there was no point of selling it. They had to just walk off.

This story constructs the soldier as a symbol of the naiveté of the previous generation who went "home" to England to fight the war. It parallels the larger cultural narrative in Australia that used the Anzac soldier from World War I as a symbol of the entire country's naive trust of England. This trust was most poignantly betrayed in the Battle of Gallipoli, where thousands of Australian and New Zealand soldiers lost their lives in a battle that British officers knew was futile (cf. Kapferer 1988). Gallipoli was used to symbolize the larger colonial relationship with Britain, and World War I was identified as the watershed for Australians' cultural independence.

The soldiers took on an even richer symbolism as victims in some of the accounts of people in the East Melbourne Garden Club. They were thrice victimized: first by colonial relations, then by the economic failure of the depression, and finally by their generation's ignorance of their environment, which caused their crops to fail and their families to eventually abandon their land.

Margaret's story narrated what has become the quintessential Australian tale, obsessively recounted by the Australian film industry. However, hers was rather novel in that it also accounted for the conditions that have compromised the ecological balance in Australia. For her, the imbalance ("the fall") was a consequence of the uninformed actions of her parents and previous generations of people who approached farming or planting in Australia as if it were a place interchangeable with any other place. Theirs was a failure to recognize a distinct identity for Australia. They planted what the market would support, irrigated for citrus plants, and did not conceive of an underlayer of hostile substance like salt. The death of the orange trees in Margaret's story suggests a misapplication of European expectations toward the land, with dire consequences for the people themselves and for the earth. In the following passage, Eva confirms some of the damage done to the environment from such poor farming strategies in Australia.

> But when the soldiers came and settled the land, they cleared it. Nobody understood about soil erosion in those days. And I certainly remember the dust storms and the sand storms. They'd go on for days because they had cleared the land and there was nothing to hold the soil down.

Both women identified their relationship with the landscape in Australia and the choices that they made about their gardens as a progression from the attitudes of their parents' generation. Now they could see the beauty of things indigenous to Australia, where their parents' generation could only see shimmering stones and failed expectations.

However, using native plants symbolically in this way has the added function of establishing a "natural" link between white Australians and the Australian landscape/continent. It adds another layer to land politics in Australia. Spatial activity and discourse around native vegetation narrated a story of how white Australians were dispossessed and injured by colonial imperialism in Australia, a claim that, in turn, stood alongside Aboriginal claims of oppression by colonial forces. And, importantly, these practices marked a distinction between the practices of British imperialism, which had all sorts of misconceptions about the land, and the good intentions and victimization of contemporary (white) Australians.

The practices of community groups and bush gardeners also defined a new role for contemporary, enlightened Australians. Rather than being the colonizers of the Australian continent, their spatial practices reposition them as stewards of the unique Australian environment. As Graeme Law asserts, "Once we become aware of our role as stewards of this earth, then region appropriateness of garden style is not a choice but a responsibility" (1999, xii). Here Law suggests that being stewards of the Australian continent leads settler Australians to see the importance of and enact the native garden aesthetic. However, reversing Law's causation provides insight into the significance of these social practices. That is, identifying and enacting the "responsibility" of replanting indigenous vegetation in Australia functions to refashion these settler Australians into stewards of the earth and, more specifically, of the Australian continent. Redefining settler Australians as stewards poses them in a relationship to the territory of Australia significantly different from the imperial relationship earlier generations had. "Stewardship" is one way of imagining the relationship between people, culture, and territory in the reterritorialization of the nation. The spatial practices of people who are engaged in redeeming the "indigenous" landscape in Australia are the means by which people redefine their own relationship with the land that they claim for their nation and are a way of redefining their relationship to a colonial past.

The case made for planting native vegetation as an act of responsibility toward the environment and as a sign of a healthy sense of place and national identity was difficult for people to contest. Even gardeners who were not, themselves, interested in promoting native Australian vegetation could recite the reasons why one would plant indigenous species. The power of the native garden discourse was underscored in my interactions with one set of gardeners in East Melbourne.

James and Vivian had an English cottage–style garden in front of their Victorian terrace house that garnered a great deal of envy from others in their community. Their front garden was no bigger than 15 feet by 30 feet. True to the cottage garden style, their front path snaked its way through clusters of flowering bushes such as daisies, yellow and white roses, and a variety of purples and pinks among the pansy, lavender, and iris beds. Nothing was organized in neat rows or with any sense of symmetry. Rather, one got the feeling of walking through a miniature country field. James joked that one of his all-time favorite birthday presents was a big sack of manure that he had received from a friend, which he happily put to use in the garden.

They had more left-leaning political views than many other people in the relatively wealthy suburb of East Melbourne. They were very positive about multiculturalism and had a great deal of sympathy for the political claims asserted in the name of Aboriginal rights. Given their overall political orientation, it was not particularly surprising during the tour of their garden that James and Vivian would suggest that the idea of promoting native birds and indigenous grasses was a good idea. What was more surprising was that a discussion of native gardens prompted them to defend their right to have an English cottage garden.

AC: Talking about that balance makes me think about some of those groups, like in the Dandenong Ranges or local communities, that are pulling up exotic plants and trying to plant what is indigenous to Australia.

JAMES: That's right. Trying to get the natives back in the country.

AC: Do you think that is an important thing to do or that it's being a little too drastic, or . . .

JAMES: Ah, if people want to do it. Native grasses and things.

VIVIAN: Native grass and things like that that have disappeared. Yes, I can see doing it if you're interested, but, I don't see the need for all of us to do that.

JAMES: No, I don't either. Like I say, if they want to do it, that's fair enough. I certainly don't say that they shouldn't be doing it.

VIVIAN: No, if they want to do it. And a lot of people are interested in both, both the native and the exotics.

JAMES: The other thing too. I can see how if they don't have these native grasses growing, then the owls will disappear.

VIVIAN: And a lot of things hold the soil together.

JAMES: Yes, stops erosion.

VIVIAN: Yes, I can see the reason. But if you only have a little bit of ground like we have, I think probably you're entitled to grow what you like [laughs]. Yes, I am not a native fanatic really; although there are some beautiful ones.

There was not a lot of language available for people to criticize the politics of the native Australian gardens, nor language with which to defend their own decision to plant a "homesick" English cottage garden. The most common form of criticism of the native Australian garden movement came in the form of attacks on the nationalist overtones of its political program. In the passage above, Vivian accuses native proponents of being "fanatic," in a way much like another club member, Edith, when she referred to native garden proponents as "hung up on purity." In a similar vein, garden expert and author Christopher Lloyd criticized what he saw as "a strong element of jingoism in this let's-stick-to-our-own-plants-school."[11]

James and Vivian were familiar with the argument for the bush garden aesthetic, although they had never been involved in such community activities themselves. Their familiarity with the logic behind planting native species suggests how widespread such arguments had become in Australia. What is more, their quick defense of their choice not to plant native plants and grasses suggests how hegemonic the association between native vegetation, environmental responsibility, and national identity had become.

## HETEROTOPIC GARDENS

The nationalism that was often interwoven in practices to redeem the native vegetation of Australia was noted and critiqued by Eva, a fellow East Melbourne Garden Club member. In the passage that follows, Eva is critical of what she saw as excessive nationalism and egoism of the push for native gardens.

EVA:   There will be *whole* gardens that are *only* natives. People are so infused with such egos that they can reel off every botanical name.

AC:   What's behind that fervor?

EVA:   Oh, I think it's part of a huge upsurge of nationalism in the early 70s that affected a lot of people: "Because we were Australian, we were best." And that was interesting because we were out of Australia for five years and in which time there was a change in government. After many, many years of the Liberal government, the Labor government was in, and that was Whitlam. And so we came back to this totally different country from the one we had left. And that was fascinating. And along with it, there was a huge upsurge in things Australian, and I am sure that was part of it. So there were a lot of huge garden projects going on, a huge upsurge in native gardens. And I think a lot of that had real value in attracting the native birds.

AC:   Is there a part of that that makes you a little bit uneasy?

EVA:   Well, yes. Because the interesting thing about the British expatriots is that they really worked for many, many years; they imported, they weeded an enormous amount of plants

without any regard for the Australian environment. And
that's their [the Digger's Club] critique of the Australian native movement. They think it's *naive* to transplant Australian
natives just because they are Australian natives. And they
transport plants from one end of the country to the other, because they are Australian natives and they look attractive . . .
So you have the Australian native garden movement on one
end of the spectrum and on the other end is the English cottage garden.

As Eva acknowledges, to a certain extent her environmental and
gardening philosophy overlapped with promoters of the Australian
native garden movement. She was aware of the environmental damage done as part of the project to colonize Australia and commented
later in the discussion on the absurdity of Australians who, as recently as her parents' generation, had no sense of their own location.
Like many people involved in replanting Australian natives, Eva was
interested in planting species that would thrive in this environment
and attract native birds back to the cities.

However, she critiqued the nationalist symbolism that had been
grafted onto native species in Australia. She argued that too often
people took the national boundaries of Australia as meaningful
ecological boundaries. For Eva, taking a species that is at home in
the dry conditions of Western Australia and planting it in a cold,
wet Tasmanian garden would make as little sense as the behavior
of earlier generations of Australians who labored to grow English
roses in the outback of South Australia. Because Australia is the only
nation-state that is its own continent, it is perhaps easier to conflate
ecological borders with national borders. However, Eva argued, in
concert with the Diggers Club,[12] that putting the issues in terms of
"Australian natives" led many people to make the ecological mistake
of planting a species in the wrong environment, simply because it
was an "Australian" native and it was going into "Australian" soil.
For Eva such practices were problematic because they ignored the
fact that there are many different ecological environments within
Australia.

Eva's own garden, which surrounded her double-fronted Victorian house in Richmond, resembled a cottage garden in many respects. It was asymmetrical with clusters of flowering bushes, flowerbeds, and plants in pots on the porch. Although she worked full

time and was required to travel for her job, she happily devoted the time necessary to maintain an elaborate garden. She noted that her current garden presented her with more challenges than the garden that she had cultivated in her last house in the eastern suburbs. The limited space and the greater use of potted plants in gardens in the inner suburbs required greater diligence on the part of the gardener. As a case in point, on the Sunday when we met to discuss her garden, she confided that she had been a little concerned all weekend about a small tree she had on her front veranda that seemed to be unwell, yet mystified her as to what was ailing it.

She ordered most of her plants from the Diggers' Club seed catalogue, which helped her choose plants from a variety of places around the world, yet which would suit the climate and soil in Melbourne. Eva's philosophy is summed up in the following passage where she discussed a program of changing one's goals away from the fleeting experience of the English cottage garden,

> They [the Diggers Club] look very much at what is possible within the environment, the microcosm of the climate that we have, what's not flowering. Yes, you can have daffodils coming up . . . but they

*Figure 11. Eva's heterotopic garden, planted with species compatible with Melbourne's climate and environment in an effort to redress damage from earlier generations of Australians.*

are such fleeting experiences. You are much better to be looking at, "how can we have an attractive garden all year round, with color, with flowers?" So they import stuff from around the world, from different countries with similar types of climates. Now I find that really interesting, something that I've really worked toward in my garden.

Eva and the Diggers' Club focused on what the "microcosm of the climate" could maintain instead of fetishizing national boundaries. However, Eva was similar to native garden "fanatics" insofar as her garden was a vehicle for her to construct the kind of world she would like to inhabit. Her garden enabled her to counter the mistakes of previous generations and create an almost utopian space within Australia, not unlike the utopian visions constructed about Australia in the nineteenth century.

In its original form, Australia as utopia was built around themes of nature, both animal life and natural landscape. As mentioned in the introduction, Australia as Arcadia has historically been one of many possible discourses available to people in and out of Australia in constructing national identity. While the nineteenth-century utopian vision of the Australian landscape was oriented to redeeming an ill-treated English working class in industrial Britain, the state to which Eva strove to return society, in her discourse about the Australian environment, was oriented to balancing and nourishing the elements of nature.

Eva promoted the utopian goal of returning to a former state of nature before the fall. In this case, the fall was caused by colonial environmental practices. The original sin was the impractical desire of colonialists to maintain an English cottage garden on an arid continent. But colonial practices in Australia also expressed a deeper pathology of asserting one's power over the environment instead of respecting the earth. Furthermore, this fall from grace was reproduced in contemporary society in the ongoing use of chemicals in the garden and through the act of planting vegetation inappropriate for the environment. In other parts of the conversation (not detailed here), Eva explained how people use artificial fertilizers because the soil has been destroyed by the removal of Australian natives. She noted, like many of the defenders of Australian native landscape design, that native species and plants compatible with the region were important not only because they were capable of surviving the Australian climate, but because they kept the topsoil in place. The native plants, in turn, attracted native birds that would control the insect population by feeding on them. Therefore, native plants were the first step to countering contemporary usage of pesticide as well as for keeping the topsoil in place. In the larger scope of things, they were the first step in returning ecological balance to the environment and countering some of the damage of colonialism.

However, as fantastical visions of an ideal society, utopias are typically not visions that are enacted on physical space, but rather usually circulate through philosophical or literary writings. Therefore, Eva's spatial practice might instead be best characterized as what Foucault calls a "heterotopia." Foucault explains:

> There are also, probably in every culture, in every civilization, real places—places that do exist and that are formed in the very foundation of society—which are something like counter-sites, a kind of effectively enacted utopia in which the real sites, all the other real sites that can be found within the culture, are simultaneously represented, contested, and inverted. Places of this kind are outside of all places, even though it may be possible to indicate their location in reality. (1986, 24)

Foucault recalls the fact that in many historical eras, the garden has functioned as a sacred space or as a microcosm of the world. He writes, "The garden is the smallest parcel of the world and then it is the totality of the world. The garden has been a sort of happy, universalizing heterotopia since the beginning of antiquity (our modern zoological gardens spring from that source)" (1986, 25).

Eva, and many other gardeners in this chapter, used the garden to think through social and ecological relations and to restructure them in ways that seemed more politically just. The larger relationship of dependency between people and nature, the relationship between bird life, insects, and flora are represented and, importantly, reordered in idealized form within the garden. What is more, colonial relations are reordered through the production of the garden. Although the Diggers differentiated themselves from more nationally oriented native gardeners, the two groups are similar insofar as they reorganize and reimagine their relationship to empire within the space of the garden. Rejecting the fragile camellia was a means of reordering imperial space and negating the imposition of colonial power on the natural world. Again, Foucault's notion of heterotopias is suggestive for understanding the spatial practices of the gardeners in this study as a form of political agency. He writes of heterotopias, "Their role is to create a space that is other, another real space, as perfect, as meticulous, as well arranged as ours is messy, ill constructed, and jumbled. This latter type would be the heterotopia, not of illusion, but of compensation" (1986, 27).

Gardens in Australia were not solely places of retreat, but were also engagements that allowed people to compensate for political imperfections and messiness, and to reorder colonial, national, and ecological relations. They were a form of spatial, political engagement.

## THE SPATIAL DIVISION OF GARDENS: CULTURAL HIERARCHY AND NATION

Vegetation was used in a number of contexts outside of the East Melbourne Garden Club and community groups to define Australianness and assert a vision for the nation-state. Through debates about vegetation in the city parks and along city streets, people produced narratives about national identity and about the natural connection between people, culture, and territory in Australia.

When we step back from individual gardens and community groups and examine the spatial arrangement of gardens (both native and exotic) and public landscape planning within the larger city of Melbourne, certain patterns begin to emerge. Homes in what were considered the "inner suburbs" were predominantly surrounded by "exotic" gardens (containing nonindigenous plants). Whether or not they were self-consciously constructed as English cottage gardens, the domestic gardens in East Melbourne primarily contained imported species such as roses, daisies, geraniums, weeping violets, and impatiens. Many members of the garden club explained their choice of garden type as a matter of wanting to maintain consistency with their Victorian homes. The garden style should match the house style, a principle also espoused by the official recommendations of the East Melbourne Group[13] in their suburb. The garden club members who propagated natives did so either as part of the community groups in the outer suburbs who were replacing exotics with natives, or in their second home, away from the city. Some had native trees, ferns, or bushes at their beach house or farm; rarely did these properties have formal gardens.[14]

This spatial division of gardens—exotics closer to the city and native vegetation farther out—was also reproduced at the level of public parks and gardens. Melbourne residents took pride in the fact that their city had many splendid gardens throughout the central areas of the city. The centralized location of these gardens meant that people passed through well-developed and maintained gardens like the Fitzroy Gardens or the Exhibition Gardens along their route to work or in getting from one part of the city to another. In urban gardens like these, nearly all the welcome shade in summer and colorful displays in autumn were provided by exotic trees. Additionally, the very structure of strong central pathways through the park, bordered by tall, leafy elms, oaks, or plane trees, interspersed occasionally by beds of flowers standing alone or surrounding a fountain, was reminiscent of European park planning. European species were also used in public squares and along the streets in the cultural and business districts of the city center.

The parks and gardens were used in a variety of unstructured ways. On a number of occasions while I sat in one of the public gardens scribbling notes from morning interviews, I shared the space with office workers and manual laborers on a lunchtime break, teenagers caught up in passionate embrace, people engaged on their cellular phones as they walked briskly past, and combinations of people of all ages, gender, and ethnicity meandering amiably. Additionally, many of these public spaces had playing fields (sports) of various sorts that facilitated the year-round pursuit of sports. The abundance of parks and gardens in Melbourne earned Victoria the reputation of being the "garden state."[15]

However, few of the many formal public gardens in Melbourne's inner suburban district were native gardens. Maranoa was one of the rare native gardens located near the city, but even this garden was about ten miles out of the center, in Camberwell. Early in the 1990s, public pressure was exerted on the Department of Parks and Gardens and public officials to replace many of the imported species of trees in a Royal Park with native trees, making it one of the few parks in the inner suburbs that included substantial native vegetation. In general, the public parks and street vegetation increased in native content the farther one moved away from the city center.

It was common sense to many Australians that native plants were better suited to the larger spaces of the outer suburbs, beachfront, and bush. However, an increasing number of people challenged the exclusion of native plants, especially trees, from the urban parks and formal avenues of the city. People outside of the East Melbourne Garden Club also asserted the symbolic connection between indigenous vegetation and a new, indigenous identity for settler Australians. The transformation of Royal Park was an example of public groups exerting pressure to replace European trees with "natives" in inner suburban parks. Proponents and adversaries of the plan to sponsor the Grand Prix also picked up on the moral authority Australian natives had acquired with the public and used it in their response to the controversial changes the state was making in Albert Park (also located in the inner suburban district). Opponents of the car race used a major newspaper to highlight the desecration of the Australian natives: "Even a magnificent red gum that existed before European settlement was not spared . . . They were unmoved by hundreds of years of tree growth instantly annihilated by the chain saw."[16]

*Figure 12. A member of the East Melbourne Garden Club touring the Maranoa Gardens (in a Melbourne metropolitan area), one of Australia's oldest gardens featuring Australian native vegetation.*

Proponents of the Grand Prix emphasized the removal of European trees, which would, happily, be replaced by Australian natives. One defender of the planned park gentrification argued:

> Some elm trees are under threat. Big deal. This introduced English species, which the Dutch beetle of the same name has targeted, are nice enough but will make way for a hundred-fold increase in Australian natives. You know, gums of the "shadow" and "ghost" variety, that were meant to be here in the first place, and that artists like Hans Heysen immortalised overseas. In fact, three hundred have been planted already.[17]

Political contenders on both sides of the battle over the use of Albert Park reproduced much of the discourse about natives that I heard from community group members and among East Melbourne gardeners. They borrowed and reproduced the moral integrity assigned to native vegetation. Both sides tried to cash in on the popular symbolic association between native vegetation and a contemporary Australian citizenry. They hinted that since their political vision for the park (and city) would foster native vegetation, then the political vision they promoted was necessarily in the best interest of the people.

In the newspaper editorial quoted above, Australian-ness, morality, and high culture are intertwined. The writer placed Australian natives on moral high ground and supported the moral righteousness of the native by connecting it to high culture. The intrinsic beauty, valor, and suitability of the gum tree (eucalyptus) for Albert Park was signaled by its ability to survive natural assaults (Dutch elm disease) and also by its history as the subject of formal painting. This writer's argument about natural selection echoed the logic of native garden proponents. However, in this political polemic, the writer also elevated the moral and national importance of Australian natives by associating them with high culture.

The intersection of native vegetation, high culture, and Australian national identity was not isolated to this incident. Several years earlier, many members of the city had been engaged in debate over the redevelopment of a different city space. In August 1992, 103 plane trees were scheduled to be planted along Swanston Street Walk to try to revitalize that area of the central business district. Swanston Street emanated out from the Shrine of Remembrance, perhaps the city's most significant public monument, in the way that the Champs Elysée acts as a central axis leading to and away from the Arc de Triomphe.[18] The city council, with the support of the public, intended to create a more "upscale" atmosphere in a street that contained many low-budget retail businesses. The city also planned to place sculptures along Swanston Street to encourage the development of cafes and expensive stores. When the council's decision was announced, a lively debate erupted in the city hall and on the editorial pages of the *Age* newspaper in response to the council's choice of plane trees over Australian eucalypts. What follows is a series of selections taken from articles devoted to this debate that appeared in the city's prominent newspaper. I have italicized parts of people's argument that illustrate how people intertwined native species with a sense of national identity and use them to symbolize a break with a previous national "false consciousness" in Australia. The rancor of the letters highlights the pervasiveness of imagining national subjectivity through spatial practice (landscape design in this case) and the extent to which people outside of the East Melbourne community used native vegetation for symbolic purposes.

> Swanston Street will be graced with the first of 103 European plane trees later this week after the Melbourne City Council last night *quelled a nationalistic uprising for eucalypts.* (*Age,* August 11, 1992)

> The Premier, Mrs. Kirner, expressed her displeasure with the council's decision. Mrs. Kirner, who had requested that the council seriously consider native trees, said last night: "I look forward to the day that we in Melbourne recognize that *our environmental heritage is Australian, not European"* (*Age,* August 11, 1992)

> With Swanston Walk about to receive its first plane tree, the Australian Conservation Foundation has accused the Melbourne City Council of *"clinging to European values"* by rejecting eucalypts. The foundation's Victorian campaign coordinator, Mr. Peter Allan, said yesterday that the council "lacked vision" by not grasping a historical chance to *create a streetscape that was identifiably Australian.* (*Age,* August 12, 1992)

> Councilor Jack Lynch said he believed the council could not be accused of *an anti-Australian-native bias.* (*Age,* August 12, 1992)

But Councilor Lorna Hannon, who voted for natives, said yesterday that while the promise of new native trees in Lonsdale Street was welcome, she was bitterly disappointed with the vote for planes . . . "I had my heart set on Swanston Walk with those great blue-green eucalypts growing. *I imagined our city with our own plants.* I think the council will deeply regret this decision." (*Age*, August 12, 1992)

*It's a poet's tree* and ought to have a more dignified name. Gum tree! It does not fit it at all. It's a wonderful tree—a decorator's tree. (Walter Burley Griffin, 1913)

Observers of the current debate about the trees in Swanston Street Walk must be aware by now that there appear to be few poets among the administration at the City of Melbourne. (*Age*, July 17, 1992)

The dispute over appropriate trees for Swanston Street Walk is set to grow today with the Melbourne City Council threatening to use contract labor if union members refuse to plant the council's choice—plane trees. (*Age*, August 13, 1992)

What this whole debate has exposed is the lack of knowledge we have about our native trees, and how *we haven't yet made up our minds if Melbourne is a European or Australian city.* (Dr. Moore, Head of Burnly Horticultural College, *Age*, July 16, 1992)

When I think of Paris and London, I think of plane trees. Whether or not these are what we want for Swanston Street, in terms of city character the die is firmly set. The decision to plant planes in Swanston Street Walk *make historic sense*; it continues a trend begun long ago. (*Age*, July 17, 1992)

Those attacking the government's decision about Swanston Street Walk used tactics in legitimizing their claims similar to those employed in the debate about staging the Grand Prix in Albert Park. Here too people used Australian natives in their construction of a proper moral order. Proponents of eucalypts in Swanston Street used this occasion to criticize the practice of imagining Australian cities (and the nation) as a European place. They argued that Australian cities were invented, through landscape and architecture design, as European. Advocates of native trees quickly drew parallels between European vegetation and a continued misunderstanding of

*Figure 13. Swanston Street, a central axis in the central business district of Melbourne. Despite a push for indigenous eucalyptus trees, the street was planted with nonnative trees and designed with a "European feel."*

Australia as European (located in Europe). They minimized the importance of British political institutions and cultural forms for Australia, while stressing (inventing) the importance of "environmental heritage."

Thus, native vegetation proponents constructed an ancientness and heritage for the Australian nation through claims to an *environmental heritage*. They connected the present society and generation of Australians to their territory and to past generations through the environment. As discussed in more detail in the introduction, Anderson's historical analysis of nationalism highlights the need for all nations to link generations across time and space. Narrating backward in time and linking the present nation with past generations of people gives the nation legitimation in its ancientness. Additionally, we could read the notion of an environmental heritage as a form of Hobsbawm and Ranger's notion of the "invention of tradition" (1983) insofar as it helped make the relatively "young" Australian nation appear inevitable and unwavering.

The debates over which trees to plant in Swanston Street typified the way tradition is invented out of the particular needs of the contemporary nation. Fifty years earlier, there was not a shared sense that eucalyptus trees and the natural environment were something that connected Australians to earlier generations of people living on the continent. Rather, the environment was represented as something that threatened Europeans and rendered them vulnerable in an unfamiliar place. In more contemporary accounts, such as the positions held concerning the Swanston Street renewal, the environment functions as a form of blood and stock connecting all Australians. This narration of heritage provided a way of imagining that white Australians are connected farther back than just colonial settlement of the continent; an environmental heritage connects white Australians back to Aboriginal occupants. Heritage in this context was not the colonial houses or British traditions. Instead, the vegetation and environment represented the ancientness of the nation and established a unique bond between its people.

As historian David Lowenthal argues, all nations produce a form of heritage that highlights certain trajectories and ignores others. It is not the inventedness of heritage that is unique or problematic in the Australian context. But because heritage is taken to be something neutral that we merely honor, as presented in the debates about

Swanston Street, we must be especially careful to remain cognizant of its constructedness and continue to ask what is made possible by the articulation of one vision of heritage over another. It is easy to see how the two main perspectives on the issue of plane versus eucalyptus trees for Swanston Street dovetailed with Republican debates about whether or not Australians should define themselves independently from the British. Again, as at other points in Australia's history, people were attempting to define their nation by shaping the landscape and thinking about its identity in relation to the geographies of Britain and Europe.

Less obvious, perhaps, is how the invention of a relatively contemporary narrative about an environmental heritage helps to reposition white Australians in relation to Aboriginal people. Conceiving of an "environmental heritage" implies that colonial settlement was not the moment at which white history in Australia began. Consequently, the historical link between white Australians and British imperial history is obscured, and instead people emphasize the historical connection with a politically ennobled history of nature on the Australian continent. Thus, an environmental heritage for Australians helped white Australians narrate a connection to past generations and the territory of the Australian continent that predated colonial occupation. It consequently helped to redefine white Australians as true heirs to the Australian continent, rather than as the heirs of British colonial power.

The notion of an environmental heritage also comes out of contemporary and international environmentalist ideas about the interconnectedness of humans and nature. The idea that nations are not only connected to the natural environment but also are descendants of an environmental heritage only makes sense after Aldo Leopold's call to "think like a mountain" in 1923 (cf. Nash 1989). Here we see a fascinating development of the articulation of nation. There is still pressure on individual nations to establish a connection between people, culture, and territory; and nation is still being imagined in relation to a horizontal connection to others within a territory as well as across generations. However, the very process of delineating Australian-ness as something distinct from other nation-states is done through the use of a highly international discourse of environmentalism.

Another strategy for developing a national identity independent of Britain that appeared in the debates around public gardens in Melbourne was the move to elevate Australian native vegetation to the status of high art. In the Swanston Street debate, one proponent of eucalyptus trees recalled how architect Walter Burley Griffin (and Marion Mahony Griffin) recognized the objective beauty of native vegetation and used it as the basis for his "city beautiful" urban design in Canberra at the beginning of the twentieth century. The newspaper-writing advocate of natives, like people in the community group regenerating the bush and like East Melbourne admirers of Heidelberg-style landscape art, moved to redeem Australian native vegetation by seeing it as beautiful, instead of as scraggly, as the colonials had. The newspaper contributor asserted Australian nature as high culture: the eucalyptus was worthy of a poet's and designer's attention and it was elegant enough to use along the city's central axis.

The language and metaphors employed in the battle over the redevelopment of Swanston Street and of Albert Park suggest that debates over vegetation were intertwined with considerations of cultural hierarchy. In many societies, high culture and status have been associated historically with the city, both symbolically and spatially. That is, things connected with power and importance, such as commerce, politics, high culture, and men have been associated with the city. Conversely, women, the domestic, leisure, and kitsch culture have been symbolically associated with and segregated to spaces outside of the city (in the country or suburbs).[19]

The spatial organization of landscape design in Melbourne (which regularly placed native species outside of the city and European species in the urban center and along the central axes of the financial district) reflected the historical status of Australian native vegetation as low culture. Proponents of eucalyptus trees in the Swanston Street debate were challenging the cultural hierarchy that had historically treated British cultural forms as high art and used them to symbolize things that society deemed important. Here again, people in Australia were challenging the colonial domination of Britain over Australia by reversing the spatial and cultural hierarchy of things that are Australian (gum trees) and things that are European (plane trees) in Australia. We see a persistent move to revalue Australian nature as high culture, and thus accord it the importance needed to rival English cultural forms in the imagining of Australian national identity. It was interesting that at the end of the twentieth century people still announced the beauty of the Australian landscape as if it were a radical, countercultural idea. Yet, as we saw in the previous chapter, even more culturally conservative members of Australian society had elevated the Australian landscape to high art in their drawing rooms, suggesting that recognition of the beauty of the Australian landscape was hardly a counterhegemonic act.

In a country where many were questioning their colonial relationship to Great Britain and attempting to articulate an independent Australian identity, the landscape served as a promising symbol for new nationalism. If Australian culture had been designated as low culture and subordinate to British culture since the Australian state's inception, then new cultural forms had to be constructed and placed firmly within the sphere of high culture. Nature had the double advantage of being shared and being "ancient." However, nations and national identity are created in the cultural realm and in governmental spheres. Nature is something always mediated by culture and historical context (see Wilson 1992); thus, creating a national identity out of Australian nature meant transforming it into a particular cultural fact. Therefore, it is important to understand how specific cultural frameworks were shaping people's relationship to the natural environment and how they could change with political and social shifts.

The movement of Australian native vegetation away from its representation as threatening Other to its representation as (high) art was also a spatial movement away from the bush (countryside) and into the city. The creation of gardens was an important step in re-imaging the environment as a form of art. The native garden movement was very instrumental in changing the cultural and political status of the native landscape. One gardener associated the changed cultural status of Australian natives with the moment when it became thinkable to put them in a vase.

The consumer success of luxury products that emphasize their origins in the Australian landscape further testified to the fact that Australian nature had entered the sphere of high culture and the domain of urban, cosmopolitan living. For example, before the 1980s, the middle class primarily consumed French and Italian wines and European gourmet foods. Beginning in the 1980s, the Australian wine industry began to boom, supported by both a strong Australian consumer base and international sales. Well-known Australian chefs like Stephanie Alexander promoted Australian gourmet items, such as Tasmanian cheeses. Additionally, the environment was commodified for national and international consumption by cosmetic companies like Red Earth and by the Australian fashion industry. These "natural" products, consumed predominantly by the middle class, enabled the international commodification of "Australia." Additionally, since the moral symbolism associated with native products was intertwined with an international discourse of environmentalism, they could be marketed more easily to middle-class consumers in other countries. Nonetheless, although these products were exported, in Australia they were part of a larger production of political subjectivity based on the idea "recognition" of a "unique" and "beautiful" Australian environment.

The association between the nation-state and natural environment was strongly reinforced by the construction of a new Parliamentary Building in Canberra in 1988, a national icon that traded heavily on images and symbols of the landscape and animals.[20] The use of the environment and Aboriginal art as symbols for the new Parliament Building furthered the status of Australian nature, again suggesting the hegemonic status of "recognizing" the worth of the Australian natural environment. The Parliament Building incorporated the Australian natural environment in a way that associated it with high art by linking it to internationally acclaimed architecture and making it the subject of mosaics and tapestries created by renowned Australian artists (settler and Aboriginal).[21]

We see that in its cultural ascendancy to the position of high culture, nature becomes viable material for national symbols. Australian culture, to the extent that it was imagined in terms of low culture like "singlets" (men's underwear) and barbecues, could not serve as the raw material out of which to build a national subjectivity. Yet, with the redemption of Australian nature, Australians could challenge the former colonial hierarchy that positioned Australian culture as vulgar and parochial and British culture as worthy of national symbolism for Australia. The transformation of Australian nature into high culture helped to produce an alternative set of symbols and allowed people to renarrate their once subservient relationship with Britain.

Figure 14. Mosaic (in tile) by Aboriginal artist Michael Nelson Tjakamarra commissioned for the New Parliament Building in 1992. The following year Tjakamarra removed the center tile of the mosaic in protest of the government's neglect of Aboriginal issues.

## CULTIVATING WHITE INDIGENEITY

Historian Tom Griffiths describes the activities of amateur historians and naturalists in Australia in the nineteenth and early twentieth centuries in order to argue that these activities were a means by which people attempted to define their relationship with place and with the Aboriginal people they were displacing. He builds on Bernard Smith's argument in his 1980 Boyer Lectures that the melancholy that settler Australians projected onto the Australian landscape was as much about fear and guilt in relation to their displacement of Aboriginal people as it was about homesickness (for England) and loneliness. Griffiths examines the efforts of amateur naturalists to understand how people negotiated their complex positionality in Australia. In describing the European-Australians' rituals of place and the specific work of the Field Naturalists Club of Victoria, Griffiths explains, "They aimed to secure the land emotionally and spiritually for the settler society. They played out in space a larger cultural negotiation between the imported and the indigenous, between European intellectual 'modernism' and Australian environmental 'primitivism'" (1996, 151). Griffiths's analysis provides a useful way of understanding some of the cultural work achieved through the twentieth-century gardening and landscape practices discussed in this chapter.

In describing naturalist clubs in Victoria, such as the Bread and Cheese Club, the Victorian Aboriginal Group, and the Anthropological Society of Victoria, Griffiths explains, "Aboriginal words and symbols increasingly became part of the 'appropriate speech' of the native born in the early twentieth century, and were used to define a white indigenous culture" (1996, 173). That is, people began to incorporate Aboriginal names and meanings into their European organization and understanding of space. They increasingly used Aboriginality to demarcate their white, settler production of space in Australia, fusing Aboriginal identity with their own spatial practice. One example of this can be found in the activities and writings of Stan Mitchell. Mitchell wrote *Stone Age Craftsmen* (1949) and worked in some instances with the Royal Geographical Society to preserve Aboriginal constructed spaces such as canoe trees, roadside trees, and rock art. Griffiths notes about Mitchell, "He believed strongly in the tourist potential of Aboriginal landscapes and in the restoration of Aboriginal names so as to 'give the place a definite character of its own which would possibly be unique in the world'"

(1996, 155). The appropriation of Aboriginal history, identity, and place making in activities such as Mitchell's were methods for creating a settler construction of place.

Griffiths's history helps us put the activities and narratives of indigenous gardening proponents into historical context. In some important ways, the activities of people promoting and planting Australian native vegetation continue to define settler Australians' place in relation to the land they occupy and, importantly, in relation to political critics who increasingly challenged Aboriginal dispossession by European settlement. Griffiths's analysis suggests that the gardeners whom I analyzed at the end of the twentieth century were part of a larger historical process by which white Australians have attempted to define themselves by imagining links with things Aboriginal. He describes a strategy that became increasingly popular as the century wore on for defining place and reconciling settler Australians' relation to the people they had displaced.

Making a similar point, Andrew Lattas notes that the increased usage of indigenous cultural signifiers in popular culture to define settler identity and mark their relationship to place in the 1930s gained even greater currency in the 1970s. Aboriginality became even more useful to white Australian society with the rise of nationalism and the economic necessity of defining Australia as an international tourist destination.[22]

> This rehabilitation of Aboriginality must be understood in the context of the resurgence of Australian nationalism. Cultural nationalists of the 1930s had sought to recruit the Aborigines in the task of constituting Australia's difference from the mother country. More powerfully, those of the 1970s and 1980s, including the designers of the Bicentennial, again drew upon this resource, to establish difference (not least for tourists), and add depths to a shallow colonial history. (1992, 166)

Lattas highlights the long history of white Australians' thinking their relationship to Britain in relation to Aboriginal identity. For many years, white Australians narrated their whiteness and European-ness; that is, they marked their *identification with* Britain by differentiating themselves from Aboriginal people. Yet at a certain historical point, in the 1930s and then since the 1970s, as Lattas argues, white Australians have again drawn heavily on Aboriginal identity. However, this time, they use Aboriginal identity to define or signal their *difference from* Britain.

Additionally, by the end of the twentieth century we begin to see Aboriginal identity used more consistently to define and elongate national history. This shift is particularly visible in the practices of Australian museums. Earlier in the century, museums exhibited Aboriginal artifacts and remains in natural history displays. Tony Bennet comments that the practice of including Aboriginal history within natural history functioned to provide a transition in history between nature and culture for Australians (1995, 150–51). Placing Aboriginal cultural objects within museum displays on nature positioned Aborigines to serve as an ecological link between the Australian environment (landscape and animals) and the coming of European civilization. These practices powerfully reflected and reinforced the logic of *terra nullius,* since positioning Aboriginal culture as partially located in nature (state of nature) underscored the "logic" of denying Aboriginal people land and a subject position within the social contract.

Eventually Aboriginal culture was represented in ways other than as a component of nature. Bennet examined the 1982 *Plan for the Development of the Museum of Australia* for how it illustrates how Aboriginal culture and history have been newly incorporated into national history. It highlights the way in which the natural landscape, Aboriginal culture, and contemporary "multicultural" settler national culture became fused in the 1980s. It claims,

> Much of the history of Australia—the driest continent—has been shaped by its climate, its geographical antiquity, its vast distances and its island isolation. Because of this, its flora and fauna are unique, and the same timeworn landscape conceals ancient life forms and enormous mineral resources.
>
> Australia's human history is ancient and distinctive. Aboriginal people populated Australia early in the colonising surge of modern peoples across the world. Over a period of at least 40,000 years, the Aboriginal people developed a spiritually complex society with an exceptional emphasis upon ritual life and attachment to place. Through time, Aboriginal societies modified to the environment and, in their turn, adapted to it with considerable regional variation.
>
> As the nation approaches the bicentenary of European settlement it has become a complex multicultural society. The continuing

story of the transformation of Australia from a country of hunter-gatherers to an industrial nation is one of tragedy, persistence and innovation. It should be told with vigor and objectivity, using our collective heritage to promote the consciousness and self-knowledge which foster a mature national identity. (Museum of Australia 1982, as quoted in Bennet 1995)

Although Aboriginal culture continues to be a transition between nature and European modernity in this later account of Australia's origin, the museum's statement now emphasizes the parallels between Aboriginal culture (as a multicultural collective and as an outcome of adapting to a unique environment) and Anglo-Celtic/Euro-Australians' history on the "driest continent."

Bennet argues that at the end of the twentieth century, settler Australians used Aboriginal culture to connect the Australian nation with a "deep past," one that extends beyond the date of 1788 to the prehistoric era (1995, 150–51). The museum's discourse suggests that the settler claim to land, like Aboriginal society, is part of a continuing process of the "colonising surge of modern people across the world" as well as of adapting to and modifying the environment ("Aboriginal people modified the environment and, in their turn, adapted to it with considerable regional variation"). And, as Bennet points out, the conceptualization of history "enables the discourse of multiculturalism to be back-projected into the midst of time where it finds its support in the regional variation of Aboriginal culture" (1995, 151). In other words, recent discourses about Aboriginal culture place it within a larger national story of an "Australian" society defined by its relationship to the "unique" environment and by its multiculturalism.

Obviously, the proponents of native vegetation in Australia were engaged in a somewhat different project than museum curators of Aboriginal history. One was concerned with nature, the other with people, after all. But they are connected, however, in that both are cultural articulations of how a relationship with the "Australian" landscape defines Australian subjectivity. And while the museum explicates the relationship between Aboriginal people and settler culture more overtly, its vision seems to be implied in the logic of the native garden movement. The project statement of the Australian History Museum explicitly claims settler Australians to be part of an historical legacy of people adapting to the unique natural landscape of the continent, in which Aboriginal societies preceded them. In gardening discourse, some linked their activities to Aboriginal people, as East Melbourne Garden Club member Margaret did when she lamented that settler Australians could have learned so much about the land if they had listened to Aboriginal people. But even when the links to Aboriginal people were left implied, the practices of those who cultivated Australian native landscapes were physically enacting the continuity of societies adapting to the unique Australian landscape that the museum described. More specifically, by physically engaging with the landscape in a way that was sensitive to the environment, settler Australians placed themselves within a tradition that was imagined to also characterize Aboriginal spatial practices.

Examining the meanings people give to their engagement with Australian indigeneity also allows us to see how Aboriginality is deeply connected to settler Australians' renegotiation of their colonial relationship with *Britain* and to their reconceptualization of the whiteness of Australian national subjectivity. Since a significant means by which settler Australians historically defined themselves as civilized and as British was to negate their connections to non-whites, it is perhaps not surprising that a shift in identification with Britishness following World War II would also prompt a shift in identification with Aboriginality. Defining place has been a necessary project for many Australians in understanding themselves in the world and in defining their political community. Griffiths's historical analysis reminds us that this has been an ongoing project in Australia.

However, in the late twentieth century, at a historical moment when Aboriginal land rights politics challenged settler Australians' legal and ethical claims to land, these activities in defining place also became the site where people tried to articulate their relationship to the Australian continent. The High Court Mabo and Wik decisions intensified an existing need for settler Australians to define their connection to the Australian continent.

When the High Court ruled in 1992 that Aboriginal people had a legitimate claim on the land, settler Australians were dramatically repositioned as invaders, as people who took the land from people who were already on it. Since 1992, many Australians have rejected an image of themselves as colonizers by asserting that they were not responsible for things done by earlier generations. People (including Prime Minister Howard) have called this new understanding of the history of contact a "black armband" view of history in a not-so-subtle move to represent facts about the dispossession of Aborigines as exaggerated. Such denials are one form of settler Australian response to the threat posed by the Mabo decision to white Australia's imagined relationship to the continent of Australia.

However, more generally, the Mabo and Wik decisions have put settler Australians in a bind because, in order to narrate their nation, they need to imagine a connection with past generations. And they need a rationale for how they legitimately occupy the land and can claim the continent as their home. While the displacement of Aborigines was always a fact white Australians needed to reconcile with their self-image as democratic and progressive, the rejection of *terra nullius* in 1992 made it less possible for white Australians to narrate their history as one of civilized, noble European colonials or even as well-intentioned political exiles from industrial Britain making their way in an unfamiliar land. And, importantly, the Mabo and Wik decisions gave Aboriginal people more political power to pursue litigation, which in turn has kept the issue of colonial dispossession in the foreground of national politics in Australia.

Redefining their relationship to the Australian continent as one of stewardship and their link to the past as "environmental heritage" has helped settler Australians begin to redefine their political subjectivity and renew their claim to territory in Australia. Such a move allows Australians to distance themselves from British colonialism and establish a connection (claim) to the land premised on something other than colonial conquest. It has allowed white Australians to reterritorialize their nation and culture by premising the imagined community on a relationship to the more politically neutral environment. As stewards, they distinguish their nation from British colonialism; they instead associate their lineage to other Australians and to Aborigines in particular, who also have a relationship with the "unique" Australian landscape.

A kind of white indigeneity is possible once settler Australians have redefined their relationship to the land as one of a spiritually informed stewardship, as opposed to one of colonial exploitation. About the development of such an identity Griffiths writes:

Through their history-making, Europeans sought to take hold of the land emotionally and spiritually, and they could not help but deny, displace and sometimes accommodate Aboriginal perceptions of place. They were feeling their way toward the realisation that becoming Australian would, in some senses, mean becoming Aboriginal. (1996, 5)

Griffiths's assertion that the process of defining a relationship to place logically led settler Australians to imagine themselves in terms of a kind of Aboriginality for themselves is a reasonable one. However, in this chapter I have tried to understand the profound political function of the "realization" of a white indigeneity. The construction of a kind of white indigeneity by non-Aboriginal Australians in a myriad of disparate spatial practices has in fact served certain cultural and political needs. This is not to say that people self-consciously chose to identify with Aboriginal people in order to achieve political ends. Rather, some of the contradictions and necessities of the settler Australians' position have led to a more widespread "recognition" or imagining of new forms of identity premised on a connection to, rather than rejection of, Aboriginal subjectivity and culture. My concern with Griffiths's language here is that he risks reproducing the common sense asserted by many non-Aboriginal Australians, one that claims that defining a sense of national belonging in Australia means "realizing" one's indigeneity (through the connection to the natural environment). It is important to remember that people narrate their claims and connection to national space in a range of ways throughout the world. White Australians could and have narrated (experienced) their connection to the nation-state in many other ways besides through a "stewardship" of the natural landscape. While people have to narrate nation in a way that legitimates claims to land and resources, it is not necessary for this to be done by "discovering" one's true relationship and environmental responsibility to the native vegetation. Rather than taking the "realisation" that becoming Australian "would, in some senses, mean becoming Aboriginal" as manifest destiny, we need to denaturalize this process. We need to try to understand the historical and political context out of which such a structure of national feeling develops and to take care to be cognizant of what such a structure of feeling makes possible politically.

Wanting to imagine one's nation as a legitimate "home" and wanting a positive collective identity is understandable. However, there are potential political repercussions to these spatial practices that may yet be realized. To the extent that an "environmental heritage" allows white settlers to feel like spectators, or even fellow victims, of colonial practices that have displaced Aboriginal people from the land, this new national discourse is potentially politically regressive. A set of practices and narratives that allows the dominant group to feel entitled once again to a disproportional amount of land and power in Australia, without interrogating the history that allowed them that privilege, is of course highly troubling. Put simply, such spatial practices can too easily facilitate the recuperation of power and moral authority. There are many potentially socially progressive, even radical, elements to the discourse and spatial practices around redeeming the Australian landscape. However, there remains a deafening silence about what it means for white Australians to be stewards of the Australian environment in the wake of the Mabo decision and in relation to the colonial critique that Aboriginal groups have been making about the continuing unjust policies of the settler nation-state. Only by more actively bringing these two conversations together, thinking them in relation to each other, can these spatial practices ensure that they fully avoid the bankrupt morality they purport to reject.

# 3

## Policing the Body Politic: Mapping Bodies and Space in Fitzroy

The intersection of geography, criminality, and national identity is a particularly rich nexus when considering Australia. Historically, these issues played an important role in defining Australian national identity and Australia's relationship to the British Empire in its transition from a penal colony to a nation-state in 1901. We will see that these three issues continue to animate Australians' renegotiation of their relationship to Britain, albeit in new ways, and inform some of the ways people are defining Australia's proximity to Asia.

The Fitzroy Police Station community delineated political identity in everyday place making. And because the police function as agents for the state, much of their place making functioned to define and regulate political subjectivity in Australia. Building on Michel Foucault's analysis of the Panopticon (1979) as a metaphor for the process by which modern subjectivity is produced and regulated by the state through practices of surveillance, the next two chapters examine surveillance and the regulation of space as important practices for defining the boundaries of national belonging. These practices work alongside discourses of criminality in defining a moral national and supranational community at a time when the identity and legitimacy of the Anglo-Australian state have been challenged by Aboriginal land rights and by a redefinition of Australia's relationship to Asia.

Fitzroy,[1] the district for which the police were responsible, was an inner suburb with a great deal of diversity. It was one of the most densely populated suburbs in Australia, and its population reflected a diverse mixture of race, ethnicity, sexual orientation, and economic class. In part, this was because it was a community in transition. For most of the twentieth century Fitzroy had been a working-class urban neighborhood in which Aboriginal and poor Anglo-Celtic Australians had historically had a sizable presence. It became more diverse in the 1950s because members of most migrant groups were housed in publicly assisted housing units in Fitzroy, along with low-income Anglo-Celtic and Aboriginal Australians. By the 1970s, Fitzroy was home to 70 percent of Melbourne's Greek population. Further, the suburb later drew a lot of the Vietnamese immigrants who came to Australia in larger numbers in the 1980s and 1990s. Throughout the century Fitzroy had a lively economy of ethnic shops, bars, unpretentious cafés, and illegal activities.

Beginning in the 1980s, middle- and upper-middle-class Anglo-Celtic Australians began renovating the Victorian houses in Fitzroy that had served as boardinghouses for several decades. Although there had always been some wealthy residents in North Fitzroy, the rapid gentrification that began in full force in the 1980s exacerbated the contrast in wealth in Fitzroy. It meant that some of the wealthiest people in the city lived next to some of the poorest in South Fitzroy. By the end of the twentieth century, many of the Greek and Italian immigrants who came to Australia in the 1950s had moved out of Fitzroy into larger houses in the inner suburbs north of the central business district or had relocated to the "greener" suburbs farther out of the city to the east. Low-income Anglo-Celtic residents, those Kooris[2] who had not been driven out by escalating prices in Fitzroy, and first-generation immigrants, most commonly from Vietnam, increasingly occupied the low-income public housing.

Transnational flows of capital, people, and culture were very much evident in Fitzroy. At the south end of Brunswick Street, the main commercial axis in Fitzroy, an African restaurant was immediate neighbor to a Vietnamese grocery that advertised Asian "health food" to expand its customer base beyond the Vietnamese immigrants who lived in the public housing high-rise across the street. The futon shop sold ambiance and Eastern bedding made in Taiwan to Anglo-Celtic and second-generation Greek and Italian immigrants studying at Melbourne University. Within the space of three blocks one could buy Italian and Greek pastry, Greek gyros,

Turkish coffee, or an Indian dinner. Perpendicular to Brunswick Street, on Johnston Street, was a very fashionable Latin district of restaurants and bars. "Mini Spain" coexisted with an overpriced New York bagel shop and a music store that specialized in "world music" and bellowed reggae and Spanish guitar onto Johnston Street during the day.

The Fitzroy Police Station, consisting of approximately forty-six uniformed officers[3] and a plainclothes detective unit of approximately twelve detectives, was located just off Brunswick Street at the south end of the suburb. One side of the station faced the area of the suburb that contained many of the fashionable restaurants and shops on Brunswick Street. The other side looked out onto the government-subsidized public housing high-rises, which the officers usually called "the caves." Fitzroy had the reputation of being one of the busier stations in Melbourne, in large part because of the suburb's steady drug economy as well as the high number of house and car burglaries ("burgs").

The police's spatial practice provides us insight into the way the spatial is an important dimension of state power. Spatial practices of the police regulate the population as well as define modern political subjectivity. And much of the political power of the state takes the form of regulating the minute movements of the body as well as people's physical movement through space. One of the ways in which Aboriginal land rights threatened the territorial definition of the Australian state is the challenge it has posed to the Euro-Australian nation-state's spatial practices. This threat takes the form of everyday resistance ("tactics" as de Certeau would call them) and the persistence of alternative means of constructing space. The persistence of more traditional Aboriginal notions of space undermines the power of the modern state insofar as Aborigines use collective memory and spiritual meaning to differentiate space, rather than visual markers that can be monitored by the modern Australian settler state.

In order to appreciate how Aboriginal practices disrupt the state's territorial power and self-definition, we must first explore the means by which the police reproduced state power through their everyday, professional place-making practice. Then, by looking at everyday Aboriginal practices of resistance in Fitzroy and considering the more general threat of land rights litigation, we will consider how the territorialization of the Australian nation-state has been challenged at this historical moment. Police spatial practices high-light how the police function as agents in reproducing spatial forms of state power, but the ethnographic material also illustrates how, at other times, their practices are best read as more spontaneous re-sponses to the threat of deterritorialization by Aboriginal and Asian groups in particular.

## POLICE STRATEGIES

Understanding the relation of the Fitzroy police officers' spatial prac-tices to the construction of the nation-state involves understanding the development in the West at the end of the eighteenth century of what Foucault calls "disciplinary" societies. Foucault writes that among other changes, the Enlightenment marked a change in how philosophers were thinking about the nature of crime. Foucault notes this intellectual shift in the philosophy of punishment in such thinkers as Rousseau, Cesare de Beccaria, Jeremy Bentham, and J. P. Brissot de Warville. Their theoretical reworking of penal law rejected the idea of crime as a transgression against natural law. Rather, crime was "something that harms society; it is a social in-jury, a trouble, a disturbance for the whole of society" (Foucault 2000b, 55). Thinkers at this time began to conceive of crime as a breach of the social contract, rather than as a moral sin.

Foucault discusses the rise of the "age of social control" that came to dominate in modern society (ibid.). With the reframing of crime as a violation of the social contract, French and English govern-ments became oriented to something that exceeds merely punishing a particular transgression. Government became more concerned to predict and prevent deviancy. Foucault explains:

> Thus, toward the end of the nineteenth century the great idea of criminology and penal theory was the scandalous idea, in terms of penal theory, of *dangerousness*. The idea of *dangerousness* meant that the individual must be considered by society at the level of his potentialities, and not at the level of his actions; not at the level of actual violations of an actual law, but *at the level of the behavioral potentialities they represented*. (ibid., 57)

As such, policing developed into a form of protecting the social con-tract by means of surveillance and the anticipation of deviancy, rather than simply by serving as an instrument for punishing crimes that had already taken place.

In another essay, Foucault writes that the police signified a program of governmental rationality through their control of space. Police surveillance of potential dangerousness in the dystopic urban landscape and social control through urban design was to become a model for governing the entire nation-state (2000a, 351). Foucault qualifies his analysis by saying that this ideal was achieved much more so by the French than the English legal system. Additionally, both England and France were limited in achieving this normative idea of governing by the development of certain strains within liberalism that provided a critique of "too much government," on the grounds that it led to ineffective governing.

Foucault's analysis of police practice in modern governance and as a disciplinary mode of power is useful for an understanding of the operations of the Fitzroy Police at the end of the twentieth century. An ethnographic analysis of their policing illustrates the many ways in which the Fitzroy police were engaged in rationalizing and mapping potential deviancy through the control and monitoring of bodies in the city's geography.[4] I pursue this analysis in two chapters in this study. The present chapter (chapter 3) highlights the use of mapping and technology to anticipate and taxonomize deviancy. The chapter that follows (chapter 4) considers how the designation by police of certain groups as criminal or deviant has been used repeatedly to define the imagined borders of the nation.

Much of what the Fitzroy police did as part of their professional activities could be classified as spatial activity. Law and order in Western democracies largely involves controlling space. As Steve Herbert writes in his ethnography of the Los Angeles Police Department, "Social power relies fundamentally upon territoriality. It is certainly the case that the police would be largely impotent without the capacity to create and enforce boundaries, to restrict people's mobility in and around certain areas" (1997, 11; see also Sack 1993).

In Fitzroy, the police's mandate, as a branch of the larger bureaucracy of the state, literally involved "keeping order"; that is, it entailed maintaining control of people in the space in which the police had authority. The police were central to the power of the state, not so much because of their embodiment of the state legitimate monopoly on violence, as a Weberian analysis might characterize them, but because state power depends on spatial control of the population (de Certeau 1984; Foucault 1979).

Because of their connection to hegemonic power, the landscapes that the police produced, reinforced, and regulated in their district of Fitzroy are best understood as what de Certeau has called "strategies."

> Strategies are actions which, thanks to the establishment of a place of power (the property of a proper), elaborate theoretical places (systems and totalizing discourses) capable of articulating an ensemble of physical places in which forces are distributed . . . They thus privilege spatial relationships. At the very least they attempt to reduce temporal relations to spatial ones through the analytical attribution of a proper place to each element and through the combinatory organization of the movements specific to units or groups of units. The model was military before it became "scientific." (1988, 84, 38)

For de Certeau, strategies are a means of exerting power or dominance by controlling space. They are the imposition of space over time.

The police's strategies with their district took numerous forms. Officers who were not assigned to patrol duties for a particular shift were engaged in numerous practices within the station building that spatially defined and regulated their district. Two officers at the rank of constable (constable or senior constable) were assigned to overseeing the Watch House, which was the central office space, serving members of the public who came into the station. The Watch House keeper and Watch House assistant also provided the link between patrolling officers and other officers at the station who might need to contact them. They were also at times an intermediary between the central dispatcher (D-24) for the district and the patrol cars working out of the station. Officers in the Watch House would also oversee the distribution of necessary equipment for officers leaving the station (radios, kit for the car, guns, and handcuffs).

Also at the station would be officers occupied with writing up reports or doing other paperwork related to their processing of "crooks."[5] This group would include personnel at the constable level and sergeants,[6] one of whom would simultaneously be responsible for managing the patrol activities of the station for a shift.[7] Although the activities within the station were often auxiliary, they contributed to the larger purpose of defining where people were in their district, what they did, and with whom they associated. All of this information allows the police to control Fitzroy better by mapping bodies and activities in relation to the physical landscape.

Figure 15. The Fitzroy Police Station. In the background are the public subsidized housing commission high-rise apartment buildings (dubbed "the caves" by the police).

Most of the spatial practices addressed in this chapter concern the activities of people on patrol outside the station; these practices took the form of car and foot patrols around the district for which they were responsible.[8] For each shift (approximately nine hours), there was typically one police car in operation at all times, with the addition of a van on some day shifts. Each vehicle was occupied by two uniformed officers (usually a constable and senior constable). Additionally, on occasion during the day, there would be a team of two "connies" (constables) on foot or bicycle. Their presence was meant to prevent crime, as much as it was intended to respond to it, by displaying the police's awareness of mundane activities and changes in their district.

The physical composition of particular areas of the station building also spoke of the centrality of spatial practices and mapping to police work in Fitzroy. The Watch House contained maps of Fitzroy and surrounding areas and held computers with the LEAP computer database that, as I will elaborate later in this chapter, mapped the physical, social, and spatial profiles of many people and activities in Melbourne. LEAP was an acronym for the Law Enforcement

Assistance Program, the computer software the Victorian police used on license from the computer company GTE GIS, who owned the program. This software was modified from a U.S. law enforcement software package and first used in Victoria in 1985. As of January 2004, the Victoria auditor-general's office estimated the Victorian police had invested $A50 million in the LEAP system and were seeking to purchase the program.

The mess (station kitchen/dining room) was the site of an important apparatus for policing. On the table at which officers would regularly eat or talk over coffee would be several copies of a photocopied bulletin (a 5 to 10 page booklet) that contained the profile of particular people about whom officers should be especially aware during that week. These bulletins were produced by the District Information Centre (DIC), which was located in the central administrative offices of the Victoria Police. The bulletins were compiled from information that district police officers had submitted to the central database of the Victoria Police Department, and they highlighted ongoing criminal activity (someone suspected of repeated robberies, for instance) or people involved in a case that the detectives of one of the urban stations were working to solve.[9]

The bulletins were one of the more formal or official ways in which people and activities at the station were mapped. They lay on the mess table with the day's newspapers for officers to pick up and glance at regularly as a means of tracking certain activities and people within Melbourne. But they complemented the ongoing, less formal commentary or storytelling in which officers engaged at the station and in the patrol cars. This "oral tradition" among the police constituted a very important means of spatially understanding and controlling the district.[10] The Watch House and the mess were key sites for the informal exchange of information between officers about incidents that had occurred recently in the community (serious and humorous) and for casual conversations about various personal or professional topics.

The police constructed and controlled their landscape, in part, through discourse. They did this through the stories they told about people and events within their district and with their descriptions of local and national geography. De Certeau argues eloquently that stories constitute spatial activity when he writes:

In Modern Athens, the vehicles of mass transportation are called *metaphorai*. To go to work or come home, one takes a "metaphor"— a bus or a train. Stories could also take this noble name: every day, they traverse and organize places; they select and link them together; they make sentences and itineraries out of them. They are spatial trajectories . . . Stories thus carry out a labor that constantly transforms places[11] into spaces or spaces into place. (1984, 117, 118)

Through narrative, people give meaning to space. They might do this by the simple act of giving directions, which shape another's experience and order physical space in a certain way—leading one past a lovely garden and away from a street congested with traffic noise or a "dangerous" neighborhood, for instance. And people constitute the meaning and reality of a landscape through stories or discussions about people, places, and activities. In Fitzroy, most of any given patrol shift was spent driving around, talking to people about their activities and about the activities of other people. And the officers, who always went out in pairs, would always talk with each other about their district. These discussions were vital to policing and territorialized the local landscape of Fitzroy.

These discussions often took the shape of people just passing the time of day and catching up on neighborhood gossip. Often the brief stories would point to the way crooks are "DAD," dumb as dogshit. On one occasion in the mess at the station, an officer commented that a particular drug dealer familiar to Fitzroy officers seemed to be dealing in a new location. Or on another occasion, while driving through the district, one officer commented to his partner that he had not seen "Deb the nuffy"[12] around in a while. This comment opened up an exchange of information on Deb and prompted the more senior officer to name other psychologically disturbed people in Fitzroy with whom the police dealt on a regular basis. This casual exchange, for instance, conveyed very important information. It was important because the police perceived nuffies to be some of the most dangerous people with whom they worked because of how unpredictable nuffies often were. Most of the police shootings of members of the public in Victoria were of mentally disturbed people. Therefore, such casual conversations as the two officers had about "Deb" created a mental map for the officers of where and who the nuffies were in Fitzroy that may well inform how an officer responds to a particular situation in the future.

These spontaneous exchanges suggest that the police informally tracked a variety of people in their landscape above and beyond law-breakers. The officers did not seem particularly ambitious about spreading this information. Rather, their practices had more of the quality of gossip or of friends catching each other up on what has been happening after a separation. Nevertheless, these practices were very important for effective policing.

Stories told about various people or incidents in the station's history were a principal means by which newcomers to the station learned the social and spatial lay of the land. This often happened while new officers were driving around with more experienced police. Despite many flaws in his leadership abilities, one of the senior sergeants at the station was considered by many of the officers to be very valuable because he had an expansive knowledge about Fitzroy from which more junior officers regularly benefited. It was considered an asset that the senior sergeant recognized and spoke with so many people (merchants and crooks alike) when he walked down the busy commercial axis of Brunswick Street. The officers who served under him read this as a form of policing knowledge that came from experience rather than from theories or textbooks. At one point in a conversation with me over beers, a constable who was completing his term as a trainee at the station stopped himself midway through a story about the station and exclaimed, "Listen to me! I sound like one of the older members with all of these stories. I haven't been in long enough to have many stories." The constable's self-censorship indicated that, in addition to teaching new officers the landscape of Fitzroy, stories were also a sign of status that comes with experience and authority. Given the antagonism between Aboriginal people and the police, which I will discuss in more detail later, there is an ironic similarity between the relationship of authority and storytelling in the Fitzroy policing community and traditional Aboriginal communities. Both groups have traditions that authorize certain individuals to tell stories about the community or past events; for both groups, the authority to have and tell stories comes with experience or the status of being an elder in the community.[13]

The practice of policing through storytelling was especially clear while riding with Senior Constable Farley, one of the officers who had worked in Fitzroy for a number of years and had an impressive cognitive map of the social and physical landscape of the district. In the car were two officers, a student doing a criminology course (Danny), and me. Senior Constable Farley was driving and Constable Denton was in the front passenger seat. Danny was a student from the Royal Melbourne Institute of Technology who was required to intern with a police station as part of the requirements of his criminology course. He planned to enter the police force as soon as he finished his degree.

The officers drove up beside a milk bar[14] located on the ground floor of the Atherton Gardens Estate housing commission flats.[15] The two officers commented that police station personnel were aware that this milk bar was a site where drug transactions took place. Representatives from the Atherton Garden Estates community group had also identified this area as a place for drug transactions in the community security meeting Constable Denton and I had attended earlier that morning. From our view in the car we could observe a steady flow of traffic in and out of the milk bar, in addition to a man and woman standing in front of the milk bar smoking. The people surrounding the Atherton milk bar were dressed in weathered jeans and casual shirts (flannel shirts or sweatshirts, etc.). The glances people stole at the patrol car as it got closer to the store conveyed their awareness of being watched by the police. Nevertheless, people moved in and out of the milk bar or continued to smoke and talk as if they were unconcerned about the police officers' gaze.

Inside of the car, Senior Constable Farley's attention was fixed on a white woman who appeared to be between twenty-five and thirty years old. As we drove closer, he kept trying to recall the woman's name and the context in which he knew her. Finally he brought the car to a stop right next to the man and woman. At close range, one could read a man's name tattooed across the woman's knuckles on her left hand. Farley asked the woman if he knew her. She smiled, perhaps at the seeming naiveté of Farley's question, perhaps out of embarrassment, or perhaps in recognition of the beginning of a game of cat and mouse; she replied that she did not think so. As she smiled, she revealed her missing and decayed teeth. Suddenly, Farley remembered the context from which he knew her. He reminded the tattooed woman that he had been called to the scene when she had overdosed over in Richmond several years before and had to be rushed to the hospital. She conceded in a good-natured manner that yes, that was right. Farley at that point asked her to remind him of her name and to tell him the name of her boyfriend next to her.

Farley's casual, yet confident request for more information from the woman upon remembering such an intimate detail about her seemed to imply that additional information was his reward for such a good memory or for caring enough to remember her for years. It positioned the woman as potentially rude if she refused to tell him her name and to introduce him to her boyfriend in the face of Farley's generous memory of her hardship. Of course, Farley (and probably the woman herself) was acutely aware that the police were authorized to bring anyone who appeared suspicious into the station for formal question. Refusing to provide information requested by an officer on the street could qualify as suspicious and result in the person being brought into the station to answer the officer's questions. Most people chose to provide the limited information requested by a patrolling officer on the street rather than be taken to the station.

Farley proceeded to ask the woman what she had been up to and had her boyfriend here (gesturing to the man standing next to her) been "bashing her up" (hitting her). Farley seemingly asked this question because the woman's two front teeth were missing and the rest were in bad decay. She laughed in response and proceeded to explain that she and her boyfriend, "Frank," had been out of the state for a while but were back living in Melbourne now. And she added that her boyfriend had been good to her lately; the boyfriend next to her nodded in agreement.

Farley then turned his attention on the boyfriend and inquired if he had a brother. The man replied cautiously that yes he did, but his brother was in jail in New South Wales at the moment. He explained that his brother had gone to New South Wales to get his daughter; however, since he was wanted on charges for something else, the New South Wales police arrested him. Farley and the man both laughed with a little superiority at how stupid it was for the brother to go to New South Wales when he was wanted on charges. Farley then said amiably, "I should get your new address now that you're back in town." The boyfriend replied, "Yeah, sure. No problem. We got nothing to hide; things are going well for us right now," and proceeded to dictate his new address slowly enough to allow Farley to record it on his running sheet.[16]

As we drove away, Farley told the rest of us in the car that he would enter the addresses into the computer database when he got back to the station to update the police records. In response to my compliment on his memory, he said that it was good to be able to remember people and things about them. "If you know some things already, then they will tell you more and won't give the police such a hard time about supplying information." I asked whether he knew anything about the tattoos on the woman's hand, since the name did not correspond to her boyfriend's name. Farley said that the "tats" spelled the name of a former boyfriend who had died a few years back in a car accident. Farley also said that he knew that the boyfriend with her today had not bashed the woman in the mouth because he could recognize that the tooth decay was a result of methadone, which addicts take in treatment programs to get off of drugs. The methadone is very sweet and rots people's teeth. Danny, the intern in the car, replied that they should just brush their teeth more regularly. Farley responded to Danny's zeal with a rather perfunctory condemnation of the hygiene of the lower class. Without much energy behind his moral proclamation, he concluded the exchange with Danny by saying that "these people are not like other people in brushing their teeth or anything else."

This encounter between the police and people within their district tells of how the practice of collecting names, addresses, and details about people's social networks and habits was an intricate part of policing. Farley was able to establish a connection and relationship with the woman by reminiscing about other shared experiences, in this case the woman's drug overdose. It was interesting that in their conversation, Farley almost seemed to position himself as the protective older brother concerned to be sure that she was safe. But as his comments about her teeth indicated, Farley quickly assessed the woman's status and asked questions that would allow him to update the station's records about her and to more effectively place her in his map of the social and physical movements of the people in Fitzroy. In a sense, police conversations with the public frequently resembled neighbors gossiping about others' foolishness and what is new in their lives. Farley used this conversation as a means of learning more about the woman's relationships, to gain information about the man she was with, and to the extent possible, to assess the likelihood that she might be involved in any past or future criminal activity. In this way, Senior Constable Farley took care to map out who was part of the Fitzroy landscape and how they related to other people and activities.

Senior Constable Farley's policing skills also provide insight into the way the body was mapped in relation to (potential) criminality. Farley used signs on the woman's body to map her activities and history. Her tattooed knuckles told of her past relationship and provided an easy means of identifying her in the future. Her teeth betrayed the woman's drug addiction and her attempts to give it up. The body itself was a landscape that provided clues to past or potential criminality. Tattoos and poor hygiene flagged a history of criminality and its potential development, prompting Farley to record the woman on his map of crime in Fitzroy.

The policing practices in this example illustrate Foucault's description of governance through surveillance that developed out of the redefinition of criminality as a violation of the social contract. The shift that began during the Enlightenment, which Foucault describes, was also visible in policing practices on the streets of Fitzroy at the end of the twentieth century. He writes that policing strategies came to aim

> to ensure the control of individuals—which was no longer a penal reaction to what they had done but, rather, a control of their future behavior while this was still taking form ... The control of individuals, this sort of punitive penal control of individuals at the level of their potentialities, could not be performed by the judiciary itself; it was to be done by a series of authorities other than the judiciary, such as the police and a whole network of institutions of surveillance and correction. (2000a, 56)

The details of individual bodies allowed Fitzroy police officers to pinpoint individuals within the larger social landscape for future monitoring or arrest. The stories around such markers that were circulated among officers at the station associated meaning with these markers of individual identity and social networks in order to produce a distinctive landscape in Fitzroy.

## NORMATIVE LANDSCAPES

Fitzroy police officers had a normative sense of who should be where in Fitzroy; this sense governed how they categorized normal versus antisocial behavior, and it guided their regulation of the latter. In this sense, they literally created social order (ordered the social) through their movements and normative notions about the social and physical landscape of their district.

These movements and beliefs can be better understood by once again drawing on Bourdieu's concept of the habitus. They were a system of "durable, transposable dispositions . . . structuring practices and representations which can be objectively 'regulated' and 'regular' without in any way being the product of obedience to rules . . . collectively orchestrated without being the product of the orchestrating action of a conductor" (Bourdieu 1995, 72; see also Mauss's discussion of "body techniques," 1992).

The habitus of the Fitzroy officers and the normative landscape they produced reflected the purpose of the state to a certain extent. But they were also configured by the particularities of the officers' social location and, to a certain degree, by their individual values.

There were many possible ways in which the police officers might have constructed Fitzroy through their discourse and behaviors. Numerous narratives about Fitzroy were available for the police to borrow. For instance, one common descriptor of it by nonpolice was as an extremely fashionable suburb, a place where one could experience the best of Australia's multiculturalism through ethnic restaurants, specialty stores, and the diverse population. Fitzroy was also spoken of in other social circles as an investor's dream, where one could find Victorian cottages in need of restoration or rundown boarding houses and slowly renovate them for resale or for personal use. And some residents of the public housing commission high-rises characterized Fitzroy as a territory to be defended against complete gentrification.

Members of the police station did not reproduce any of these versions of Fitzroy. Instead, they constructed a dystopic image of the suburb. This was not because their experiences of this landscape were exclusively negative; in fact, police members had many friendly encounters on any given day. Their landscape was shaped by regular interactions with local business people who "took care of the members." This meant that the proprietors offered the police discounts, or in the case of food and alcohol, gave things to police officers without charge. The friendly relations also encouraged officers to remain in Fitzroy and socialize as a group after finishing their shift at the station. They enjoyed a warm welcome and friendly conversation with owners, managers, and staff when they came by to talk during working hours or to drink when off duty.

Perhaps because of their relationship with retailers, the police officers' landscape, even while on duty, was very much shaped by consumer interests. Day shifts in the police car often included some shopping and attending to errands. Police members swapped information about crooks as they looked out the window of the car while passing through different areas, but just as regularly they exchanged tips on good deals on cellular phones, electronics, and car services. Thus, their landscape was not comprised exclusively of hostile people and incidents of crime. In fact, they were popular members of an active social world in Fitzroy. And both inside and outside of Fitzroy, they could let a fellow cop or security officer know that they were "on the job" (i.e., in the police force) to qualify for special treatment.

Despite this, most officers recoiled at the thought of living in Fitzroy. Most took pride in the fact that they lived at least half an hour's commute from the station. In fact, some spoke of the foolishness of one constable who had recently bought a house several blocks from the station. The common reason they gave for their view was that they did not want to live close to the crooks they dealt with on a daily basis, and they perceived Fitzroy to be too crowded and too urban. Senior Constable Drake described his last station assignment (Carlton Police Station) as particularly stressful because he also lived in Carlton (a fashionable urban neighborhood) with his wife, who was a lawyer.[17] He said he hated this arrangement because there were times when "crooks" would follow him home from work to try to intimidate him. He "took care of it" by confronting them and then "standing over them for a while so they got the message."[18] Part of the disadvantage of this arrangement for Drake seemed to be that it did not allow him to keep distinct spatial boundaries between his home life and professional life in the way officers who lived in the outer suburbs could. Repeatedly, officers told me that they almost never spoke to their wives or families about their jobs. The male officers claimed that their wives "got bored" with hearing the same kinds of stories over and over, and they found the way their husbands could make jokes about death and other serious topics to be offensive.[19] Some officers, including Drake, also claimed that their wives did not want to see them as the people they had to be to do their jobs effectively.

For Senior Constable Drake, it was harder to keep professional and familial landscapes and their corresponding identities separate when assigned to a station in his own suburb. Drake underscored the disadvantages of working too close to home by telling me about an evening when he and his wife interrupted someone trying to break into their car, which was parked on a street near their house. Drake immediately grabbed the man and told him that he could co-operate by coming to the police station to be charged or have Drake beat him up. The man chose the latter option and Drake made good on his ultimatum. Drake explained to me that if he had not delivered some kind of punishment, the guy would no doubt return another day to finish the job of stealing the car. However, Drake's wife refused to speak to him for several days. Drake concluded that he reduced his contact with crooks and reduced his wife's anger when he lived and worked in different suburbs.

These kinds of stories were some of the direct ways officers constructed Fitzroy and the inner suburbs more generally as an undesirable place, despite the many positive aspects of their time in Fitzroy. They also constructed Fitzroy as a dystopia through their practice of calling it "the village." This term was used sarcastically as a way of signaling Fitzroy as a community gone awry. Their landscape indeed was similar to a village in that they repeatedly dealt with a certain group of people and insofar as they policed by collecting stories or gossip from the locals. However, the locals of this anti-village were not the butcher, the baker, and the candlestick maker. Rather, they were the nuffies (psychologically disturbed people), the "scrotes" (people of "low-class origins"), the "dockers" (talented crooks with "good form"), the drug dealers, the wife beaters, and the "battlers" (people who try to carry out a task against the odds and perhaps fail, but do so with dignity).

Despite the many pleasant relationships and situations the officers experienced in Fitzroy that I observed, when officers set out to give me a tour of their professional landscape they always took me to see "unappealing" things (e.g., the prostitute district, a woman who weighed two hundred pounds, or the homosexual club scene) or socially maladjusted people. Of course, part of this inclination toward the "depressing" or "shocking" might have been to see how I (someone who was not a cop—a woman, an academic) would react to the "real world" (my terminology). And perhaps they were partly motivated by a desire to be helpful, that is, to provide someone who had traveled halfway around the world to study their environment something worth writing about.

Yet, far from disliking their position in Fitzroy, the police officers reveled in the depressing quality of their landscape and celebrated the dystopia through their humor. When two officers discussed a crime, a third would often add casually with feigned naiveté, "I hear there's a bit of crime in Fitzroy." This would cue another officer to exclaim with irony, "No. Rumor. It's all rumor." This repeated performance depended on the idea that it was so obvious that Fitzroy was riddled with crime that it was funny to suggest that one could be unaware of the fact. On another occasion, after listening to a woman report the details of being harassed by a stranger, Senior Constable Chapman responded ironically, "Welcome to Fitzroy!" suggesting by her comment that being in Fitzroy means dealing with stalkers and other undesirables.

And, far from being something that upset them or suggested inefficient policing on their part, Fitzroy's degeneracy was a point of pride for the officers. Officers said that one year in Fitzroy was equivalent to three years of experience in an outer suburb and five years in a country station. In other words, conditions in Fitzroy made them better cops. Discussion of how much crime and "low life" existed in Fitzroy and their tours of the dystopic social landscape afforded the officers a way of talking about their skill and credentials as police officers.[20] They allowed officers to build their identity as police around positive qualities like perseverance, being "normal" themselves, and toughness. Thus, officers filtered out some experiences and emphasized others to create a landscape that was reasonably in touch with the objective world, yet also fulfilled their need for a positive professional identity.

Additionally, the process of imaging Fitzroy in a particular way was also a component of how the police regulated their district. Officers had a normative sense of who should be where in Fitzroy, what was "normal" and acceptable. People and things that deviated from the police officers' normative landscape caught their attention and invited investigation. For instance, the "scrotes" were expected to be in the more southern end of Fitzroy, near the public housing commission high-rises, or in other pockets of the suburb near subsidized housing. The middle and upper middle classes had more latitude in where they might be expected to wander, but generally they were expected to be in North Fitzroy (the high income end of the suburb) and near the restaurants and pubs on Brunswick Street.

People on bail were subjected to intense surveillance of the police since they were required to come to the station regularly to sign the bail book. On the first visit, the police typically took the person's photo with a Polaroid camera (if they did not already have a photo on file) as a means of making the task of tracking their movement and behaviors that much easier in the future.

The officers tracked people across time and space as part of their policing strategies (in de Certeau's sense of strategy). For example, one night the police were required to track down an Aboriginal man who was accused of stealing the jacket of a "trendy" (the police's term for a person who follows fashion trends) in the Napier Hotel (a pub) while the two were playing pool. They began their search by determining, with the aid of their computer system,[21] in which hostel the Aboriginal man supposedly lived and by drawing on their accumulated knowledge of which pubs Aborigines were known to frequent at that time of the evening. These steps narrowed their search of Fitzroy to specific places, sparing them the futility of patrolling the district without more specific direction.

The normative landscape the police had and enforced was often reductive; scholars have written about how police expectations of crime among people of color often leads to the overpolicing of those communities and to a higher rate of arrests of people of color (see Chan 1996; Hogg 1991; J. Marcus 1991; Hogg and Carrington 1998). These normative landscapes or the cognitive maps[22] allowed the police a shorthand for noting people and events that were "out of order." This was a large component of their crime prevention because it meant that they stopped "suspicious" people and thus limited these people's sense of ease to be in certain areas of the district. It also meant that the police were more present in areas like South Fitzroy or the Atherton Garden Estates buildings (which they were required to walk through at least once a shift).

De Certeau emphasizes the supremacy of space over time in his concept of strategy. He notes that resistance is the often short-lived victory of time over space. Yet, while resistance might be more about opportunity and thus spontaneity, de Certeau perhaps overemphasizes the tradeoff between space and time in spatial practices.

By emphasizing the supremacy of one over the other, de Certeau loses sight of the way time is an important component of space. For instance, in police practices, such as in the steps the officers took to apprehend the Koori man accused of stealing the leather jacket, time was a significant dimension of space. Their strategies for regulating the man's behavior depended on their sensitivity to how time altered or redefined spatial landscapes. The police were aware that the parks that Kooris might frequent at 3:00 p.m., closer to the busy commercial district of Brunswick Street, were altered with time, rendering them a different social and economic space at 1:00 a.m. According to police cognitive maps, at 1:00 a.m. the park would function instead as a location of drug trafficking among first-generation Asian immigrants and their white, working-class clients. In turn, at this hour, Aboriginal landscapes in Fitzroy would be comprised of a certain constellation of domestic sites, the few pubs in Fitzroy in which Kooris were welcome (according to Fitzroy officers) and two or three hostels.

Many policing situations allowed for alternative ways of interpreting the action and motives of the people involved; in these incidences, the normative landscapes of the Fitzroy officers shaped their perception of undesirable behaviors and people. For instance, while driving around during one shift, the officers pulled over to talk to a white man standing in the rain outside a row of expensive, renovated Victorian houses in the southern end of Fitzroy.[23] The late hour (around 11:00 p.m.) and the fact that this man was in his twenties, part of the age group that commits most of the crime in Melbourne, made him immediately suspicious to the officers. When asked by Acting Sergeant Burns for some type of identification, he could produce none. People were not required to carry identification in Victoria even though they were legally obligated to give the police their name and address when asked. The young man explained that he lived in the countryside but was visiting his mother whose house was in front of us. When Acting Sergeant Burns asked him why he was standing outside in the rain the man replied that he had mistakenly locked himself outside. He did not want to ring the bell and wake his mother "out of respect for her."

In the face of such an illogical explanation, Burns instructed, "Without turning around, tell us the address of your mother's house." Acting as if he did not hear the officer's clear instructions, the young man turned around and read the house number on the front of the building. Burns rolled his eyes in disgust at the man's antics and instructed him to provide his address in the countryside. While recording this on his police running sheet, Burns cautioned the young man that if this house were burgled tonight, or ever, he would be the first person for whom the police would come looking.

With this warning, the officers left the young man to stand in the rain. I observed to Officer Burns as we drove away that he had acted as if he thought the man was lying and questioned what he thought the man really had been doing in the rain. Burns shook his head and assessed was that the young guy was just a "fool" and was probably standing outside his girlfriend's house to see if she was with "some other guy."

This incident illustrates how the regulation of territory functioned in the police's activities. They circulated the territory of their district and regulated who could move without restraint and under what conditions within their district, based on their normative sense of their landscape. For instance, in contrast, a middle-class couple talking in the rain would be less likely to attract police notice or prompt a warning.

This example of the young man in the rain also highlights how the construction of landscapes is not always a conscious one. The police's normative landscape was as much about what the police officers defined as normal as about what they defined as abnormal. For instance, a given behavior, loitering in the rain on a dark night, was worthy of police interrogation when it was read as a potential crime against property. The same behavior, when it was no longer read as crime against property, but instead was read as the unsolicited attention of a man (a "fool") toward a woman, was no longer categorized as a social problem and was no longer worthy of police investigation and prevention. That is, the police officers made choices about their responses based on what they categorized as antisocial behavior versus "normal" behavior. Furthermore, because the police influenced who could remain on the street comfortably, their perception of their landscape—what they saw as acceptable versus unacceptable—functioned to construct the character and identity of Fitzroy.

## TECHNOLOGIES OF POLICING

Although much of the way in which police mapped and reproduced information about their district was through informal discussions and unsystematic movement through the Fitzroy landscape, their practices were part of a more formal system of spatially demarcating the district. The informal became more systematic when the officers translated the random conversations they had and observations they made while on patrol into detailed social and physical maps for the state. Officers were supposed to record every police action they performed and every "suspicious" person with whom they spoke while on a car or van patrol. This record, the running sheet, facilitated the systematic recording of people and activities that went on day and night in Fitzroy, and it provided a record of the police's patrol activities for station management. When members of a car patrol were not answering specific calls, they would randomly stop and talk to people who caught their attention, much like they did with the young man in the rain.

In practice, the police exercised a lot of discretion as to whom they recorded. They typically did not record shop owners' names on the running sheet when they stopped to chat. However, they used their official mandate as their justification for gathering the names of many groups of people or random walkers with whom they stopped to talk. For instance, when out on a car patrol one evening, two officers from the Carlton Station stopped to talk with

*Figure 16. Two Fitzroy police officers searching an abandoned car.*

a group of boys in their late teens who were standing near some parked cars.[24] They were on Faraday Street, one of several streets that comprised a busy restaurant and cafe district of Carlton, an inner suburb that bordered Fitzroy. The senior officer of the car, Senior Constable Emily Clancy, made small talk with the boys, asking them about which shops they frequented and warning them that the police were concerned that the arcade owner was dealing drugs. She concluded the conversation by explaining that she was obligated by station policy to record their names and addresses.

While she was gathering their names, she verbally noted when someone was not from the immediate area and asked how he came to be in this suburb. She also inquired about the ethnicity of various names. None of the boys resisted giving their names and addresses. The information garnered through these conversations usually became part of the archive of the police's computer system. The extensiveness of the information in the police's database depended in large part on how conscientious individual officers were about transferring information from the running sheet into the computer the next time they served a shift in the station. The Victoria Police had plans to eventually equip all of the patrol cars with laptops that would enable officers to enter running sheet information directly into the police database while on car patrol.[25]

The running sheets were a prime mode of establishing where people were in the social and spatial landscape of Fitzroy. As police officers performed their car patrols, they constantly assessed situations for potentially unproductive behavior. The Carlton officers on this particular evening noted the ethnically diverse group of teenage boys as potentially antisocial. Their ethnicity, age, gender, and numbers, combined with their spatial-temporal location, signaled potential deviance to the police. They were potential customers of the drug seller in the video arcade, and they were potentially involved in gang activities. Including them in the state's map allowed the police to better analyze the nature of these individuals' behaviors and friendships and to judge whether they were potentially a threat to the community (i.e., the social contract).

The police helped produce a rational spatial order using LEAP. LEAP was the centralized database program modified from a U.S. law enforcement software package and could be accessed from each station. Police members would enter into the computer the name of anyone to whom they spoke on the street who had given them cause to track them. However, people might also be recorded in the computer system for many reasons other than encountering a police officer on the street. Anyone who had a bureaucratic relationship with the state, such as a driver's licenses, car registration, or bicycle registration, might be in the LEAP system. Of course, people who committed a crime had extensive details on record, including their fingerprints. And, a detailed entry would also be in the database for a person who had been the victim of a crime or for people who had witnessed a crime. Additionally, in October 1999, the state government provided $A55 million to set up a database that recorded the DNA of people convicted of a certain crimes (e.g., drug trafficking, homicide, sex offenses, burglaries, theft). Upon conviction, an application would be made to the court for a DNA sample to be provided to the police and recorded as part of their LEAP database. The court had also approved the collection of DNA samples from people serving sentences in prison at the commencement of the program.

The LEAP system was a basic question and answer program. In addition to using the category of name to call up information, officers might use categories such as fingerprints, utilities, incident, or location. Besides providing access to a particular address, the computer system could also provide details about the area in which a given person might socialize or work, who else is associated with that geographical area, what type of crime has happened there, who else lives with a particular individual, or whom a person was dating the last time the police had information on him or her. The DIC managed the system as a whole. Details about unresolved crimes and particular people or activities that concerned the police would be published and distributed through the bulletins that circulated in the mess rooms of all of the stations potentially affected by the information.

Some of the seasoned officers complained that the computerized system did not allow them to record their instincts or hunches, which were believed to be important for effective policing. They explained that freedom of information laws in Australia allowed members of the public to request access to the information about them on the police's LEAP system. Consequently, some police members perceived themselves as obligated to be much more conservative about the impressions they recorded about the individuals they processed or encountered on the streets. This need for caution was a prime example of why most officers complained about "libertarians" who were concerned to defend civil liberties against government. Officers complained that such civil rights made the job they were trying to do for the public that much more difficult. They also believed that civil liberties provided crooks with a lot of loopholes for evading just punishment.

Nevertheless, on the whole, most officers in Fitzroy seemed to appreciate the LEAP system. Officers also commented that collecting names and some general information on people allowed the police to effectively monitor the activities in the district. Constable Clancy explained that having the names of the group of boys with whom she spoke in Carlton, for instance, helped the police maintain a sense of where people were at various times of the day and night. This would allow the police to help determine suspects for crimes that happened in the suburb at any particular time of day or night. In discussing the use of police mapping, Clancy stressed how it gave the police the ability to clear innocent people of suspicion of crimes.

Of course, the computer system also provided the state with a great deal of power. The running sheet was the intersection of the police's place making and the state's practice of disciplining the population by tracking and individualizing bodies in space. The running sheet was an important technology for ordering criminality, corporeality, and spatial meaning. The police were essential agents for regulating the population at the level of the individual body. They did so by mapping the body in relation to markers such as tattoos, deformities, and addictions in order to track people across space and time.

Police mapping is a particularly rich example of Michel Foucault's concept of disciplinary power. Disciplinary power produces the individual as a distinct identity in an effort to regulate people at the more intimate level of bodies and behaviors in industrial societies with large populations. Foucault characterizes this effective and distinctly modern exercise of power:

> Each individual has his own place; and each place its individual. Avoid distributions in groups; break up collective dispositions; analyze confused, massive or transient pluralities. Disciplinary space tends to be divided into as many sections as there are bodies or elements to be distributed. One must eliminate the effects of imprecise distribution, the uncontrolled disappearance of individuals, their diffuse circulation,

their unusable and dangerous coagulation; it was a tactic of anti-desertion, anti-vagabondage, anti-concentration. (1979, 143)

Foucault notes that the body has been used in the exercise of domination in many historical eras; however, the Enlightenment marked the beginning of the operation of power "at the level of the mechanism itself—movements, gestures, attitudes, rapidity: an infinitesimal power over the active body" (137).

Historian Alain Corbin examines some of the many practices in the late eighteenth century and the nineteenth century that helped produce the individual as a distinct concept and as a key category in governing (1987). He describes how more widespread use of full-length mirrors and portraiture among the general population in France fostered a new sensitivity to individual identity. The development and use of a wider variety of first names, which replaced the practice of naming children after a godparent, also helped to make the individual thinkable as a particular form of subjectivity. In other words, the individual became recognizable during the Enlightenment in a way it had not been in previous eras. In addition, the expansion of literacy and of bureaucratic organization during the nineteenth century made it easier to require people to produce documents of identification and personal information such as their age and address, which in previous eras was not common among the larger population of peasants. All these practices contributed to a new sense of the individual as a meaningful mode of subjectivity or personhood.

The historical details also illustrate for us how state bureaucratic practices have historically been central to the development of the category of the individual and how individualizing has helped the state govern more effectively.[26] Not only did state practices *depend* on the creation of a sense of individual identification among the population, but they helped *produce* this modern form of subjectivity by reinforcing the idea of individuality in their regulatory practices. In this respect, the Fitzroy Police illustrate Foucault's point that the individual is key to the control of the population in the modern era; their technologies of policing construct and fix the individual in space in the metropolitan center, despite the difficulty an urban, industrial population poses for governing.

Additionally, the LEAP system in Fitzroy was an interesting technological form of what Foucault called panopticonism. Foucault conceived of Jeremy Bentham's design for the panopticon prison as a paradigmatic example of the nature of contemporary power in the modern era (from the late eighteenth century to the present). Bentham's idea of the panopticon entailed a central guard tower that allowed the guards to survey all the prisoners who occupied the cells that surrounded the central tower like the spokes of a wheel. Brightly lit cells allowed for further visibility and control of the prisoner by the guard. Important in the architecture of the panopticon is the fact that the prisoners could not see the guard and therefore could never be certain whether or not they were being monitored. This system was designed to create a sense of constant surveillance among the prisoners that would eventually prompt them to begin to self-monitor their own behavior. Foucault argues that Bentham's original design for the panopticon embodies a "type of power that is basically the society we are familiar with at present, a utopia that was actually realized" (2000a, 58).

In Australia, the LEAP system functioned as a form of panopticism in that it worked as a kind of ever-present gaze that constituted a new form of disciplinary knowledge for the state. Further, much like Foucault observed, "This knowledge was no longer organized around the questions: 'What was done? Who did it?' It was no longer organized in terms of presence and absence, of existence and nonexistence; it was organized around the norm, in terms of what was normal or not, correct or not, in terms of what one must do or not do" (59).

The LEAP system was also an example of the fact that panopticism as a form of power does not rely exclusively on enclosing people in prisons, sanitariums, or classrooms in order to exercise domination; it is much more flexible. The machinery of power functions through the act of *partitioning*, of locating individuals in space (Foucault 1979, 143). Foucault details the discipline of partitioning in the following passage:

> Its aim was to establish presences and absences, to know where and how to locate individuals, to set up useful communications, to interrupt others, to be able at each moment to supervise the conduct of each individual, to assess it, to judge it, to calculate its qualities or merits. It was procedure, therefore, aimed at knowing, mastering and using. (143)

The running sheets and the LEAP database facilitated the process of partitioning in Fitzroy. As instruments, they permitted the police (and state more generally) to individualize the citizenry by calculating who was in which spaces in Fitzroy and under what circumstances.

Individuals were produced and monitored through seemingly banal bureaucratic technologies. Like any good government office, the Victoria Police Department's bureaucracy involved a plethora of forms that the officers filled out after a crime. The "offender" form was an important tool for gathering and consolidating information on individuals. With this form, the department gathered a great many details about people's physical appearance, personal habits, and personal landscape. To fill out these forms properly, officers needed to detail such things as hair color, length, and style; facial hair; eye color; glasses; speech; complexion; build; distinguishing features such as acne, deformities, body piercing, scars, or "mentally handicapped." In general, these details about physical appearance were very useful to the police for identifying people (without even having to get out of the police car) and tracking them across time.

Constable Moser underscored the potential of this system for me one night as he compiled the paperwork required for a shoplifting arrest. The store security guard had caught the man stealing a "torch" (flashlight) from K-Mart worth $A2.75. To begin, the constable filled in all the boxes he could, simply by looking at the "shoppy" (shoplifter). This included asking the man to open his mouth so he could study the appearance of the man's teeth. Through his interaction with the "shoppy" in filling out these forms, Moser learned more about the man's habits and friendships. He asked the man how often he saw his children and ex-wife, where he socialized, what pubs he drank in, what brand of cigarettes he smoked, and whether he had a job. He recorded all the information on the lines provided for "antecedent information."

Later, Moser explained that this information might come in handy sometime in the future in ways he could not necessarily fully anticipate. For instance, details like the brand of cigarettes a "crook" smokes might be useful (especially if an unusual brand) if a corpse were found with a branded cigarette butt near it; this information could help them narrow down suspects. Moser also explained that he would have written in even greater detail if the crime had been more serious. He might fill the entire reverse side of the form with a floor plan of a person's house, noting the type of locks on the door, places through which an escape could be made, the kind of things on the walls, who his "mates" were, who his girlfriend was, what habits he might have when committing a crime (such as if he tends to use a knife or always entered through a window). The constable would find out the names and ages of a crook's children and how often he sees them. Then, if the police were looking for that person and knew that he saw his children regularly, the police would know it would be only a matter of time before the crook showed up at his children's house. The officer would find out whether the crook used drugs and what kind of habit he had. Knowing what kind of habit the crook had, for instance, would enable police to calculate how much money he would need a week to support his habit and might cue the police to expect him to commit a burglary.[27]

Moser's description of procedure indicates the level of detail, from the quality of a man's relationship to his children to the brand of cigarettes he smokes, involved in police spatial practices. The greater the possibility that the police might want to censor a person, the more energy they put into individuating the suspect. Of course, we must keep in mind that different officers demonstrated varying degrees of competency in using the mapping system of the police force to its fullest potential. For instance, there was a lot of variation in the level of detail a particular officer might collect about a person or his or her social network, and there was variation in how much information was transferred from paper reports into the LEAP system.

This analysis of policing technologies is intended less to produce a sense of paranoia for the reader concerning one's own regulation by the state and is more concerned with better understanding the form of governmentality that is employed by the state, whether it is executed to its fullest potential by particular police officers or not. The recording of behaviors, landscapes (individual, domestic, and affective), and body markings is important for a system that rationalizes space as it permits the state to regulate people with increasing precision.

## ABORIGINAL SLIPPAGES

The police "rationalized" space by mapping individual bodies and behaviors onto the physical city. Correspondingly, the very design of the city itself, a grid formation, came out of an Enlightenment impulse to rationalize society. As a colonial space, Melbourne was designed following Governor Darling's 1829 Regulations, which mandated that all Australian townships be structured in rectangular form.[28] As Paul Carter points out, "One constant feature of the grid plan is its association with the notion of authority or the idea of control: 'A straight street lends itself to control from without'" (1988, 210, and quoting from Stanislawski 1946). The grid territorialized Australia by connecting its colonial cities back to an imperial source on a number of levels at once. Reproducing the British grid city was a means of reinventing Australia as a British place and of erasing Aboriginal meaning and presence from the landscape (see also Jacobs 1996).

But it was more than just the *look* (the aesthetic of a European urban grid design) of Melbourne that created a modern, European identity for Australia. The use of the grid and spatialized modes of power was part of how Australia operated as a modern European state. In other words, it was not only the aesthetics of the grid city that territorialized Australia as a Western place, but also the process of power that defined the nation-state in a particular way and that continued to be reproduced in contemporary police practices.

Botanical taxonomies were another means of rationalizing space in colonial Australia. William Lines makes this point in relation to the botanical collecting that Molloy undertook in the Western Australian colony of Vasse in the mid-nineteenth century for James Mangles in Britain:

> As an unwitting agent of modernity, Molloy helped bring Western taxonomy to the Australian bush, to the sacred landscape of the Aborigines. The imposition of the science of order intruded yet another boundary between the settlers and the world around them, a boundary not at all apparent to the Aborigines. (1994, 262)

Botanical, scientific classification was a means of ordering and regulating territory in Australia. Like the grid, it was a form of modern power insofar as it constructed the natural Australian landscape in terms of European scientific categories that came to dominate over Aboriginal spatial meaning.

Despite the dedication of individual police officers in contemporary Australia and their elaborate systems for mapping, the police, and by extension the state, never achieve total control of the population. As they did with other groups in Fitzroy, the police employed spatial technologies for tracking Kooris in their community. Pettman makes the point that "in reality Aborigines are constantly and disproportionately subject to state surveillance and control as welfare recipients, and through policing, court action and imprisonment" (1988, 6). This characterization also held true for Kooris in Fitzroy. Despite this fact, Fitzroy police officers had a difficult time fixing Aboriginal bodies in time and space.

The police's spatial and political relationship with Aboriginal people was apparent, in part, by how it differed from their relations with non-Aboriginal people in Fitzroy. For example, the Fitzroy officers typically had an easy time finding non-Aboriginal people to help the police fill out a lineup when they had an eyewitness to a crime. Curious about people's willingness to give up their time to serve in a police lineup, I asked one Anglo-Celtic Australian man who had spontaneously hopped into the police patrol car to be taken to the station why he had agreed to participate in the police lineup. The man, in his early twenties, laughed at my question and said that it would be a great story to tell his mates later that night. In fact, he had just seen a Seinfeld episode several weeks back in which Kramer was used as an extra in such a lineup. Kramer had been identified (of course) as the person who committed the crime, even though he was not guilty. Despite the Australian man's pleasure in constructing his experience as risking a fate similar to Kramer's, he obviously had a lot of faith in the state's systems to individuate accurately enough so that only the guilty person would be identified for a crime.

This was not true for Aboriginal people in Fitzroy. Aboriginal people never volunteered for police lineups. This was consistent with their general unwillingness to help facilitate police control of their spaces and behaviors. Their refusal functioned at some level as a refusal to let the state individuate them. But perhaps it also indicated an anxiety that the state was still far too imperfect at individualizing black bodies.

Additionally, Aboriginal people in this context regularly defied the established norms for the proper way to use public space that the police were constantly trying to reinforce. Much of the everyday struggles between Aboriginal people in Fitzroy and the police were about the police's inability to incorporate them successfully into their systems and to get them to behave according to middle-class norms of proper public behavior.

This dynamic was illustrated in countless encounters between the police and Koori people in Fitzroy. For instance, during one afternoon car patrol, the two officers decided to perform their required survey of the grounds of the Atherton Estates by driving the patrol car (somewhat disrespectfully) across the lawn surrounding the high-rise apartment buildings that comprised the estate. Included in this routine police surveillance of the public housing commission estate was the area dubbed the "sacred site" by the officers at the station. It was labeled as such because Aboriginal people were known by the police to socialize in this ten foot by ten foot area. Some officers cited the fact that Aboriginal people "got away" with having bonfires in this area as further evidence of the special privileges they received, despite Aborigines' claim to being disadvantaged as a racial group. On this afternoon, Senior Constable Thompson stopped the patrol car to watch a man who appeared to be Koori urinating in a bush near the "Sacred Site." When the man finished zipping up his fly, Thompson motioned him to approach our car. Without getting out of the driver's seat, Thompson asked him his name and where he lived, in order to record the information on his running sheet. The Koori man told Thompson with cautious civility that he lived in the public housing commission apartments located in Collingwood (an inner suburb close to Fitzroy). Before he drove away, Thompson concluded the brief exchange by telling the man that it was wrong to urinate in public.

Once out of hearing range of the man, Thompson told the second officer and me that the Aboriginal man would be surprised to discover that he was summoned to appear in court for charges that Thompson would make concerning his "pissing" in public. He recited out loud what he would tell the judge in court: he would tell him that there were women and children playing in the area, that police had told the man that his behavior was wrong, and that the officers had told him that he would be receiving a summons. Thompson seemed somewhat boastful about making an assertion that was true on only one account. Upon returning to the station, Thompson looked through photos of people arrested at the station in the past and confirmed the man's name and address.

This incident illustrates the more generalized pattern I observed among this policing community: when officers had discretion over simply providing a warning versus enforcing a more severe punishment, in relation to Aboriginal offenses they often chose the latter. Additionally, it captures the overdetermined nature of so many police–Koori encounters in Fitzroy. Many officers seemed to understand their harshness to Aboriginal people as a form of compensation for the "special treatment" they received from the government. It was an unfortunate irony, lost on the officers at the station, that many of the "special" protections Aboriginal people received were aimed at protecting them from police hostility. In a sad catch-22, police personnel in turn often used these "special" protections to justify further hostility toward Aboriginal people.

Behaviors performed by Aboriginal Australians (labeled inappropriate by the mainstream society), as well as Aboriginal lack of cooperation with the Fitzroy police, can be read at a certain level as practical strategies for survival. As Andrew Lattas remarks about such behaviors by Aboriginal people in Australia, "At great cost to themselves, they defiantly mark out the lack of total European control over Aboriginal existence" (1993, 3).

Norbert Elias's work (1994) lays out the way in which class identity and state control historically have been predicated on norms of hygiene and "civilized" behavior. The police functioned as the unit that enforced the larger, ongoing civilizing process in the state's relationship with Aboriginal Australians. The civilizing process was fully underway at the level of etiquette (reinforcing norms of quietness, sobriety, respect for authority, etc.) and it was underway insofar as the police attempted to map Aboriginal bodies and make them more accountable to the state. If we understand the state's control to be in large part predicated on the keeping of a certain spatial order, then the characterization by a number of other scholars of Aboriginal behaviors of drunkenness and disorderliness as oppositional is a useful one (see Lattas 1993; Cowlishaw 1990, 1988).[29] Anthropologist Andrew Lattas makes the point: "Symbols of disorderliness can become symbols of resistance to an order which is experienced as oppressive in its attention to regulating the minute aspects of one's body and being. This is not to romanticise drunkenness but to explore the meanings it assumes in the embodied context of Aboriginal-European relations" (1993, 252; see also Langton 1993).

Slippages that Kooris in Melbourne effected in police spatial practices were a form of what de Certeau calls "tactics." As de Certeau describes them:

A tactic is a calculated action determined by the absence of a proper locus . . . It operates in isolated actions, blow by blow. It takes advantage of "opportunities" and depends on them, being without any base where it could stockpile its winnings, build up its own position, and plan raids. What it wins, it cannot keep . . . In short, a tactic is an art of the weak. (1984, 36–37)

Given that modern forms of power attempt to rationalize people's behavior through maps that seek out patterns and locate behaviors and bodies onto the city grid, Aboriginal behaviors often frustrated the efficacy of the police's spatial production of landscape. Officers regularly returned to the station annoyed that an address they had collected from a "crook" proved to be fictional. Aboriginal people in particular were likely to provide a false address or be particularly difficult for the police to locate because they moved among several addresses. They might move among an Aboriginal hostel, relatives in one of the city suburbs, and relatives in the country, for instance. Thus, there was a whole series of fictional geographies that people improvised as a means of resisting the rationalization of space and the rationalization of their lives. Often the police interpreted these slippages or tactics as signs of Aboriginal irresponsibility (see Creamer 1988). The police were not able (or interested) in finding patterns to this movement, but rather explained it in terms of culturally derivative irrationality and irresponsibility (the "walkabout"). This situation translated into less control of Aboriginal bodies than the police might otherwise have had.

At times, the ability of Koori people in Fitzroy to find opportunities to locate themselves beyond the purview of the police was a consequence of earlier racist policies in Australia. For instance, the spatial practices of Aboriginal people were made even more complex by the fact that many Aboriginal people had the same last name, such as "Morgan," although were not necessarily related. This fact was a result of the assimilation policies in Australia documented in the *Report of the National Inquiry into the Separation of Aboriginal and Torres Strait Islander Children from Their Families* (Human Rights and Equal Opportunity Commission 1996, based on a 1995 national inquiry). During the era of assimilation in Australia (from the late 1930s until the late 1960s), Aboriginal children of mixed racial heritage (European and Aboriginal) were forcibly removed from their Aboriginal mothers and put in the custody of the state (in orphanages and foster families). The children were given Anglo-Celtic names to replace their Aboriginal names. At the end of the century, such policies resulted in Aboriginal people whose names did not necessarily mark their Aboriginality easily for the police. Furthermore, they meant that Aboriginal people could and did use their European and Aboriginal names tactically in their dealings with the police.

The contentious relationship between Aboriginal people in Australia and the police has been well documented by this point. The Royal Commission into Aboriginal Deaths in Custody (Commonwealth of Australia 1991) examined the causes and conditions of police detention of Aborigines nationally that had led to Aboriginal deaths while in police custody at a much greater rate than for non-Aborigines. The commission was prompted by the disturbing fact that from 1980 to 1988, 60 percent of Aboriginal deaths in police custody happened not in prison but while in the custody of police stations, and many had involved the death of unconvicted prisoners held on remand (30 percent). The report found that Aborigines were held in custody at much higher rates for relatively petty offenses and that often Aborigines were held for behaviors that fell into the category of drunkenness and other public order offenses. Their rate of detention was about twenty-seven times the rate of non-Aborigines, and their rate for repeat detention was 22.5 percent compared with 14 percent for non-Aborigines. The findings in the commission report corroborated other analyses that demonstrated that Aborigines were among the group most frequently denied bail or unable to meet bail conditions.

These statistics prompted discussion of how police practices documented by the government report figure into larger patterns of colonial practices toward Aborigines in Australia. They have opened up discussions about what Gillian Cowlishaw has described as "regular, active and aggressive expressions of enmity towards Aborigines in rural Australia" (see 1993 and 1988) and as has been examined in the work of numerous scholars (see Carrington 1991; Cowlishaw 1999; Cowlishaw and Morris 1997; Cunneen 2001; Cunneen and Libesman 1995; Bessant et al. 1995). The commission report spurred a number of policy changes that affected stations like Fitzroy. For instance, Fitzroy officers were required to contact the Sobering Up Center for Aborigines whenever they arrested an Aboriginal person for drunkenness. The aim of this social service was to limit the amount of time Aboriginal people spent in police custody. Further, free legal aid was provided through Aboriginal Legal Services, also located in Fitzroy. Nevertheless, the number of Aboriginal deaths in custody in Australia and jailing for crimes like public drunkenness continued to climb even higher in the years following the commission findings.

This history of the police and Aboriginal people in Australia greatly shaped the interaction between these two communities in Fitzroy. The Aboriginal community at times needed to call on the police to help contain a situation and to protect people. However, people in the Koori community were reluctant to involve the police for fear that the incident could result in another unnecessary Aboriginal death in police custody. For example, one afternoon the Fitzroy station received a call from Aboriginal Health Services, which was located on Nicholson Street, several blocks from the Fitzroy Station. Senior Constable Peters and Constable Ashford responded to the health agency's call for the restraint of a psychologically disturbed (nuffy) Koori patient who was running through the building screaming, barging into people's offices, and generally frightening people at the Aboriginal Health Services.

The two officers returned to the police station a half an hour later, very angry. The officers were frustrated because when they arrived in response to the call, the patient had already left the building, and no one at the Aboriginal Health Services would give them any information to help the officers identify and locate the Koori man who had disrupted the health service agency. Peters and Ashford concluded in frustration once back at the station Watch House that "they just hate white people over there!"

Later, I had the opportunity to discuss this incident with a friend, a non-Aboriginal employee of the Aboriginal Health Services who had observed the incident described above. Holly confirmed that the two officers had arrived at the facility to find that the Aboriginal patient had left and no one would provide them with information about who the patient was. Exasperated, the officers told the Aboriginal and non-Aboriginal staff that they had received three other calls to which they were required to respond, along with the Aboriginal Health Services' call. They warned the staff that they would not respond to further calls from Aboriginal Health Services if no one was going to cooperate with them once they arrived.

Holly further explained to me that the staff had been very ambivalent about how to respond to the police when they arrived. They wanted to prevent such an episode in the future and therefore were tempted to tell the police who the patient was. However, their fear for the patient's safety won out in the end and motivated their collective silence. The staff was all too aware and concerned that the previous year a Koori psychiatric patient had been shot and killed by the police.

A similar resistance to cooperating with the police took place among another group of Kooris unaffiliated with the Aboriginal Health Services. After two Koori men had been in a fight that resulted in one of them receiving several stab wounds, the wounded man nevertheless refused to provide any information to the police about his assailant. A lawyer at the Aboriginal Legal Aid Office in Fitzroy explained to me that people in the Aboriginal community viewed the legal system as discriminatory toward Aboriginal people and were therefore reluctant to turn in another Aborigine, even if they had been victimized by him or her. Although there had been many witnesses to the stabbing incident, none of the witnesses would provide a statement to the police. In the end, the Koori man who had been stabbed supplied the police with an obviously false explanation for his wounds, which functioned to emphasize for the officers the noncooperation of the Koori community. He told the police that he had fallen on his knife—twice—rather than legitimate police involvement in the Aboriginal community in any way.

The information from the report on Aboriginal deaths in (police) custody alone might explain the suspicion that Aboriginal people had toward the police in Fitzroy. Additionally, however, many of the stories that are included in the report on the separation of Aboriginal and Torres Strait Islander children from their families describe the role of the police for most of the twentieth century in forcibly removing children from their Aboriginal mothers. The following excerpt from one such story in what has become known as the "Stolen Children Report" (Human Rights and Equal Opportunity Commission 1996) gives a sense of the complicated and painful historical relationship that existed between the police and many Aboriginal communities in Australia.

> I was at the post office with my Mum and Auntie [and cousin]. They put us in the police ute [utility vehicle] and said they were taking us

to Broome. They put the mums in there as well. But when we'd gone [about ten miles] they stopped and threw the mothers out of the car. We jumped on our mothers' backs, crying, trying not to be left behind. But the policemen pulled us off and threw us back into the car. They pushed the mothers away and drove off, while our mothers were chasing the car, running and crying after us. We were screaming in the back of that car. When we got to Broome they put me and my cousin in the Broome lock up. We were only ten years old.[30]

While perhaps not as volatile as in rural communities, the history of animosity between the Aboriginal community and the Fitzroy police seemed to be reproduced daily insofar as their spatial practices represented radically opposed political goals. The police were positioned by the state to track people and make the landscape visible and rational in its order. Kooris in Melbourne were positioned by the history of racism in Australia to keep beyond the eye of state power.

De Certeau's discussion of memory and landscape is suggestive for understanding how Aboriginal spatial practice has threatened the territoriality of the Australian nation-state more broadly. He highlights memory as a spatial practice that challenges modern modes of power because it renders landscapes partially invisible, and therefore unavailable for surveillance.

> Memories tie us to that place . . . There is no place that is not haunted by many different spirits hidden there in silence, spirits one can "invoke" or not. Haunted places are the only ones people can live in— and this inverts the schema of the *Panopticon*. (de Certeau 1984, 108)

De Certeau is referring to past personal history and to childhood in particular. For him, these personal histories have power because they organize space in ways that are invisible to the state and are therefore destabilizing on some level.

It is a little difficult to imagine a significant threat to state authority posed by Proust's childhood memories in their spatial structuring of the gardens at Combray. At this point in his theory, de Certeau remains more focused on the individual than on larger social structures or groups. However, de Certeau's point is still suggestive; Aboriginal spatial practices that draw upon the Dreamtime offer a compelling example of how landscapes that are partially invisible to the state could radically destabilize the logic of power through surveillance.[31] Aboriginal Dreamtime cosmology structures space. It structures people's relationship to each other as well as to other elements of the universe, such as the landscape, animals, and spirits, via creation mythology. Aboriginal Dreaming as spatial practice draws upon memory and histories passed down through generations; thus they are not fully transparent to people outside of a specific community.

Jane Jacobs argues that Aboriginal meaning and use of space in Australia is threatening to the rational order used to organize and define space in the West because it mixes the secular and the spiritual; Western cities in particular are predicated on a division between the two (1996). I would also suggest that traditional Aboriginal spatial practice is a persistent alternative construction and system of meaning for space. Well over a century after colonial settlement, Aboriginal people still assert their priorities and reality in relation to the territory of continental Australia through their persistent involvement and adaptation of traditional Aboriginal Dreamtime stories about the land (see Jacobs 1988; Jordon 1988; Creamer 1988; Povinelli 1993; Bird 1992; Myers 1986). In this respect, Aboriginal spatial practice resists the panoptic logic of state control. Aboriginal people construct space in ways that are only partially visible to settler Australians; their traditional spatial practices involve histories, spirits, and relations with animals and the landscape that are not easily quantifiable and are inaccessible to people not authorized to know them.

As Jacobs notes, part of the work of the state in ensuring its hegemony has been to make these sacred stories visible (1996). Disclosing Aboriginal stories about the land has been part of the terms of (possibly) gaining state recognized ownership for Aboriginal people of a particular territory. This point is well illustrated in the Hindmarsh Bridge controversy in 1995. In the legal dispute over permission to build the Hindmarsh Bridge in South Australia, women Ngarrindjeri elders were required to provide sacred information concerning the fertility significance of the bridge site for Aboriginal people. They were required to disclose this information to the office of the Minister for Aboriginal Affairs (MP Tickner, Labour Party) in 1994 in order to obtain a heritage ban on the site. Female staff members in Tickner's office were in charge of collecting the sacred information since Aboriginal custom stipulated that only women could have access to this knowledge. The Adelaide Federal Court nonetheless overturned Minister Tickner's decision to issue a heritage ban for twenty-five years by deeming him negligent for "denying himself the full details of the sacred claim by not reading the information in the envelopes."[32] Of course, availing himself to the "full details of the sacred claim" would have meant that Tickner read the sacred information provided by the Aboriginal women that Ngarrindjeri law prevented him or any other male from doing. With this decision, the court, in essence, negated Aboriginal power to impose their own meaning on the land and tried to force Aboriginal people to make all of their sacred constructions of the land visible to the state.

In a highly political twist of events, even though the Ngarrindjeri women did not reveal the secret woman's knowledge to inappropriate people (men), members of the settler Australian government nevertheless did it for them. In January 1995, the Ngarrindjeri women's testimony on the sacred meaning of the site was mistakenly directed to the Shadow Minister for the Environment (Ian McLachlan, Liberal Party) instead of being delivered to Sean McLaughlin, a senior advisor to the Minister of Aboriginal Affairs. Despite being clearly marked "Confidential. To be read by women only," the envelopes containing sacred women's knowledge were opened, photocopied, and distributed to politicians, journalists, and the solicitors acting against the Commonwealth's motion to provide heritage protection for the Aboriginal site. This disturbing incident illustrates how in contemporary political battles between Aboriginal groups and the state (and corporations), making Aboriginal spatial meaning visible is an important means by which Aboriginal culture is undermined and their claims to the land invalidated. This incident also suggests how this process happens at many different levels of the government.

With her ethnographic material on government self-determinacy programs among the Rembarrnga people, Gillian Cowlishaw underscores the problem of Aboriginal meaning and culture not being visible enough or fully understood by white Australians. While acknowledging Said and Bhabha's arguments that part of the operation of colonial governmentality was the practice of codifying and rendering alternative cultures "knowable and visible" (Bhabha 1983, 23), Gillian Cowlishaw asserts that, in Australia, this has not been the case. She argues that in Australia, governing Aborigines "depends on its opposite, that is, a refusal to come close to or become familiar with the reality of indigenous experience" (1998, 155). She illustrates this point with ethnographic description of contemporary, keen white government men who end up reproducing Rembarrnga (Aboriginal) marginality through their refusal to accommodate differences presented by Aboriginal oral tradition, illiteracy, or decision-making processes. She explains, "For instance, on the one hand Aboriginal ceremonial life was treated with formal deference but given no space to operate; on the other hand the stark difference of illiteracy could not be mentioned. Illiteracy is construed as a shameful lack rather than as an alternative cultural realm of morality" (147).

However, Cowlishaw's argument that governmental policies for economic self-reliance in Aboriginal communities ironically require the production of an Aboriginal subjectivity in the mold of the bourgeois ideal actually supports my argument in this section. Cowlishaw argues that it is not so much ignorance or racism that explains the failure of contemporary progressive governmental policies (for self-determinacy) toward Aborigines. She insists that we need to recognize how the cultural domain of the governmental administrators structures self-determination programs. Cowlishaw argues:

> Recognizing 'the community' entailed the *production* of communities as suitable recipients of state funding. Certain kinds of subjects had to be produced who would take part in the procedures that the state demanded. The bourgeois ideal of autonomous, self-willed subjects took a particular form in this field of governing Aboriginality. (150)

Further, she explains that self-determination programs are still grounded in a cosmology that privileges history as progress, an epistemology that posits knowledge as technique, and "an ontology premised on being as apparent and visible" (151). With this observation, Cowlishaw, in effect, describes the organizing principles of modernity and the ways in which they disempower many Aborigines. Cowlishaw's analysis suggests how Aboriginal groups have been disempowered by the fact that their cultural practices are not recognized, let alone accommodated, by federal programs for self-determination. What she stops short of saying is that such forms of epistemology and ontology are the structure that modern power takes. We could also say about Cowlishaw's ethnographic material that the ontology the federal administrators are importing into Aboriginal communities— as a Trojan horse of sorts—is part of the means by which the modern state governs.

My point is that encounters such as that with the keen, white governmental officials Cowlishaw describes do more than ignore Aboriginal forms of meaning and communication as Cowlishaw posits. Above and beyond that, they impose Western modes of action that require argumentation and "proof." As in the case of the Hindmarsh Bridge case, Aboriginal groups are forced to make their knowledge "apparent and visible" if they are to receive government resources. Thus, the imposition of an ontology premised on the visible is not just a cultural difference between (modern) Western culture and Aboriginal cultural forms. This ontology is central to modern modes of power and governmentality. Specifically, this mandate to make meanings and knowledge visible to the government is an important process by which settler Australians have responded to the challenges that Aboriginal land rights pose to the territorialization of the Australian settler state.

In the localized context of Fitzroy, Aboriginal tactics of evading police control of space posed a problem in that a central function of the police was to reproduce a visible social order through their technologies of surveillance. Additionally, Aboriginal land rights claims, on the whole, offended the police in Fitzroy. In a larger sense, Aboriginal land rights claims threatened the police officers in ways much like they threatened white Australians and the settler state as a whole. One officer described his cynicism toward Aboriginal land rights politics during a taped interview; his perspective echoed comments other people at the station made more informally. Senior Constable Matthews explained:

> There's been a lot of claims, but there hasn't been many accepted. Unfortunately, mainly, the Aboriginals when they made the claims, they only made claims to land that was worth a lot of money, always in a high profile area. Well, I think it was very—a lot of Australian people were disheartened because they could see that they were a bit [inaudible] in that sense, you know. And I think a lot of people got very skeptical because of that.[33]

The Fitzroy officers responded to the deterritorialization that Aboriginal land rights represented in unofficial, more spontaneous ways. Symbolic contestation over land rights infused many of the everyday negotiations between Fitzroy officers and Aboriginal people in the community (who in the main were not part of any official land rights claims). Police officers countered Aboriginal resistance by overpolicing their communities and making them more visible. They also did so by rhetorically substituting and punishing the "antisocial" tactics of Koori people in Fitzroy (drinking, urinating in public, etc.) in place of the more profound, deeply threatening spatial practices Aboriginal culture and land rights claims presented the nation.

In Fitzroy, police officers did not just overpolice Aboriginal zones of sociability and housing, but they framed their own practices in terms of a rejection of more liberal governmental policies toward Aboriginal land rights. For instance, one senior constable recounted that when she was processing the paperwork and interview with a Koori man who was brought into the station for theft, he informed her repeatedly that all this land on which they walk in Fitzroy was Aboriginal land. They were on land that rightfully belonged to him and Aboriginal people in general. The senior constable was annoyed at the irrelevance of his statements to her need to process him on the charges for which he was apprehended. She described this incident to me in a discussion at a later date as a classic example of Aboriginal people wanting everything in unreasonable terms, despite the "special treatment" they already received.[34] This senior constable argued that she had numerous Aboriginal friends, but could not comprehend a reason for Aboriginal people who had broken the law to lay claim to land that was very valuable (such as the land under the Fitzroy Station) in discussions about other things like why they had shoplifted or urinated on Brunswick Street.

In addition, officers were quick to note that Aboriginal people already received much more government "special treatment" compared with other ethnic minorities, and yet their crime rate and the general health of their communities in Fitzroy were far worse than other ethnic groups who received less government help. When dealing with the Koori man she was arresting, the senior constable expressed her disrespect and alienation from the political policies involving Aboriginal people by informing the man that "yes, this is all your land and I have a detention cell that you can have back right now."

In a similar gesture, the officers at the Fitzroy Station nicknamed the park around the Atherton Garden Estates (public housing) where Aboriginal people drank and socialized, the "sacred site." This renaming was an act by which police officers countered Aboriginal claims to land based on traditional ownership and religious significance to their culture. Their use of the term "sacred site" suggested that that which Aborigines tried to pass off as sacred was really just drunkenness and disorderly conduct. In these mundane practices, officers engaged with public, national debates through everyday, symbolic acts in Fitzroy.

All too often when analyzing police practices, scholars individualize the power of the state in the form of the police officers who enact them, as if there were complete synchronicity between the state and the people who work for the police force. For instance, in his analysis of the state's policing of Aborigines, Andrew Lattas treats the state as a uniform entity and police practices as a direct extension of state policy (1992). Ethnographic analysis of police practices provides insight into the ways in which members of the police contest governmental policy in their practices or reflect cosmologies of the larger middle class, rather than simply reflecting the state.

In their everyday practices of overpolicing Aboriginal spaces and cynically rearticulating Aboriginal claims to land, individual Fitzroy officers engaged in contestation concerning legitimate control of the Australian continent that has been called into question by Aboriginal land rights claims. They used sarcasm and renaming as a means to

*Figure 17. The park beside the public housing apartments that Fitzroy police officers unofficially referred to as the "sacred site."*

reassert the legitimacy of white Australians' control of land in Australia and to challenge the policies of the federal government.[35]

To conclude, understanding the way in which the nation is deterritorialized gives us insight into a particular moment in Australian history and to how territorial redefinition of nation is particularly overdetermined at this historical juncture. But these processes hold larger lessons about the way in which indigenous people potentially threaten the modern nation-state. The dimension I have stressed in this chapter is less about how the settler state narrates the connection between people, culture, and territory than about an equally important dimension of space and the politics of nations. The practices of the Fitzroy police help us see how territorializing the everyday landscape is a means of defining people's political subjectivity within the modern state as well as for understanding some of the institutional means by which the state's identity and power are spatially produced.

Spatial practice is an important component in legitimating the political authority or control of the state over a territory. But it is also crucial for regulating the citizenry within the national territory. I have highlighted the threat that Aboriginal political activity has created in challenging the political system because this is an important dimension in the current urgency the Australian state faces in relegitimating its control and in reproducing its systems for regulating the citizenry. However, there is no reason to believe that other groups, in their political engagement with state powers around the world, do not engage in spatial practices of resistance in ways parallel to Aboriginal people in Australia. De Certeau's work stressed tactics as a primary means of resistance more generally, as a means of inscribing a different reality onto the world and of defying modes of power that depend on spatial control. The ethnographic material in this chapter enables us to see how the reproduction of power and challenges to that power happen in very localized, mundane contexts and take place within numerous landscapes such as the body, the city, and the imagination.

# 4

# The Poor White Trash of Asia: Criminality and Australia in the International Landscape

Foreign Minister Gareth Evans was determined to put Australia on the map. Literally. He arrived in Brunei in late July for talks centered around the annual ASEAN [Association of Southeast Asian Nations] for foreign ministers' meeting armed with a new map depicting the land Down Under as smack in the heart of the East Asian Hemisphere.

The persuasive diplomat failed to convert everyone to his world view, however. "If I look at a map, I will immediately say that Australia is not part of Asia," Malaysia's Foreign Minister Datuk Abdullah Ahmad Badawi said under questioning from Australian journalists. "You don't know your geography." (Hiebert 1995, 26)

The nation-state's geographical relationship to political communities *beyond* its borders is an important component in defining the collective political identity of the people *within* national borders. Australia's identity has been defined through spatial practices that position the Australian nation-state in the larger international community. This chapter analyzes how people's efforts to define the nation, historically and today, are strongly linked to positioning Australia geographically in the international landscape. This process is undertaken both within Australia by nationals and by nonnationals beyond its borders. Historically, people have defined Australia's identity as a modern nation and as a white nation by locating it internationally. The influence of supranational identities on the Australian colonial settlements is easy to imagine. However, the contemporary place-making and narrative practices of the Fitzroy police help us understand how defining the nation in Australia today still involves positioning it in the international community—in relation to the West and to Asia in particular. The ethnographic material also illustrates how this process is achieved through every-day practices.

Furthermore, reading the ethnographic data in relation to history shows how criminality and moral behavior have been important categories for defining Australia's location and collective identity. Originally, criminality and "low-class" behavior were a way by which the British defined the physical, national, and moral borders between Australia and Britain. The narrative construction of Australians as criminals and as vulgar was a means by which the British middle class located Australia on the other side of the world, despite attempts by many Australians to construct it as intimately connected to Britain. This history casts interesting shadows on contemporary police practices that define Asian immigrants as outsiders in the national community because of their supposed criminality and dirtiness. This chapter explores how people deploy the link between nation, lawfulness, and morality to reconfirm Australia's location in the West. The history also provides a context for better understanding how Australia is territorialized not only by nationals but also by people in other nation-states. Historically, Australia has been defined in particular ways and positioned as outside the privileged space of British nationalism by the British middle and upper class in England. Yet, the comments of Lee Kuan Yew and others provide a contemporary example of how Australia's geography and national identity continue to be constructed from outside as well as contested from inside.

Australia's national identity may be particularly intertwined with its geographical location in the international community and is therefore an especially rich example for our purposes. However, this chapter illustrates that the qualities that are used to define the nation, such as modernity, morality, or whiteness, are also instrumental for defining supranational communities like "Asia" and "the West." Further, the fact that other nation-states such as Great Britain and Singapore participate in defining Australia's geography as not overlapping with their own imagined communities suggests that others use international geography to define their own national identities. The chapter thus provides a useful framework for understanding more broadly the processes by which geography is imagined and defines national identity within the international geography.

## POLICING DIRTY SPACES AND POLITICAL CATEGORIES

Routine patrols of the public housing commission high-rise apartments ("the caves") where many Vietnamese immigrants lived in Fitzroy usually elicited some comment from Fitzroy police officers about hygiene. Officers warned me as we approached the building, for instance, that the elevators or apartments would smell disgusting because of the strange odors that "Asian food" gave off. They made frequent and disparaging comments about the litter left in elevators; instead of perceiving the litter as a sign of the complacency of the residents in general, officers interpreted the litter as a cultural fact about Asians specifically.[1] Senior Constable Matthews was probably more direct but not uncharacteristic when he shook his head in the elevators and pronounced, "Asians are dirty, dirty people."

This condemnation extended beyond the particular Asian residents who lived in public housing. Police officers recounted stories they had heard about how "Asians" behaved at the Crown Casino in Melbourne. Many people, Melburnians more generally and Fitzroy officers in particular, took it as a cultural fact that Asians were pathological gamblers and would even abandon their children in cars for hours in pursuit of their unchecked habit. Throughout 1995, the media also regularly reinforced this cultural "truth." On occasion officers noted with regret that police officers sometimes gambled away their entire pay packet, but this was never interpreted as a truth about all police officers. However, for many people with whom I spoke, the incidences of impropriety around gambling by Asians in Melbourne were framed as an issue of cultural difference about Asians that threatened the city more generally. At the police station, I was told about excesses of Asian gambling that linked to hygiene. One story posited that Asians were such intense gamblers that they would "piss and shit right there at the table" rather than take a break from the game. Filth was associated with Asian-ness in phantasmal ways through stories that seemed exaggerated and unrealistic given the strength of security on duty in the casino at all times. That story caught my attention not because I had a lot of faith in its accuracy, nor because I was convinced that the narrator

*Figure 18. "The caves" (public housing commission apartments) in Fitzroy.*

himself believed it. Rather, the story was an example of how issues of hygiene and filth extended to people who were not necessarily first-generation immigrants or in the lower class.

The police officers' nonnarrative practices were consistent with their commentary about Asian filth; however, their practices also conveyed a fear of contamination. In addition to commenting on the dirtiness of Asians, officers avoided touching anything in the building with their bare hands, instead using protective gloves on occasion or, more commonly, using their pen to punch elevator buttons or open up fire extinguisher doors looking for hidden syringes. Their behavior articulated a sense of danger from contamination within a zone that was designated as Asian.

Mary Douglas's work on purity and danger encourages us to read the marginalization of "dirty" things and people as a process of negotiating social categories. She writes:

> If we can abstract pathogenicity and hygiene from our notion of dirt, we are left with the old definition of dirt as matter out of place. This is a very suggestive approach. It implies two conditions: a set of ordered relations and a contravention of that order. Dirt then, is never a unique, isolated event. Where there is dirt there is system. Dirt is the by-product of a systematic ordering and classification of matter, in so far as ordering involves rejecting inappropriate elements. This idea of dirt takes us straight into the field of symbolism and promises a link-up with more obvious symbolic systems of purity . . . Uncleanness or dirt is that which must not be included if a pattern is to be maintained (1966, 36 and 41).

Put simply, Mary Douglas argues that dirtiness is not an objective fact. It is a characteristic assigned to things, people, or behaviors that contradict a constructed social order and thus threaten the hegemony or naturalness of that social order. She explains that things that challenge our individual and collective schema or categorical system are dealt with in a variety of ways. They might be interpreted in such a way as to be made to fit an existing category. Or they may be avoided altogether, physically controlled, used as a catalyst to transform existing categories, or labeled dangerous.

Individuals tend to be better able to adjust their categories or schema in the face of something that does not fit their ordering of the world than can societies at large. However, public values and categories mediate individuals' sense of reality. As Douglas details:

But its public character makes its categories more rigid. A private person may revise his pattern of assumptions or not. It is a private matter. But cultural categories are public matters. They cannot so easily be subject to revision. Yet they cannot neglect the challenge of aberrant forms. (1966, 39)

Thus, public categories, which structure private perceptions to a large extent, are conservative in the face of challenge and, as such, they tend to be defended with more rigidity and fervor.

The treatment of Asians as contaminating and dirty is an example of the social control exercised against people who violate social categories. Immigrants in many contexts and historical periods have been stigmatized as unclean because, by their very definition, immigrants challenge the division between inside and outside or us and them of an imagined community. And in the era of the nation-state, immigrants challenge what anthropologist Liisa Malkki (1995) calls the national order of things. Although we can identify a more general pattern of hostility toward immigrants, it is still important to examine specific contexts to understand the particular divisions or categories that the immigrant is contaminating by his or her very presence. It is also interesting that in Melbourne, a city with many different immigrant groups, it was only Asian immigrants who were labeled dirty. What specifically did Asian immigrants threaten?

One way to understand police anxiety about Asian "filth" is by examining how Asians disrupted key categories that have been used to define Australian identity in the past. The presence of Asian immigrants in large numbers—the visibility of their bodies—blurred the historical divisions between East and West and between civilized and uncivilized. Of course these divisions have always been highly artificial and empirically false.[2] However, before the large influx of Vietnamese in the late 1970s and more recent immigrant groups from other parts of Asia, there was less to challenge these categories that defined Australia in opposition to Asia. Asian bodies on the streets of Fitzroy functioned to destabilize historical categories. But other factors also destabilize the dichotomy between East and West and Asia and Australia. These include government rhetoric about Australia's rightful place in Asia and the increased flow of capital, business people, and tourists between Australia and the Asian region. At a historical moment when these categories were under transformation, Asian bodies were immediate evidence of the erosion of categorical and geographical lines that had defined Australian identity in the past. Ang and Stratton comment on the anxiety generated by shifting relations between Australia and Asia:

> In the era of global capitalism, the Australian nation-state finds itself more and more economically dependent on the NIEs (newly industrialized economies) of East Asia. This development has led to the perception of, and anxiety about, an unprecedented overturning of given hierarchies, where "Asia," previously the powerless Other, now takes on the position of a commanding center in relation to which "Australia" is (economically) marginalized. At the same time, Australia remains similarly peripheral to "the West," of which it nevertheless remains, historically and to a large extent culturally, a part. The "West" provides "Australia" with a rich source of (cultural) power which continues to produce a sense of superiority vis-à-vis "Asia," a superiority however which is now ridden with anxiety— as expressed in the ominous economic projection that if Australia doesn't change, it risks becoming, in the words of Singapore's Senior Minister and long-term Prime Minister, Lee Kuan Yew, "the poor white trash of Asia." (1996, 29)

Ang and Stratton very nicely summarize the shifting cultural terrain that makes up the larger context in which we need to place police spatial practices. Shifts in the global political economy in the second half of the twentieth century mean that former international cultural and economic hierarchies have shifted. In terms of economics, Australia is now marginal to, even dependent upon, Asia. And while Australia was marginal to Western nations, its historical and cultural association with the West had given Australians a sense of superiority over Asia. The realignment of the international landscape and new Asian prosperity have created anxiety for many Australians since their status, identity, and future economic prospects have been unsettled by these transformations.

The public discourse about Asian hygiene at the casino and police officers' heightened caution about contamination was a localized response to shifts in key social categories and hierarchies. Because the presence of Asian immigrants threatened the categories many Australians used to define themselves and their location in the world, immigrants were perceived and treated as polluting and dangerous to society. The threat they played on a symbolic level to the body politic was expressed in terms of a perceived threat to the individual, physical body. As Douglas insists, "We cannot possibly interpret rituals concerning excreta, breast milk, saliva and the rest unless we are prepared to see in the body a symbol of society, and to see the powers and dangers credited to social structure reproduced in small on the human body" (1966, 116).

Asian immigrants challenged historical notions of Australian-ness. Their presence, combined with Australia's increasing economic dependence on Asia, undercuts the key differences used in the past to imagine Australian identity. Of course Australia may eventually be territorialized as an Asian nation; these spatial categories are so-cially produced and are therefore open to renegotiation. However, during the renegotiation of national geography and identity that served as a backdrop to police spatial practices, we see people projecting their heightened sense of racial, geographical, and political instability onto Asian immigrants. They transferred the danger of unstable social categories onto a different form of danger, in this case, danger to one's health and personal comfort. In highlighting the Otherness of Asian immigrants through their spatial practices, police officers (re)territorialized Australia as part of the West.

## NARRATIVES OF CRIMINALITY

In numerous national contexts, ideas about criminality have been used to delineate the inside and outside of the national community. The nation has been conceptualized as a moral space or commu-nity that is endangered by the lawlessness of certain groups. The national collective is defined in opposition to the qualities associ-ated with criminals. One particularly rich analysis of the construc-tion of nation in opposition to lawlessness is Paul Gilroy's *Ain't No Black in the Union Jack* (1987). In his study of the public attention directed at black criminality in Great Britain, he argues that this discourse operates for many as a means to negotiate postcolonial re-lations within the metropolitan center. Further, criminality is used to explain the decline of British imperial status. Gilroy posits that criminality gets intertwined with nation because its laws often sym-bolize the nation. He writes, "The subject of law is also the subject of the nation. Law is primarily a national institution, and adherence to its rule symbolizes the imagined community of the nation and expresses the fundamental unity and equality of its citizens" (74).

Britain has a particularly long history of defining the nation in opposition to criminality since, as Gilroy argues:

> The process in which the nation state was formed in Britain in the eighteenth and nineteenth centuries also provided the context in which modern legal institutions grew and developed . . . The identification of law with national interests, and of criminality with un-English qualities, dates from this process of state formation and has a long history which remains relevant to the analysis of 'race' and crime history today. (77)

In the eighteenth and nineteenth centuries, the British nation-state literally excluded people designated as lawless from the national community by transporting them to the American colonies and to Australia. More recently, entire racial categories are designated as outside of the national community not through exile but through discourses about culture, race, and crime. While discourses of criminality circulate transnationally and function to mark the outside edges of national community, Gilroy astutely insists that nationalist discourses must be understood in their local manifestations because particular social and political relations are being negotiated through them. In other words, we need to understand the particular cultural context in which the criminality and moral degeneracy of certain groups are positioned as a threat to the nation.

Along with inheriting Britain's legal institutions, Australians reproduced the association of nation with lawfulness. This trend is perhaps a consequence of the Australian middle class's over-identification with British class hierarchies (see Hughes 1988). But it is not enough to say that discourses of criminality have been a way for people to give voice to racism in Australia. Nor is it enough to say that they articulate what Ghassan Hage (1998) has called a general fear of loss of control to nonwhite immigrants because these discourses were primarily directed toward one group—Asian Australians. If this category were merely a means of defining Australia through the exclusion of nonwhites, then there are groups within Australia, such as Aboriginal people, whom we might also expect to be defined in relation to criminality and as a threat to the nation. Thus, we need to look in more detail at what the discourse around Asian criminality in Australia makes possible.

Much as scholars have observed about other police departments (cf. Lardner and Reppetto 2000), the Fitzroy officers had an unofficial taxonomy of "typical" crimes that corresponded to various ethnic categories. However, the crime of other groups was not cited as threatening to the nation-state in the way "Asian crime" was a distinct threat. Other racial groups were associated with a certain kind of criminality. For instance, people from Southern Europe or Middle Eastern background, categorized as "Europeans," were expected to commit crimes resulting from their "hot tempers." One officer described crimes typical of this ethnic population as cases involving "weird murder-suicides and such." During car patrols, officers always pointed out in both Fitzroy and its neighboring station, Carlton, the area of the district where the young European boys, the "petrol-heads," would drag race. The police perceived drag racing as an activity through which young Italian men demonstrated their machismo. The police considered these young men who also tended to be disrespectful to the police to be hypermasculine, an almost pathological version of something that was otherwise considered normal or good. Nevertheless, although officers used these drag racing incidents to illustrate the nature of young European (read: Mediterranean) men in Australia, they were not a significant criminal problem or a threat to the nation.

As mentioned in the previous chapter, Aboriginal people frustrated Fitzroy police efforts to rationalize space and thus challenged modern, Western modes of power. And while police personnel did have narratives about the nature of Aboriginal criminality, the officers did not present their criminality as a problem for the state. That is, discourses of Aboriginal criminality were not used to define Australian political subjectivity. For instance, one senior sergeant described Aboriginal criminality in the following terms:

> Well, just their values in life; what they think is important in life. They don't care so much about their own or other people's property or wealth or whatever. Whilst Australians, we've just about had it as this excellent welfare state. They'll [Aborigines] ask for it [welfare], and if they don't get it, they'll say "okay, I'll have to ask for it again next week" and hardly care, it seems. And that's a bit hard to deal with. Their attitudes to criminal things have a lot to do with possession of property and stealing out there.

The senior sergeant drew distinctions between "Australians" and Aborigines, but did not identify their criminality as something that threatens the national community. If anything, it was their "noble savage" qualities (no appreciation of property or work) that characterized Aboriginal difference and influenced their "attitude" toward the welfare state. Alcoholism and disregard for property set Aboriginal people apart and accounted for their marginality. At the Fitzroy station, these values, in turn, informed Aboriginal criminal practices, but criminality did not define Aboriginal culture. Thus, it was not the case that all nonwhites were defined in terms of their criminality. In fact the criminality of other racial or ethnic groups was used to underscore the exceptional quality of Asian criminality. One senior sergeant explained:

> Aboriginal crime is a different attitude than Asians—there is nothing like their [Asian] malice in Aboriginal crime . . . their true criminality by malice, and definition of malice, is very low in the Aboriginal community.

The Victorian Police Department even had a separate "Asian squad," which was a subsection of the police force that addressed Asian crime.[3] The presence of this Asian squad indicates how Asian criminality was a category in and of itself and required a special wing of the police force in order to address it. As observed in the previous chapter, the police seldom made moral judgments about criminal behavior yet police officers regularly described Asian crime as deeply threatening to the nation-state and as a reflection of lower moral standards. As with a number of issues, the police were surprisingly uniform in their assessment. People in this site repeatedly stated that Asians,[4] especially those living in "the caves,"[5] committed a greater number of and more violent crimes than other groups in Fitzroy. The police associated Asians with drug trafficking and violence. "Cultural difference," as opposed to poverty or displacement, accounted for their criminality. As Senior Sergeant Bates explained it:

> The Indochinese seem to have all sorts of different attitudes toward respect of other members in society—quite different to the Western attitudes; their attitudes of—the other major element in criminal law is bodily injury to your fellow man—violence, crimes of violence, as it seems, crimes of poverty, they have some pretty different ideas, cultural ideas, and they're a bit hard to come to terms with.

Officers attributed the Otherness of the Vietnamese to their culture in general as well as to their experiences in the Vietnam War. It was often suggested that the police could not expect the Vietnamese to respect them as authority figures after the abuse of authority they experienced in Vietnam with corrupt and violent Vietnamese police and government officials. They also suggested that criminal punishment was no deterrent because the Vietnamese had seen much worse already in their experiences with the Vietnam War. Therefore, a criminal sentence or even physical threat made by an Australian police officer would be nonthreatening in comparison.

In keeping with current trends in criminality that explain crime in terms of social factors (poverty, learned values), the officers pointed to those factors that they believed produced criminality and excessive violence in Vietnamese people. However, officers usually used social factors as a basis for defining enduring cultural truths that present a lasting threat to Australian society by Vietnamese immigrants. Despite using culture as the causal factor, difference was still discussed as if it were ahistorical and immutable, much as we see in the police officers' description of the enduring violence among the Vietnamese. Among the Fitzroy officers, Vietnamese criminality was articulated as both a product of cultural difference and history, in that people pointed to the Vietnam War as a causal factor in fostering violence in Vietnamese people. One chief inspector in the Victorian Police succinctly linked criminality, culture, and

Figure 19. Vietnamese shops on Brunswick Street in Fitzroy.

war trauma in a way that was very similar to accounts of the link at the Fitzroy Station. The *Age* newspaper described the Chief Inspector's causal analysis, which he gave at the national summit on youth and crime:

> Chief Inspector Rod Norman, of the Victorian Police youth advisory unit, told the first national summit on police and ethnic youth relations in Melbourne that bad experiences with police in other countries led ethnic youth to mistrust police in Australia, leading to strained relations. He said refugees from war-torn countries, where the army enforced law and order, sometimes saw people in uniform as a threat. "A trip to the police station was a 'one way trip' in some countries." (*Age*, 8 July 1995)

This story was typical of how antisocial behavior was accounted for as something caused by environmental factors. But at the same time, it was depicted as endemic to a culture, reproduced in the children of each generation. It was also typical of the way in which the media represented "ethnic crime" in Melbourne in such a way as to invite readers to associate it with Asian immigrants. In this case, neither the officer nor the reporter specifies which "ethnics" are so problematic for the police. However, the story provides clues ("refugees from war-torn countries") that invite the reader to make generalizations about Vietnamese and Cambodian immigrants in Australia.

Embedded in these cultural truths was the idea that Australian society was superior to Vietnamese culture. Étienne Balibar discusses the language of cultural difference as a new form of "racism without race" insofar as it achieves the same kinds of political work of reproducing the idea that there are inherent differences between different groups (Balibar and Wallerstein 1991). In this new form of cultural racism, the salient groups are still categorized by race, and they are still placed in a hierarchy of development. However, instead of explaining the genesis of these differences in terms of biology, people explain differences between whites and people of color as a product of cultural heritage. Balibar's notion of racism without race is useful for understanding how a social and cultural notion of Asian difference and its threat was articulated by the police officers.

Despite speaking of historically contingent causal factors like the Vietnam War to explain Vietnamese violence, the officers still treated the differences as fixed. In citing examples of Vietnamese criminality for instance, officers at the Fitzroy Station supplied stories about children of refugees who would have been too young to experience the Vietnam War. In these stories the children were examples of the cycle of violence within the Vietnamese-Australian community. Officers believed that the war had left a permanent trace on Vietnamese culture and threatened to disrupt the Australian society since Vietnamese adults were teaching their children antisocial behaviors. One senior constable, Sam Demitris, illustrated this common explanation for violence:

> This young Vietnamese kid came to the station from outside, and he wouldn't have been all but about six, and he said that two boys were having a [inaudible] in the street. And I said, "Well, you go and tell those guys to stop or I'll come out with the Bogeyman." Well, the little guy's going to run around—after a bit comes back with this other guy who would have been now about eight, and they run in, and the next thing, another boy runs in, two Vietnamese kids, and an Australian boy runs in with a baseball bat, and he runs into the front station with his baseball bat. He's really just a kid, and he's not all over nine too. So I jumped the counter and calmed the whole situation down.
>
> What happened was that this Australian boy, his grandmother died, and the Vietnamese boys were giving him a hard time. He wanted to belt these guys, but the fact that he came into a police station, with the baseball bat, in front of the police, didn't seem to frazzle him. Okay, because generally as a kid when I was growing up all the policemen were good for getting out of the way, okay? And that is basically the problem that they're having at home [grandmother's death] because of the two of them [Australian kids] being in association with all that sort of stuff [blatant violence].
>
> But when I turned around to the Vietnamese kids and said, "How would you feel if your grandmother or your mother passed away?" And he said, "Well, my mother and grandmother are dead."
>
> So that one I threw out. I thought, "Shoot. And he's over here, he's been over here for three or four years, and he's been looked after by his aunt, that's got a tribe of eight kids herself." So these kids have no hope, no help and hope whatever.

Sam describes a hierarchy of social breakdown through his story. Although it was the Australian boy who threatened the younger Vietnamese boys with a baseball bat, Sam nevertheless perceived the Vietnamese boys as the greater social threat. The Australian boy entering the police station with a baseball bat was understood by Sam to be the kind of thing he did as a child—seeing the police as "good for getting out of the way" and understandable because he had been motivated by grief. The violence displayed by the Australian boys was part of normal boyhood experience. Conversely, the Vietnamese children's taunting indicated social pathology. They were members of an ethnic group who had completely different values and assumptions than "Australians" and thus disheartened Sam. Their loss of family members meant that they had had "no hope" for proper socialization and compelled Sam to abandon his usual practice of teaching young boys important civic values. The difference of Vietnamese culture was indelible.

Senior Sergeant Doherty also depicted cultural difference as insurmountable when characterizing Vietnamese immigrants as "violent by nature because of all the turmoil in their country" despite their impressive work ethic. The turmoil (i.e., the Vietnam War) reflected a truth about *Vietnam*, rather than a truth about the Western states (of which Australia was one) that were complicit in creating the "turmoil" in "their" country by sending troops to the Vietnam War. Nevertheless, the violence of Vietnamese immigrants did not worry Doherty because it remained confined to the business transactions of the immigrant community. His officers were smartest to keep a "machete's distance" away and let the Vietnamese "sort it out themselves."

This notion of noninterference does not suggest police slackness so much as a perception on the part of the commanding officer that the Vietnamese community in Fitzroy was independent from the community at large. The police's responsibility seemed to be to those "Australians" affected by "Asian violence." Needless to say, such policing practices reproduced the Vietnamese immigrant community as outside of the boundaries—legal and cultural—of the imagined community of Australia. Additionally, Doherty's advice for officers to keep a "machete's distance" away from Vietnamese violence was yet another example of the kind of slide that took place in explaining Vietnamese criminality. Although Doherty cited Vietnamese violence as a consequence of social factors, he nevertheless deployed images that suggested an essential, primitive violence among Vietnamese.

This ethnographic material provides a snapshot of police attitudes toward Asian criminality at one moment in time. The police department has since begun programs in partnership with immigrant communities to foster cultural sensitivity in new recruits. Community groups were invited to explain their policing needs and officers were encouraged to learn Vietnamese and act with greater professionalism in general. In other words, perceptions of race and culture among the police are historically contingent rather than essential to their profession. More important for this study is how criminality has been used to spatially construct the nation and national identity. Asian criminality provided a vocabulary for people to negotiate the relationship of Australia to Asia. Not only did this spatial process happen in everyday contexts, it was also a means for contesting federal policies, which in this case sought to (re)locate Australia in the imagined community of Asia. So while Gareth Evans, Foreign Minister for Paul Keating, created his map of the "East Asian hemisphere" to show Australians and the ASEAN community Australia's true political geography, police officers mapped out the relationship between Asia and Australia differently. Their aversion to Asian bodies and spaces and defining crime as the latest threat Asia presents against Australia officers reinforced the borders.

The association between Asian-ness and criminality was not confined to the police. A concern about Asian criminality also circulated in the media and within the larger community. In the interview below, Emily, a member of the East Melbourne Garden Club, explained her fear that Australia would be compromised by the violence of immigrants and Vietnamese immigrants in particular:

EMILY:   I don't like people bringing their wars into our backyard. If they want to fight, they can do it over there. And I think a lot of people feel like that.

AC:   Have there been actual incidents in Melbourne of that? I mean, what makes that spring to your mind?

EMILY:   Well, I'd heard about different things on the news, and I don't know if it's just in Melbourne but, you know, in Australia. You know, like the stabbing between certain Vietnamese groups and things like that.

Media reports regularly highlighted violence as a key social problem involving Asian communities in Melbourne. Although newspaper articles might highlight how Vietnamese were victims of the new violence troubling Melbourne, for instance, they also made it clear that Asians were responsible for the violence. As a consequence, they constructed a picture of "tribal wars" being fought on Australian soil and an Asian predisposition for violence.

An article entitled "Death-Threat Terror as Gang Hits Family"[6] that appeared in Melbourne's major newspaper was typical of the way Asian criminality was represented in the media. The article strongly suggested through its mention of the victims' connection to South Vietnam and police suspicion of "mistaken identity" that Vietnamese gangs were implicated in the attack of an innocent family. In typical fashion, the media stopped short of blaming a particular ethnic group for violence, but gave "hints" as to the group responsible. In the language of this article, neither "Asian" nor "Vietnamese" was used as descriptors. But the article instead included the detail that the culprits spoke a "dialect particular to South Vietnam." This story illustrates the way in which Asian immigrants were positioned as a problem in a previously lawful country because they "import" violence and criminal networks. It directs readers to the salient features for making sense of the urban criminal landscape by invoking ethnic identity, rather than the names of rival gangs or category of crime (drug, theft, etc.). Ethnicity is the significant organizing concept.

Additionally, media representations of crime regularly presented ethnicity as something that was out of control. In the article I cited, ethnicity was presented as intertwined with senseless revenge between gangs, so out of control that it could strike innocent families asleep in their homes. In this article, as in the discourse of officers and Anglo-Celtic Australians in the city, there was a sense of tragedy that innocent people were being hurt. There was also a sense of threat that ethnic violence was on the shores of Australia, ripping apart ethnic communities and just short of potentially erupting into the lives of white Australians. In some ways, the sense of impending doom in discourses about Asian criminality in Melbourne recalled for me the stories that circulate in the United States about killer bees that will cross the Mexican border "very soon." In both cases a menacing foreign intruder was poised to destroy a peaceful society.

We cannot draw any conclusions from a few unsystematically collected newspaper articles on "Asian violence." I note such articles to make the point that the image of Asian deviance was one that also circulated outside of the police community. In part, the police helped foster its circulation because they provided causation for the media in interviews, but the media also played an independent role by subtly inviting readers to see ethnic violence as a problem in the city. The success of the media in constructing such an image was evident in the comments of people I interviewed outside of Fitzroy.

Ghassan Hage argues that strife is more newsworthy than the many peaceful ordinary behaviors of Third World–looking people in Australia (Hage's phrase) because Anglo-Celtic Australians possess a sense of white entitlement to governance of multicultural "problems." The media helped position white Australians as entitled to worry and to dictate the extent to which immigrants should assimilate. In what Ghassan Hage calls the fantasy of containment among white Australians, he explains that "the Third World–looking migrant is relegated to the position of a national object to be governed by the eternally worried White national subject. It could even be said that it is this 'right to worry' which differentiates White from non-White national subjects in Australia today" (1998, 233).

There is a more general narrative about the threat that contact with Asia has for Western subjectivity that circulates in the West through films about the Vietnam War in particular. *The Deer Hunter* and *Apocalypse Now* both narrate Asia's destructive potential for Westerners. However, in Australia, where the government and large sections of the public were linking the country's future to Asian prosperity, it was the *national subject* who was threatened by the primitive spirit of Asia. The comments of one Australian woman illustrate the link between Asia's historical threat to the Australian nation and contemporary criminality:

CLAIRE: I don't know if you're aware of this, but I mean it's still happening to a certain extent, but everyone was paranoid about the Asian invasion in Australia. A lot of Asian companies and people were investing in Australia. I guess that's why people are really paranoid about government assets being sold off. I think it even goes back to the racial thing maybe. Also it's just that element of Japan invading Australia during the war.

AC: Do you think people care about that?

CLAIRE: I myself do. I see it endlessly on television. Every major drug crime seems to have an Asian link to it. That concerns me. And some of the gangs, like the Triads and all that. The whole thing. It's along the same lines as the Mafia, where they're getting businesses to pay to be protected and that sort of stuff. Outrageous that these people would do that. And I don't want to see it happen here.

"Yellow peril" and "Asian invasion" have been the threats that Australia's location in the Pacific has had in the national imaginary, and for many years they fueled the drive to define Australia as part of Great Britain and the West (Walker 1999; Burke 2001). Historian Tom Griffiths links geography, race, and a history of fear of Asia when he describes a collective feeling of vulnerability in the first half of the twentieth century emanating from people's sense of space in Australia.

> The open spaces, it was continually argued, needed to be talked up; they needed to be developed and populated for two reasons. One was for defense of the nation, the other for defense of race. "Populate or perish!" was the cry. So few people inhabiting the vast lands closest to Asia was regarded as a precarious sort of possession, perhaps ominously reminiscent of the diffuse hunter-gatherer economy so recently supplanted. That knowledge of their own swift usurpation was haunting. (1996, 186–87)

Originally, the White Australia policy functioned to insulate the nation against the Asian region; during World War II anxiety about being subsumed by Asia was articulated in terms of the threat of a military invasion by the Japanese ("There were Japanese submarines in the Sydney Harbour!"). This anxiety about Australia being subsumed by Asia continued through the end of the twentieth century in a slightly different form.

When Labor politicians and many members of the business community were calling for greater integration into Asian economic communities, anxieties about the threat of Asia's proximity continued through a fear of being overwhelmed by Asia. For instance, former MP Pauline Hanson and the One Nation Party criticized immigration and multicultural policies that permitted Asian immigrants in particular to "form ghettos and avoid assimilating." One Nation Party literature also warned of the danger Asian criminality posed to the national body: "In our cities, girls as young as 14 sell sex for as little as $10 to buy drugs from Asian gangs" (1996, 119; see also Hage 1998). For Pauline Hanson an Asian presence on Australian shores would mean the destruction of the body politic and the individual bodies of its citizens. But anxieties about greater symbolic and material fusion with Asia also shaped the concerns of people like Claire—people who did not necessarily align themselves strongly with conservative or nationalist parties. As reflected in Claire's comments above, a collective anxiety about the threat of Asia to the Australian nation formed a subtext for many social debates in Australia—from immigration policy to privatizing state-owned utilities. Crime and concern about contamination were public discourses of which members of the Fitzroy police made use to define the parameters of national belonging and to contest the political push to imagine Australia as part of the Asian region.

Australia's economic dependence on Asian economies stood in tension with the racist ideology of Western superiority, especially over Asia, that has formed the basis of the definition of Australian national identity for many decades. Under the leadership of Liberal Party Prime Minister John Howard, there was a governmental and popular attack on the way Keating had positioned Australia in relation to Asia. As the Asian economies weakened at the end of 1997 and beginning of 1998, many were quick to cite this trend as proof that engaging further with Asia was not really in Australia's best interest. This backlash signals the heterogeneity of views about Australia's imagined proximity to Asia. It also illustrates that despite the appearance of a uniform agreement among Australians since the 1990s that Australia needs to "recognize" that it is located in the Asia Pacific, Australia's location in the international landscape is a matter of ongoing negotiation.

Of course, anyone in the least bit familiar with Australia's history cannot help but be a little surprised and perhaps even amused at the irony of criminality being used as a means for symbolic exclusion from the nation. Australia, after all, began as a penal colony. Examining the history of the intersection of criminal identity with Australian identity renders this irony perhaps a little less surprising. Briefly tracing Australian history demonstrates that the association of criminality with Australian-ness was a means of defining nation and positioning Australia internationally in its earliest formation as a European settlement and that the intersection of criminal identity, national identity, and geography has merely been reemployed in contemporary Australia to meet more recent political exigencies.

## A FEW CHAINS IN THE FAMILY

As noted in the introduction, the British initiated the association of criminality with Australian identity. For the rising British middle class in the nineteenth century, bourgeois mores and norms of lawfulness defined Britishness, while working-class culture and criminality defined the convict and free settlements of Australia. Richard White notes how the peasant/working class was blamed for its own failure in industrializing England:

> In 1852 Earl Grey, the Secretary of the State for Colonies, told Charles Dickens that emigrants were "necessarily far below the average of the working population in respect to steadiness and strictly moral conduct" . . . The logical extension of this view of the emigrant was the portrayal of Australia as simply the "dustbin of the unwanted and unsuccessful." (1981, 37–38)

Not only were the new immigrants the worst of Britain, they were also easily influenced by the convicts once they arrived in Australia (38). All in all, the various forms of moral decay were consolidated in the image of Australia.

Even though Australia's identity as a criminal society was more about the needs and the projections of Britain than it was about Australia, Australians were still affected by this assigned identity (see Hughes 1988; White 1981; Clark 1963). It was this original image of Australia as the dustbin of the unwanted and unsuccessful that the middle class in Australia had to work to offset. The Australian middle class, in the nineteenth century especially, was mainly of British descent (as opposed to Irish descent) and identified with the values of the British middle class. Therefore, the respectability of the middle class in Australia was premised on the reproduction of their Britishness. As Manning Clark writes, "They . . . wanted the recognition in England that the numerous and rapidly increasing colonial generation was just as moral and sober in their habits as the people of the mother country" (1963, 51). For many years, Anglo-Australians marked their British-style respectability through a variety of social practices such as playing cricket and serving afternoon tea and through political policies like the White Australia policy.

It is not surprising then that many generations of middle-class Australians prior to the mid-twentieth century constructed their identity in opposition to the figure of the convict. Robert Hughes explains:

The idea of the "convict stain," a moral blot soaked into our fabric, dominated all argument about Australian selfhood by the 1840s and was the main rhetorical figure used in the movement to abolish transportation. Its leaders called for an abolition, not in the name of an independent Australia, but as Britons who felt their decency impugned by the survival of convictry. (1988, xiv)

Thus, the shame associated with criminality was a significant barrier to Australians' feeling a sense of national pride and legitimacy. Hughes continues by delineating the lingering effect the social stain of convictry had on the imaging of Australia.

For decades to come, the official voices of Australia would continue to stake their claim to respectability on their Britishness. If the end of transportation had been brought about in the name of the convicts' own descendants, this might not have happened. But the fight was on behalf of free emigrants and their stock; it was this side of Australia which most fervently brandished the myth of corrupted blood and "convict evil." After abolition, you could (silently) reproach your forebears for being convicts. You could not take pride in them, or reproach England. (ibid.)

As early as 1822, abolitionists in Australia were issuing arguments to the British government to end transportation for good, but not out of a sense of the inhumanity of transportation as a form of punishment or a belief that the offspring of convicts were free of their parents' deviancy. Australian abolitionists reproduced many of the classist constructions of the criminal that circulated in nineteenth-century Britain and in the process strengthened the mythology of the "convict stain" that haunted Australian society.[7] Rather, Australian abolitionists worked to stop convict transport as a means of redefining Australia and eroding the shame associated with living in a community that included penal colonies.

Thus, Australia, as a society and as a physical location, was imbued with the shame and degeneracy the English middle class projected onto the lower (criminal) class. The border between British nationals and the unwanted elements of society (the poor, criminal, Irish political activists, etc.) was marked by physical distance (sending "misfits" across the world) and through the narrative construction of Australians as inferior. Although in the logic of imperialism, the British took for granted its political control of Australia, the

British were careful to maintain their cultural distinction. While middle-class Australians worked against the low status of their nation, they did so by trying to qualify as British. They tried to imagine Australia as an extension of Britain through cultural forms like the English cottage garden and institutions in order to define their own respectability and political importance.

The association of Britishness with respectability continued well into the twentieth century in Australia. One Australian woman, in an interview in Los Angeles, remarked upon this as she recalled her initial failure to be admitted to art school in Sydney in the early 1970s. Alice, now a successful artist and scholar, attributed her rejection to class differences and described the way class was marked on one's body in Australia.

> And then I failed the interview. It was partly because if you live in this little working class suburb near Parameta and you don't have any money and you don't go on any vacations, and you don't, kind of, do anything, and you live in your head as I did as a kid. It was very clear that there were a whole bunch of people who had very expensive portfolios. There was a kind of clearly marked class difference that you don't get here [Los Angeles] actually.
>
> It kind of plays out regionally in different ways. You can sort of see differences in people; but it's much kind of more marked across your body and your speech and your whole manner in places like Australia, which I guess is in relation to British stuff . . . you know, newscasters will speak with a slightly more clipped Australian accent that sounds a little more British.

Alice's experience indicates how the idea of English respectability functioned in Australian class relations and Australian identity well after the end of convict transportation. Her attempts at class border crossing highlighted for her how class was signaled not merely through possessions, but also through more subtle forms such as cultural knowledge and the body. Alice's working class suburb near Sydney was encoded in her speech patterns and mannerisms. Conversely, Britain and things associated with it marked a positive class status on the bodies of Australians and by referencing England even in such local spaces as a Sydney art institute or through the studied accents of community newscasters. Thus the body is a landscape on which class and national subjectivity are marked. Many Australians, particularly before the 1970s, located Australia within the imagined community of Great Britain with the cultivation of clipped speech patterns and modes of dress and through the cultivation of "good taste."

Alice's experience also suggests how cultural capital intersects with local geography. Local spaces, coded as high culture and wealth, positioned Australia as more centrally located within the British Empire and operated as a refutation of the moral and geographical differentiation Britons made between Australia and themselves. The Australian middle class located themselves socially and politically by marking moral and geographical differences between themselves and the Australian working class. Certainly there has been extensive critique of the British within Australia from the time of colonial settlement, largely by those disempowered by British privilege (e.g., convicts, Scots, Irish, working-class British). But because of the class privilege of people who identified with Britishness, British identity played into hegemonic notions of Australian national identity for many years.

Ghassan Hage also makes the point that the hyperidentification with British upper-class identity also constituted some within Australia as the "national aristocracy within the field of Whiteness." Hage argues that even people in the working classes could feel the entitlement of the governing class because of their identification with white, British cultural identity (1998, 193). This gave white Australians a sense of privilege to manage nonwhites and to set the terms (limitations) of their inclusion.

Not surprisingly, members of the Irish working class in Australia reclaimed the image of the convict much earlier than Anglo-Australians. They did so by producing folk heroes out of the figure of the bushranger, many of whom were escaped prisoners (Hughes 1988, 158). Not until the 1960s, with the publication of Manning Clark's *History of Australia* in 1962 and L. L. Robson's *Convict Settlers of Australia* in 1965, did the middle class begin to appropriate the figure of the convict into their own conceptualization of Australian identity. Although intellectuals such as Marcus Clarke, Price Warung, and G. A. Wood redefined the convict as a victim of English class oppression at the end of the nineteenth century, Clark's and Robson's histories were significant in breaking the silence around the convict for the Australian middle class (Hughes 1988, xvi). The romance of the (lawless) bushman was also taken up in artist Sidney Nolan's "Ned Kelly" series in the middle of the twentieth century.

Since the late 1960s the image of the convict has undergone a significant transformation and has become a highly respectable and romantic figure for the bulk of the Australian middle class. For instance, before the 1970s most penal institutions and late-nineteenth-century prisons were used for diverse and idiosyncratic purposes by the government, if they were used at all. Since then, they have been steadily converted into some of Australia's prime national museums. Port Arthur, Hyde Park Barracks, the Old Melbourne Gaol, are but a few examples (Bennet 1995, 154). Additionally, people who were firmly entrenched in the upper middle class in Australia such as Dora, an East Melbourne Garden Club member, were very enthusiastic about the idea of convict ancestors. The reevaluation of the convict was evident as Dora discussed her family heritage.

AC: Do you know whether they came over as settlers? I mean, if you are fourth generation, that would have put them back to one of the earlier settlers.

DORA: Well, no one really minds having a few chains and things in the family at this stage.

AC: It's almost chic now?

DORA: That's right, yes. But I've never been able to trace my roots back to any of the people who came out as convicts. No, I think most of them did just come out, you know, of their own. Whether they traveled steerage or where they traveled, I don't know; but I think most of them came out under their own steam. They weren't guests of Her Majesty or His Majesty or whatever. But I wouldn't mind if they were. I mean, nobody seems to mind that now.

Dora was so comfortable with the possibility of having convict ancestors as to be playful in her consideration of "having a few chains in the family." Britain's condemnation of the convict settlers was transformed in Dora's discussion into the ironic suggestion that the convicts were the fully accommodated guests of the King or Queen, not social deviants. At a historical juncture when many Australians wanted to differentiate Australia from Britain, the convict who was originally used by the British to mark moral, geographical, and national difference had been reemployed symbolically to mark a new difference. The convict came to be an ironic symbol of what many Australians saw as a reversal of the moral hierarchy in the postcolonial relationship between Australia and Great Britain.

In Los Angeles, Alice made a similar observation about the change in attitude among Australians toward their history as a penal colony. The fact that Dora was in her seventies and Alice was in her late thirties indicates that this perception was shared across generations in the middle class. It was not that Australians such as Alice or Dora were advocating criminal behavior. Middle-class Australians had reclaimed the figure of the convict because the criminality of the original convicts was understood in new terms. Over the last century, and especially since the 1960s, the convict has been transformed into a political hero.[8] The convicts were popularly understood as victims of class oppression in England. Australians of all social classes believed that the convicts' "crime" was to be poor and thus a threat to middle-class property owners. Convicts did not freely choose their fates, nor were they morally degenerate. Rather, they were criminals because people during the industrial revolution had so few choices, faced miserable social conditions, and received extreme sentences for petty crimes.

With this interpretation, Alice and other Australians drew inspiration from the convicts' ability to survive poverty and from their attempts to make a new life for themselves in Australia under extremely cruel circumstances. Reevaluating the convict settlers lent them social legitimacy and allowed the Australian middle class to construct a national identity from their convict history. It also allowed Australians to reposition themselves in relation to British imperialism. That is, a more romantic or compassionate understanding of the convicts also decriminalized Anglo-Celtic Australians. Their nation's collective criminality (as historically defined by the British middle class) was reinterpreted as historical, class-related, and above all an asset to Australia. Alice illustrates the link many Australians made between imagined attributes of the convicts and contemporary Australian identity.

> ALICE: And you know in Australia there is a pride about coming
> from convict stock, you know. I don't know if my family
> or my father's family were Welsh and Irish in backgrounds.
> Maybe the Irish bit, I don't know how long they were here,

but it's quite conceivable, the place has only been around
for a couple of hundred years, that they were of convict
stock, right?

And when I say that here [in the U.S.], people say, "Oh
no, I'm sure they weren't." And I'm like, "Yeah, they were."
You know, I like to present this with—It's a sort of difference
in—You know, there's a kind of pride to being something.

AC: Why would you take pride in it? [being from convict stock]

ALICE: Well, it makes you tough and resourceful and resilient and
kind of, umm—And I mean if anything else, I have a sort of
inverse snobbery, which my friends will tell you so.

AC: But you don't think you are alone in finding that sort of
amusing? To think, "Oh, I might be from convicts."

ALICE: No, that's very pervasive. That's a point of pride because
it's sort of anti-British as well. I mean, people have this very
peculiar relationship to Britain.

Alice indicates how the figure of the convict provided a national
ideal type for Australians more generally. The attributes Alice identified in the convicts helped her define particular qualities in herself
and imagine a commonality she has with other Australians. The previous embarrassment within the Australian middle class over convict
ancestry was turned on its head and came to function as a point of
pride for many people. It became a mark of respectability and social
prominence. And indeed, even among officers at the Fitzroy Police
Station, the suggestion that Australians might feel shame for their
convict past elicited wide grins and appreciative comments about the
convicts for being "antiauthority." Britishness was equated with a
cold, colonial respectability and was contrasted to the resourceful-
ness and resilience of Australians and of Irish-Australians in particular. Therefore, the reassessment of the convict allowed Australians to
reposition themselves in relation to British imperialism.

Thus, the inversion of previous codes of respectability functioned
as another form of rejection of the idea of British cultural superiority and of colonialism. Instead of drawing on native plants for their
symbolism, as the people discussed in chapter 2 had done, many
Australians mounted their rebellion through the figure of the convict. By glamorizing the convict settler, Australians contested the association of their national identity with low culture and class status.

While Australia continued to be situated in the Commonwealth, mainly through sporting competition, its imagined geography in relation to the British Empire has undergone dramatic redefinition since the 1960s. This was achieved in part through a reconceptualization of Australian criminality and in part because of a shift in the organization of the international community. The criminality originally associated with Australian identity had been revalued and became a means by which contemporary Australians highlighted their separateness from Britishness and their victimization as a colony of Britain.

However, the use of concepts of criminality and low moral standards to define the outside of the national community, ironically, came to be used within Australia to define Australian identity as distinct from Asian ethnic identity. The ethnographic material from the Fitzroy Police suggests that these concepts continued to be used to define the national in opposition to particular groups of people. While Australians were not defining national identity in opposition to the lower classes per se, as the British may have done in the eighteenth and nineteen centuries, some defined the nation in opposition to a notion of Asian deviance.

Further, as used by the British originally, discourses of criminality and deviance were used to mark international borders. Originally the British middle class used Australian deviance to define British nationalism as morally distinct and geographically distinct from Australia. Although there was a level at which colonies were encouraged to see themselves as offshoots of the mother country, the British middle class also worked to demarcate their difference from their colonies. As Australian history illustrates, notions of inherent deviance were a means by which the British nation was defined as geographically, politically, and morally distinct from Australia, despite attempts within Australia to position Australia as conterminous with Britain. More recently, notions of criminality have been used in Australia to position the nation in relation to Britishness in new ways and in relation to Asia. People used the newly claimed moral superiority of the original Australian convicts to distinguish Australia as a nation distinct from contemporary Britain elitism and the history of British colonialism. Like some Australians' use of the victimization of the environment as a sign of Australian colonial victimization, other used the figure of the convict to assert a distinct, morally pure national imaginary (of course, plenty of people used both symbols).

But the idea of criminality also allowed people within Australia to continue to mark their superiority as Westerners over Asians and to reject the positioning of Australia within the imagined community of Asia.

## THE POOR WHITE TRASH OF ASIA

The negotiations in this chapter concerning where Australia belongs were not simply a matter of Australia's unique need to position itself in the larger international landscape. Australians' need to locate their country also reflects the (re)negotiations required between states as the cold war organization of the international landscape reshuffled into geographical economic regions. Australians' quest to position Australia internationally has involved much coded negotiation over whether the new economic communities are based only on geography or whether inclusion also depends on other categories like race or civilization. For instance, the negotiations about whether some of the marginalized nation-states within Europe, like Poland, should be allowed to join the European Union has raised questions about what the terms of inclusion are for that particular supranational community.

The positioning of an individual nation-state within the international landscape has important ramifications for the state's economic and political status as well as for their symbolic clout. Therefore, aspiring to belong to an imagined supranational community can lead people within a nation-state to define their national identity in such a way that it "qualifies" them to be a member of a more powerful supranational community. Australia demonstrated an awareness of the differences one's international location can make during the colonial era through their desire to be part of the British Empire and the "West." During the nineteenth and early twentieth centuries, when Australia's best chance for inclusion into a powerful economic and cultural community was to qualify as part of these communities, Australians strove to do so. Since race and concepts of civilization have been key markers of geography, inclusion in the imagined supranational communities of the British Empire or the West also functioned to define Australia as white and civilized.

When it seemed as if membership in the imagined community of Asia could provide Australia with more opportunity and more people rejected the racism that informed the White Australia policy, many politicians and other Australians began to work to construct Australia's identity in such a way that Australia might be accepted as a part of the Asian (or ASEAN) community. In negotiations with Asian states, Australians have been highly motivated to define Asia in strictly geographical terms, even though in the past they participated in the general assumption that the region of Asia was a product of shared racial, religious, and cultural features.[9]

After many decades of the White Australia policy that heavily restricted Asian immigration, it was perhaps not surprising that some Asian political leaders were resistant to Australians' attempts in the 1990s to redefine their geography and to realign themselves with the supranational community of Southeast Asia. Some Asian leaders have restricted inclusion into their supranational community by reasserting the idea that racial, religious, and cultural similarities define geographical communities. At times Australia has been disqualified from inclusion into Asia on the grounds that Australia is indeed European and therefore would not be a natural member of ASEAN or the region more generally. When in 1995 Mahathir Mohamad (Malaysia), for instance, accused Australia of being "mentally still European" and therefore unable to participate in the true consensus-building process of ASEAN, he affirmed Australians' success in constructing themselves as European for so many decades.

Here Mahathir Mohamad also exemplifies an essentializing move to construct an imagined supranational community around qualities designated as "Asian," such as consensus building and morality. This is an example of the appropriation of an identity by a marginalized group that was originally constructed to contain and discipline a group of people. Foucault describes how the demarcation of homosexuality as a distinct identity in nineteenth-century Europe was designed to repress groups of people, but it was also used by people categorized as such to conceptualize their subjectivity in positive ways and consequently resist their disempowerment (Foucault 1990, 45–46). More recently, identified "Asian" qualities have allowed people to construct a sense of community that might facilitate economic cooperation in the region, contest Westernization, and disrupt historic racial hierarchies that posited the superiority of whiteness.

Former Prime Minister of Singapore Lee Kuan Yew also engaged in negotiation to define the international landscape and Australia's proximity to Asia in the mid-1980s when he threatened that Australia could become the "poor white trash of Asia." Considering this label in light of Australia's history and its contemporary negotiations for inclusion in Asia reveals it to be a very economical and symbolically rich assertion of the relation between Australia and Asia. For instance, it functioned to remind Australia and the world of the centrality whiteness has played in Australians' definition of their national identity in the past. Lee Kuan Yew ironically reminded, insisted even, on marking Australia as white at a historical moment when Australian leaders were becoming more silent on this point and beginning to promote their nation as multicultural (read: multiracial). Further, he inverted the historic hierarchy on which Australian identity had been premised by suggesting that while Australia might come to be included as a member of the extended family of Asian states, it would only be as a "trashy" relation unless Australians made significant changes to their society.

Of further interest is Lee Kuan Yew's use of Australia's traditional marginalization in the British Empire in order to position Australia as marginal to Asia. He recalled the terms by which Britain disciplined Australia as a nation—invoking class and moral inferiority—and ironically posited that position of class inferiority as somehow essential to Australian national identity. The central strategies Australians used to define themselves in terms of British hegemony included defining their geography as outside of Asia, defining themselves as respectable middle-class people, and "defending" their whiteness against fusion with Asia. Lee Kuan Yew seemed to be insisting that this history should not be so quickly erased simply because Australians would now like to be a part of "Asian prosperity." He thus ironically invoked the very things that Australia sought to deny in defining their nation and geography in the past—lower-class whiteness and location in Asia.

Additionally, the use of the imagery of "white trash" has yet another layer of meaning. This imagery provides insight into how the organization of nation-states in the international landscape has been constituted historically through racial hierarchies. Lee Kuan Yew's characterization of Australia as white trash was a means of shaming Australians for their racism toward Asia, but also a means of highlighting the "shame" of "downward mobility" a white Western nation risks when it starts to petition Asia for inclusion into its community. John Hartigan uses Mary Douglas's notion of "trash" as defined as "all materials that must be excluded from a cultural system in order that its modes of identity be maintained as naturalized conditions" (Hartigan 1997, 320). He explains that the label of white trash is assigned to people who violate the dominant racial order:

> In this regard, stances of the name "white trash" should be read as inscriptions of racial pollutions, moments when the decorum of the white racial order has been breached and compromised. "White trash" is used to name those bodies that exceed the class and racial etiquettes required of whites if they are to preserve the powers and privileges that accrue to them as members of the dominant racial order in this country. (ibid.)

Lee Kuan Yew artfully highlighted the way that Australia risks compromising Western, hierarchically organized, racial categories by now attempting to be part of the imagined (supranational) community of Asia. And indeed, perhaps it was to this racial "shame" that the Fitzroy police officers were responding in their spatial containment of Asian immigrants in Fitzroy. Even more, Senior Minister Lee's imagery offers a subtle critique of how a white nation petitioning for inclusion into the geographical and racial category of Asia might be read as "polluting" its whiteness and, more generally, the entire racial category. Of course, the playfulness of a political leader using such a colloquial expression in public and of assigning an identity reserved for individuals to an entire nation-state signals the irony of Lee Kuan Yew's comment. The Singaporean leader chose an expression to censor Australians, which using inversions, rendered his insult even more powerful for its subtlety. Lee reminded Australians that they had spent many years trying to avoid a diminishment in their international and personal status for associating with Asia. The irony lies in the fact that Lee underscores for Australians the "superiority" of their whiteness just at the moment when many people in Australia had become invested in altering Australia's identity and location to take advantage of Asia's economic prosperity.

## LESSONS FROM THE OUTLIER

This chapter has mapped some of the ambivalence people demonstrated within Australia in working as a nation to be accepted as a member of the Asian community. Being a member of Asia might have allowed Australia prosperity and, therefore, overall political status. But it also required people to relinquish their understanding of Western-ness and whiteness as categories that defined Australia's worth as an individual nation and, more importantly, as a member of the international hegemony. Members of Northern European or North American nation-states have been able to reconceptualize their positions in the international landscape (from being in the "West" to being part of a regional community) without having to challenge the racial hierarchy that has defined international geography since the colonial era. Canadians, for example, have been able to transform their former status as part of "the West" (which defined their geography and political identity in the cold war) into a membership within the supranational community of the North American Free Trade Agreement. They have been able to do so without having to confront the ways in which race has defined their national and supranational identity up until this time.

In contrast, the reorganization of the international landscape from an East–West split to economic regions has deterritorialized the Australian nation in profound ways. Australia was left vulnerable as a result of this reorganization, in part because nationals had worked to secure their position as part of the international hegemony in the past by being hostile to the very Asian states from which they now sought acceptance. And Australians have been faced with an especially complex process of reterritorialization because in order to become a full member of the most vibrant supranational community now left available to it, the people in Australia have had to undertake some difficult cultural and political work. Australians have been challenged to disassociate their sense of national and international superiority from notions of race and civilization in a way that people in Germany, Canada, or the United States have not. Reterritorializing Australia vis-à-vis the international community has required much renegotiation for ordinary Australians as well as for Australian leaders who define international policy.

Therefore, examining the ways in which people within Australia spatially position their nation-state internationally provides insight into how such practices are important means for defining the nation. Further, the labor Australians must do and the resistance many demonstrate to "recognizing" Australia as part of Asia indicates how international geography and the racial categories that have informed international geography in the past are undergoing transformation and renegotiation in the present era.

In casual conversations with Americans about Australia over the past several years, many Americans have informed me that Australians are particularly racist. No doubt many of the policies and social practices Australians engage in could be fairly labeled racist; however, the same criticism can also be made about Americans, Canadians, Germans, etc. What I believe the material in this chapter highlights is the way in which the organization of the international landscape naturalizes and protects the racial hierarchy that underpins many first-world national identities. Because Australia has always been on the outside looking in—on the outer perimeter of Empire, on the symbolic edge of the northern hemisphere, on the outside of Asia— historically it has responded by trying to prove its membership. This has meant touting the (often unspoken) terms of international hegemony, such as defending its identity as a white society or by boasting of a greater degree of civilization. But Australia has merely been a more visible example of a general process also engaged in by numerous other nation-states. Because the geography of the United States and Canada has always positioned them within supranational communities that define themselves as white and civilized, these states have not had to go to the extremes that Australia, located in the South Pacific, has had to in order to define itself. Acknowledging this fact is not to say that the desire to define one's nation as white is an ethically acceptable one. Certainly it is a form of racism engaged in by many Western nation-states. Instead, my aim has been to highlight how the process of "thinking the nation" through categories of race and geography is one in which most nations have participated.

While redefining their nation through its geography has been a complicated political and social process for people in Australia, the "awkwardness" of Australia's position is very useful in trying to understand the interconnections between identity, imagined geography and the nation. These spatial practices in Australia allow us to see the way in which a nation's move to position itself internationally is an important means of defining its status and identity within its borders. This process is less a matter of literal geography than a matter of using spatial and narrative practices to position the nation in an imagined international geography through terms such as race, prosperity, and civilization.

# Conclusion
## On the Margins of Nation

Despite almost thirty years of bipartisan promotion and sweeping popular support for multiculturalism as a narrative of national identity, the practices examined in this study nevertheless still assumed and reproduced a dominant white Australian national order. In this respect many of the spatial practices in East Melbourne and among the Fitzroy police illustrate and support Ghassan Hage's reading of a dominant nationalist subject position that presumes to be entitled to manage and worry about "third-world-looking people." Hage discusses how this subject position represents a kind of spatial management. One incident Hage uses in his analysis involves the police. One of his Lebanese interview subjects related his experience of having an Anglo-Australian police officer call him "a piece of shit" during a policing encounter on the street. Hage observes in his analysis that conceiving of non-Anglo-Celtic Australians as a "piece" underscores their status as removable. Hage argues that "all those who engaged in physical or verbal nationalist violence implicitly conceived of themselves as spatial managers, seeing in the Arab other a mere object to be removed from national space" (1998, 44). In Hage's discussion of spatial management, the management of others in national space is a useful way to conceive of belonging and national race relations. However, despite how central space is to the point he makes in this example, space remains metaphorical.

The spatial practices in East Melbourne and Fitzroy help us move beyond analysis that revolves around *spatial metaphors*. The ethnographic material enables us to understand how bodies are managed and nations physically constructed in everyday confrontations and cultivations. The spatial practices in this study indicate that in many ways the bodies and social position of so-called ethnic groups in Australia are being managed, despite popular support for multiculturalism. Through police regulations and surveillance, for instance, and through community regulations aimed at preserving heritage, "ethnics" are assigned and reminded of their place in the national community.

This study has tried to better understand how various social groups are treated as though they pose territorial as well as social problems for the nation. Among many other factors, immigrants and indigenous people deterritorialize the settler state with the presence of their bodies or through their persistent claims to land and rights. For example, as chapter 4 argued, Asian bodies on Fitzroy streets confuse former divisions between East and West on which previous notions of Australian identity were predicated. Similarly, the persistence of Aboriginal land claims and Aboriginal ways of organizing space (through a Dreamtime cosmology, for instance) unsettle white Australians' control of the continent. In both the East Melbourne Garden Club and the Fitzroy Police Station many people were engaged to some extent in recentering white culture. This behavior indicates the kind of social recuperation that occurs when a white majority begins to feel itself on the margin of what it considers to be its own nation or when it begins to feel threatened by the possibility of becoming the "poor white trash" of a region over which Australians have historically felt superior.

The analytical insights in this research project have been generated from the place-making practices of two distinct social locations. They are distinct not because the groups were especially unusual, but because they were particular. The Fitzroy police officers were particular in the way in which their spatial practices were deeply connected to state policy and power, for instance. Likewise, the East Melbourne gardeners occupied a distinct social class, generational perspective, and gendered location in the liberal division between public and private spheres. This study has not tried to generalize about the totality of Australia from such specific contexts. Instead it has capitalized on the details and context that ethnography affords us in order to develop our understanding of the process of politics, the relationship of territory to the nation, and the nature of modern power.

Developing our theories from the details of everyday life also allows us to understand the ways in which social identities converge and political positions can be much more complicated than purely abstract theoretical frameworks may acknowledge. For instance, this study has offered insight into the way social class and geography inform each other. Certainly, we have long taken for granted that class is reflected in the landscape: wealthy people live on one side of the tracks and the poor on the other, for instance. But in examining how people discipline urban and natural landscapes, we can see better how social class gets written onto the landscape of the physical world and onto the landscape of the body in order to mark class distinction and to define the nation. When people sought to code Australia as British, this move was accomplished through a myriad of social practices. For instance, class distinction and nation were defined through the clip of an accent, through picturesque descriptions in colonial travel writing, and through the reproduction of bourgeois cottage gardens within the rationalized grid of Melbourne's urban design. The complicated lived realities of the people in this study and the histories to which those practices corresponded illustrate how nation and geography are often overdetermined by other identities like race and gender.

Additionally, this study has explored how nation is marked on the intimate landscape of body and on local space in ways that reflect the positioning of the nation internationally. For instance, Australia is reasserted as part of the West through the identification of aberrance on Asian bodies and in behaviors. This analytical trajectory has been another way in which the study has affirmed a growing conviction in social theory that we cannot look at these categories of identity—class, nation, gender—in isolation; social identities are defined in relation to other established identities and social categories. But we are also reminded that these social identities are not simply free-floating nor are they always constructed in narrative form. Rather they are constituted by what people do to their bodies, where they place their bodies, and how they shape the landscape around them. In this respect, social identities are very much grounded.

Like every study, this analysis can lay claim to producing certain kinds of knowledge and not others. Examining the spatial production of political community out of such particular contexts is limited insofar as it does not allow us to make more general statements about how *most* Australians at the turn of the twentieth century were imagining the geography of their nation. This study does not allow us to know definitively whether most people supported the idea that Australia is a part of Asia or whether most positioned Australia someplace else in the world, as quantitative studies would seek to determine.

Instead, this project can call into question the transparency of national geography. Rather than tally up opinions, it has worked to generate insight into the process by which individuals and national communities define themselves and claim territory through an imagined relationship to place. Narratives about the relationship between a people and place, as well as practices that physically shape the landscape are means by which people appropriate territory and define the characteristics (e.g., civilized, white, native) of a people. This political process illustrates the centrality of territory and landscape to constructing and legitimizing nation-states. It also highlights the interconnections between the local and the transnational and suggests some of the ways in which individual, physical bodies are implicated in the governing and definition of the larger body politic.

Nevertheless, while this study has been indicative of how a number of social identities are constituted spatially, it has been concerned in particular with the way the identity of a political community (the nation) is produced through spatial practices. In doing so, it has considered how mundane practices, such as planting wattle trees and using pens to push elevator buttons, not only shape local landscapes but also define the nation. They not only define the nation as lawful or indigenous, for instance, but in Melbourne they were also the means by which people imagined Australia in relation to larger geographies such as "the West," the "British Empire," or "Asia."

Last, this study has been concerned to provide a historical context for the territorialization of Australia. An important reason for this concern has been to demonstrate that the compulsion Australians have felt to position their nation in some imagined international landscape is not a particular neurosis of their own. The work of Wigen and Lewis affirms that there has been a long history of people struggling to define the international landscape. Defining who is part of Europe and later the West has not been a purely esoteric exercise; it has been a means by which individual nations have attempted to align themselves favorably with the economic and political reciprocity that goes along with these "natural communities." And importantly, individual nations have needed to associate themselves with the many characteristics that have been used to define geographical difference. The characteristics that have been used to define Europe, for instance—civilized, white, rational—have been very important qualities for individual nations like Australia to be able to claim for their own national identity. As in Australia's case, the nation's geography can be used to mark the society's race, degree of civilization, or even disposition ("mentally still European"). Geography is a material reality on one level, but it is made meaningful by the qualities that are deemed to go with it. It becomes political because it is part of how people define their collective political identity and their personal identity. And, of course, geography as the marker of natural political alliances shapes the flow of material resources and goods.

Thus, placing in historical context the process by which imagined international geographies are used to position and define particular national identities helps us understand how this process of territorializing the nation is not isolated to the contemporary context. It has been a component of nation building from the outset and perhaps has even informed the construction of political communities that preceded the nation to a larger extent than we have realized. A historical perspective also helps us appreciate the intriguing position in which Australia has been. Most of us learned in grade school that Australia was the only country that occupied an entire continent. We also learned that as an island continent it had no borders to another country. Ironically, Australia as a nation-state has very much occupied a border position in the international landscape. At various times in history it lay on the border between Europe and Asia, colonizer and colonized, West and East, and more recently on the border between the West and Southeast Asia. This border status has perhaps made geography a more central feature of Australia's national identity than it has been for other nations. Yet, with an appreciation of the history of political geography and how these available historical constructs are redeployed and reshaped in contemporary spatial practices, we can understand that Australia is merely a particularly rich example of a more generalized process by which international geography defines national identity.

On a very basic level, politics is an engagement of our imaginations and passions. It is shaped from people's cosmologies, priorities, and, of course, fears. It has been easier for scholars of the political to trace the imagination as it is channeled into policies and political ideologies. But the imagination also calls into being the very world itself. We do not invent streams and mountains, but as this study has explored, these material realities are given meaning, function as objects to be claimed, and are used to justify hierarchies of political belonging as a consequence of our political imaginations.

Space and geography are not just the stakes of politics, they are also the process of politics. And as our relationship with space is restructured by highly politicized processes of globalization, displacement, and an unprecedented volume of migration, the imagination is engaged to make sense of and reorder the social landscape. However, as this study highlights, imagined geographies and spatial practices have been a component of any number of other political processes. These processes include colonialism, the establishment and legitimation of the nation-state, the process of modern governmentality and the organization of the international political landscape. The production of real and imagined landscapes is a profoundly political process and challenges us to expand our analytical frameworks to understand political cosmologies, not only as they are deployed through ideological narrative but also as they are deployed through spatial practices. Politics, as an act of shaping the world to match our desires and visions of what it should be, is, after all, an activity that stands at the nexus of our bodies, imaginations, and the material world.

# Notes

1. I frequently use the term "settler Australian" in keeping with much Australian studies scholarship. Most of the people described as settler Australians here are Anglo-Celtic; this ethnic category continues to be the largest in Australia and in both my field sites. However, I have often opted to use a more general term than Anglo-Celtic for the people I describe because their practices reflect broadly Australian behaviors and attitudes. In many cases, delineating the people involved strictly in terms of race (whiteness) seemed too confining given the way other immigrant groups (Europeans from a non-English-speaking background, for instance) participate in the same attitudes. Additionally, even though it is Anglo-Celtic Australians who are engaged in the practices described, it is the settler state and the legitimacy of postsettlement nationals that these practices confirm. However, I sometimes use the term "white Australians" deliberately to mark a social practice and participants defined in relation to the practice by their racial identity, and sometimes I employ the label "Anglo-Celtic Australians" to refer specifically to people in this ethnic category.

2. Australian Labor Party.

3. Aboriginal people now make up approximately 1 percent of the population of Australia. However, this figure is controversial since there is disagreement about who qualifies as Aboriginal.

4. The White Australia policy prohibited "non-whites" from coming to Australia. The Immigration Restriction Bill of 1901, the 1902 Pacific Labourers Act, the 1901 Commonwealth Posts and Telegraph Act, and the

237

1902 Commonwealth Franchise Act worked in concert to bar immigration of "Asiatics" (people from the Asian region) and Pacific Islanders and to deport Kanaka laborers from the Queensland sugar fields. Students, tourists, and businessmen from India and Japan were allowed to stay for a maximum of five years. These acts also established the withholding of such benefits as voting, representation by unions, job opportunities in the postal service, and availability of elderly or invalid pensions for Asiatics, Pacific Islanders, Aborigines, and half-castes.

5. International relations theorist John Ruggie characterizes the spatial order of modern nation-states as territorially disjointed, mutually exclusive, functionally similar, and sovereign with two fundamental spatial demarcations: between public and private spheres and between internal and external spheres (1998). On the whole this seems like a useful generalization. But we would of course find much variation in how the public and private sphere is defined in different national contexts. In fact, in the United States, feminist activism around issues like domestic violence or rape in marriage has made it increasingly difficult to clearly differentiate between public and private realms and illustrates how particular internal political issues within a nation-state will affect how the public is differentiated from the private.

6. Social or cultural geographers do not only deal with historical documents. Even when they are analyzing contemporary struggles over place, they typically analyze past contestation, rather than studying it ethnographically as the political struggles are under way.

7. Like Australia, other polities have aspired to be included within the geographical/cultural category of "Europe" in order to enjoy the privileges associated with that category. Eighteenth-century Russia is another state in a complicated position in relation to the "myth of continents" as Lewis and Wigen term it. See Lewis and Wigen (1997, 27) for a discussion of Russian Westernizers' efforts to have Russia classified geographically as a part of Europe. They were motivated to situate Russia within Europe as a way to define their political and cultural identity in terms of European "superiority."

8. Richard White contends that these issues were a significant factor in why the "bizarre" plants and animals became symbolic of Australia and came to appear both on governmental and commercial emblems (1981, 15).

9. Australia could potentially provide a port in which to build ships and otherwise support British battleships should tensions with France escalate over Eastern trading rights (Hughes 1988, 60).

10. Of course, despite its definition as a penal colony, the Australian colonies from their earliest development also included colonial administrators and their families as well as free settlers.

11. The term "Arcadia" originally referred to a mountainous region of

ancient Greece known for the pastoral innocence of its people, but gradually evolved into a term used in utopian discourse to describe rustic simplicity and innocence. Utopian thought flourished in eighteenth-century England. Writers such as Daniel Defoe, Jonathan Swift, and Edmund Burke used imaginary lands in their writings to criticize contemporary politics and social mores as well as to experiment with alternative possibilities. A number of social factors may have contributed to this literary and intellectual development. These include political corruption, rapid social change in the early phases of the industrial revolution, and the presence of British colonies in the nascent stage of development (Claeys 1994, xii–xiii). These colonies offered the possibility of beginning a "new" social order (through imperial domination over existing societies) as well as a place to which convicts could be deported facilitating a reordering of British society. While Australia would not be colonized until the latter part of the century, many of these social factors entered into the construction of Australia as an Arcadian alternative to England in the mid-nineteenth century.

12. Besides Dickens, several other novelists created fictional accounts of people who had attained success or transcended their working class status through emigration to Australia. Details of the story line and ambivalence about class mobility varied; however, a general theme of the possibility of redemption in the bucolic new society of Australia ran through novels such as E. B. Lytton's *The Caxtons* (1852) and its two sequels, *My Novel* (1860) and *What He Will Do With It* (1860).

13. George Marcus promotes multisited ethnography as a means of studying new and spatially complex phenomena like transnationalism, flexible specialization, or time-space compression. He writes of multisited ethnography: "It develops instead a strategy or design of research that acknowledges macrotheoretical concepts and narratives of the world system but does not rely on them for the contextual architecture framing a set of subjects. This mobile ethnography takes unexpected trajectories in tracing cultural formation across and within multiple sites of activity that destabilize the distinction, for example, between lifeworld and system" (1998, 80). Instead of treating the local and global as distinct spheres as conceptualized in the past, more and more ethnographies investigate the way in which the global is interwoven in the processes of the local and even mediates the connection between different local contexts. Yet, multisited ethnography maintains anthropology's distinct strength of facilitating insight into situated practices and cultural formations by examining them in the context of specific social and political relations.

14. The Fitzroy Police Station was made up of approximately forty-six uniformed officers and a plainclothes detective unit of about twelve detectives. It was located in the inner suburbs of the city in Melbourne's most

densely populated neighborhood. My activities within this site included observation at the station, participant observation in patrol cars, and both formal and informal interviews. Most of the officers had a high school education, although a number of officers had some university education as well. Most of the officers were under forty, lived in the outer suburbs, and were politically conservative.

15. The East Melbourne Garden Club comprised mostly older (forty-five to eighty-five) middle- and upper-middle-class Anglo-Celtic women. Men were no more than a quarter of the club and were in the main retired. The monthly meetings attracted a core group of about thirty-five people, although members created and hand delivered approximately 1200 meeting announcements each month. Since the official membership of the club was closer to seventy-five members, I interviewed a larger group than the regular attendees. Other activities included the production and distribution of announcements, lunches, attendance at other cultural events (speakers or plays), and regular social visits. I met the husbands, children, and old school friends of the members.

## 1. A PICTURESQUE NATION FOR A "BARREN" CONTINENT

1. In Australia people distinguish between inner suburbs and outer suburbs. The outer suburbs are closer to the typical definition of a suburb. The houses tend to be farther apart, population density is low, and there is less pedestrian traffic. The inner suburbs in Australia are more complex. Many contain single-family houses. However, the inner suburbs tend to have more apartments and the houses tend to be closer together than is generally associated with the suburbs. They also tend to be urban or semiurban neighborhoods with a lot of housing built before World War II and often have better access to public transportation and more pedestrian traffic.

2. It should be noted that Fitzroy and Richmond were also quickly becoming exclusive suburbs despite their low-income housing in the escalating value of historical houses in Melbourne.

3. The East Melbourne Group was an unelected community organization that developed regulations and recommendations for the suburb. Most of these took the form of building restrictions that would preserve the historical integrity of the community. People who wished to make changes to the facade of their house were required to submit building plans to the community group for approval. This group was also involved in some of the political campaigns on behalf of the community, such as the battle to prevent lights from being installed at the neighboring MCG or the effort to save the local library from being closed by the state government.

4. Examples of such landscape painting include the work of John Sell Cotman, Joseph Wright of Derby, Cornelius Varley, Myles Birket Foster, and Helen Arlingham.

5. During the Victorian era when health and sanitation conditions of the city were increasingly causing alarm, the garden was also conceived as a space that would allow women to get the fresh air increasingly believed necessary to ward off disease, but would still keep women in the private sphere. As Margo Huxley analyzes in the historical writings of Richard Aldridge, town planners viewed gardens as a vehicle for proper femininity and the health of the nation. Aldridge promoted the health benefits of gardens in the following passage: "Valuable as public gardens are they do not meet the same purpose as the home garden. The garden may not be more than a few square yards, but it nevertheless gives the wife an opportunity of enjoying pure air and direct sunshine whilst still within the area of her home. In the days of maternity, a quiet restful garden must often seem like a perfect oasis of rest and quiet to many a workman's wife" (as quoted in Huxley 1994, 166).

6. The division between public and private took on a particular importance during the industrial revolution. However, Jackson argues in his history of vernacular gardens that the garden has been an important symbol of private property in Western society since ancient Rome. Further, he posits that the garden has been the domain of women since that time as well, given that it was actually encoded as such in Roman law. He writes that the garden as domain of women continued as Northern European civilization developed in the Middle Ages. Further it was the horticultural systems developed in the peasant garden by women that eventually were extended and allowed for the cultivation of field crops (1994).

7. The philanthropic impulse is also illustrated and satirized in the novels of Margaret Wilson Oliphant (*Miss Marjoribanks*, 1865) or George Elliot (*Middlemarch*, 1872), whose heroines look lovingly at the dilapidated houses and gardens of the village peasants as potential recipients of their good intentions (Scott-James 1981).

8. Shapiro provides another interesting example from the North American context of how the destruction of meaning systems and exchange was also a means of negating indigenous spatial meaning and propriety of the land. He describes the Iroquois' use of wampum belts to record land deeds and treaties (1997, 10). Like European nonrecognition of the way the Australian Aboriginal Dreaming or systematic burning of bushland were a form of spatial order, ignoring Iroquois spatial meaning as inscribed on wampum belts was a means of producing the land as available for European appropriation. See also Shapiro's discussion of European cultural privileging of monuments and buildings versus indigenous limited clearing of the wilderness (Shapiro 1997, 23).

9. Lewis and Wigen also argued that Anglo-American geographers buttressed colonial legitimating narratives for many years by lending scientific credence to what are now widely recognized as false ideas of environmental determinism.

10. Lee takes this quote from the *Queensland Agricultural Journal*. See Lee 1996 for a full citation.

11. Georgiana Molloy to Helen Story and to Mrs. Kennedy, July 24, 1833, cited in Lines 1994.

12. See Jack Goody 1993 for a comprehensive social history of flowers.

13. This is a popular Australian expression describing the tendency of Australians to find fault with individuals who have succeeded or distinguished themselves in some positive way. By this point, many scholars have discussed the cache of an imagined male working-class Australian, be it in the form of mateship, the battler, or the stockman, in Australian national identity (see White 1981; Schaffer 1988; Kapferer 1996).

14. Scholars have made a similar point about the "heritage industry" in contemporary Britain. See, for example, Wright 1985; Corner and Harvey 1991; and Hewison 1987.

15. See also Vron Ware's analysis in *Beyond the Pale* (1992).

## 2. GOING NATIVE

1. For instance, I am aware of environmental efforts to protect native species against imported plants in California, Mexico, New Zealand, and South Africa.

2. The "bush" was the term used to describe areas outside of the city proper or pockets of natural life within the city other than regularly maintained parks.

3. William Kent 1685–1748; Capability Brown 1716–1783; and Humphry Repton 1752–1818.

4. The "homesick garden" is an expression used by Graeme Law, architect and environmental planner (1999, xi).

5. See Edna Walling's books, *Gardens in Australia* (1946), *A Gardener's Log* (1948), and The Australian Roadside (1952).

6. *Independent Press,* January 10, 1994.

7. Ghassan Hage (1998) does an analysis of environmentalist discourse as it reinforces a white nationalist fantasy that aims to tame or weed immigrant groups who threaten to cause an ecological imbalance in Australia. His analysis centers mostly on Australians for an Ecologically Sustainable Population (AESP) and does not examine the links to Aboriginal land rights politics or national place making as I am concerned to do in this study.

8. "I love a sunburnt country" is the first line of the second verse of Dorothea Mackellar's poem, *My Country*, written before World War I. The first verse of the poem describes the idealized British landscape. In the second verse Mackellar describes the beauty of the unique Australian landscape. The stanza ends with the line "the wide brown land for me." The poem is taught to schoolchildren all over Australia and continues to hold great sentimental value for many people.

9. The inner suburbs were those neighborhoods that radiated approximately fifteen miles out from the central business district. They tended to be suburbs that were settled during Melbourne's boom years in the late 1800s. Thus, Victorian- and Edwardian-style housing was most common there but heritage homes were also intermingled with other building forms such as modern apartment blocks or brick veneer tract homes. The land blocks tended to be much smaller than suburbs located farther out and, while the real estate values varied from suburb to suburb, some of the most expensive housing was located in these areas; real estate prices were climbing most rapidly in the inner suburbs.

As the population of Melbourne increased and housing prices climbed, the radius of what was considered the metropolitan area of Melbourne moved farther out. As in the inner suburbs, housing prices and class divisions also varied in the outer suburbs. However, a large section of the middle class lived in the outer suburbs, and there was less class variation within a single neighborhood than one might have found closer to the city center. Housing styles also varied, with the occasional Victorian home and California bungalow style among the predominantly brick veneer tract houses. Interestingly, a popular housing type on the outer, Eastern fringe of these suburbs was a newly constructed brick veneer house in Edwardian style, which combined the historical features of the inner suburbs with the additional yard space and newness of the outer suburbs.

10. Letter to the editor, *Age*, February 11, 1995.

11. Lloyd is quoted in Ford 1999, 60.

12. The Digger's Club was a seed catalogue company that also maintained a garden outside of Melbourne that was open to the public. "Diggers" was an interesting choice of name, given the arguments in this chapter. The name connoted the digging that gardeners do, and it recalled the utopian group in late-eighteenth-century Britain that protested the land enclosures at the beginning of the industrial revolution. However, "Diggers" also had a patriotic connotation since it was the name of Australian World War I soldiers who have an important place in certain discourses about Australian national identity. This third dimension of their name is interesting in light of the critique the Diggers (gardening group) made concerning the nationalism of some proponents of Australian native gardening.

13. As discussed in the previous chapter, the East Melbourne Group was a voluntary association first developed to protect the elms and other street vegetation in East Melbourne from government removal. The group met monthly to discuss issues concerning the neighborhood and to socialize with neighbors. Examples of other issues with which the East Melbourne Group was concerned included safety, saving the library from being amalgamated with other neighborhood libraries, and approving the construction changes residents want to make on their houses.

14. Gardens in less Anglo-dominated inner suburbs, such as Brunswick, Carlton, or Footscray, were less likely to reproduce an English cottage garden but still tended to have a greater proportion of imported species.

15. Until 1994, Victoria used the slogan The Garden State on its license plates. Former State Premier Jeff Kennet instituted the new slogan, Victoria on the Move!, a phrase more in keeping with his vision of development for Victoria.

16. *Age,* December 1994.

17. *Age,* August 11, 1992.

18. With sardonic humor not uncommon in Australia, one man commented that he thought it was rather fitting that up until recently in Melbourne's history, on one end of this major axis was the Shrine of Remembrance and on the other was the Carlton Brewery.

19. This has changed somewhat in the post-Fordist era (see Harvey 1990). In the past twenty years, industrialized centers have increasingly developed "edge cities" in which financial districts are located outside of the city centers, closer to suburban residences, and many urban centers, most notably in the United States, have become containers of the poor and the nonwhite.

20. Architects Walter and Marion Griffin furthered the project of re-imaging the Australian landscape with their initial design for the capital territory in 1913. The Griffins raised the cultural status of native vegetation by using it in their "city beautiful" design for Australia's capital city and by treating it as something a designer would use. The Griffins' use of native vegetation in the original urban design for the capital city also helped create an association between the nation and native Australian vegetation.

21. See Fiona Nicoll (1993) for an analysis of the way the artwork commissioned for the Federal Parliament Building served as a site for Aboriginal political protest.

22. Some of the amateur naturalists about whom Griffiths writes may have also constituted the group that Lattas defines as "cultural nationalists" in the 1930s. However, these two groups were not necessarily composed of the same people, despite the fact that both were, at some level, using Aboriginal identity to define settler identity in Australia.

## 3. POLICING THE BODY POLITIC

1. Fitzroy was located in the inner suburbs of Melbourne. It bordered the Central Business District, East Melbourne, Abottsford, Carlton, and Richmond.

2. "Koori" is the Aboriginal word referring to Aboriginal people who originate from the Eastern part of Australia, which includes the region in which Melbourne lies.

3. The names of police officers and of the people I interviewed outside the police station have been changed to protect their privacy. Although I have used pseudonyms in the place of their real names, I have chosen names that reflect the gender and ethnicity of each informant.

4. In his 1976 lecture series entitled "Truth and Juridical Forms," Foucault downplays the importance of space in the disciplining of the individual in the nineteenth century. He writes, "The modern society that formed at the beginning of the nineteenth century was basically indifferent or relatively indifferent to individuals' spatial ties: it was not interested in the spatial control of individuals insofar as they belonged to an estate, a locale, but only insofar as it needed people to place their time at its disposal" (2000b, 80). However, the ethnographic analysis of the Fitzroy Police as well as other studies of police practices (Herbert 1997) suggests that social control is very much dependent upon spatial control. Additionally, in later essays and interviews, Foucault himself came to argue much more strongly for the importance of the spatial dimensions of modern forms of discipline and governance. In 1982 he asserted, contrary to his earlier emphasis of time over space, that the idea of good government became much more connected to issues of the organization of cities and to architecture. He writes, "From the eighteenth century on, every discussion of politics as the art of the government of men necessarily includes a chapter or a series of chapters on urbanism, on collective facilities, on hygiene, and on private architecture. Such chapters are not found in the art of government of the sixteenth century" (2000a, 350).

5. This was the slang term universally used at the station when talking about those people accused or convicted of crimes. It was only used among other officers (and to me), but not when in the company of members of the public with whom the police interacted. Another term used less frequently was "villain." In New South Wales, would-be criminals are called "baddies," a term sometimes used in Victoria.

6. Although I am using the term "officer" to refer to all of the uniformed police personnel, the members of this station (and my impression was that this was true for the entire Victoria Police Department) used the term "member" as a general way to describe all police officers. They used "officer" to refer to people at the rank of sergeant and senior sergeant.

Uniformed officers were required to sit for exams to move to the next rank. The police drew a distinction between uniformed officers and detectives, according the latter a degree of additional respect. Detectives could be of the rank of senior constable or above. However, they generally garnered a great deal of respect from other officers because promotion to detective rank required the successful completion of what was reputed to be a very difficult exam. Detectives did not wear uniforms and enjoyed more independence than uniformed officers because they were responsible for investigating crime cases.

7. Most officers had distinct assignments on top of their regular policing duties. For example, one such assignment was the "community liaison"; this position entailed fostering partnerships for crime prevention between the police and community groups such as the neighborhood watch in various parts of Fitzroy and residential representatives from the Atherton Gardens (public housing estates next to the station). Officers carrying out these nonpatrol duties wandered in and out of the Watch House, but conducted most of their shift activities in the shared office space (sergeants' room) or in the community, as was necessary. Officers working in the station were engaged in a form of customer service to the extent to which they were responding to the issues people in the community presented them either in person or over the phone at the station. But much of what officers did when not on car patrol or some other activity that took them away from the station (testifying in court, for instance), consisted of recording the locations, activities, and information that they gathered during their car shift concerning people considered "suspicious." Or, as in the case of the Watch House keeper and assistant, their activities involved providing information and other assistance to officers on patrol to more effectively monitor the community.

8. At the time of this study, Fitzroy was part of a district that also included Collingwood, Carlton, and Melbourne (Central Business District). The organization of stations into districts was a method for sharing resources. With a similar end in mind, the Victoria Police Force has since been divided into different subgroups. As of 2004, Fitzroy was located in Region I, Division 2.

9. After 1996, the DIC began to use an e-mail system to circulate information about crooks in addition to the bulletins. The DIC sent narratives of crimes or people of whom police should be aware, but also used the e-mail system to send clips from security cameras that depicted robberies in which the perpetrator was still at large.

10. This is my phrasing. The police did not call it an oral tradition or seem particularly self-conscious of these circuits of information as an important part of their policing.

11. De Certeau (1984) makes a distinction between "place" and "space." A place is a location, an "instantaneous configuration of positions" and connotes a stability of activity and identity. Space is the effect of practices that "orient it, situate it, temporalize it . . . space is a practiced place." For further discussion of the ways these two terms differ, see 1984, 117.

12. "Nuffy" is the slang term the police used informally to refer to mentally handicapped or emotionally disturbed people.

13. For further discussion of traditional Aboriginal practices of authorized use of stories, see Myers 1986; Povinelli 1993; Bird 1992; Michaels 1994.

14. A milk bar is a small market that carries a limited stock of milk and other common household items. It is equivalent to an American convenience store. However, it is rarely a franchise.

15. The Atherton Garden Estates were built in the 1950s and consisted of three high-rise apartment buildings. They were owned by the state government and were available only to people whose income qualified them for subsidized housing. A number of the residents were concerned that the gentrification of Fitzroy would result in the Atherton Estates being demolished and their consequently being relocated out of the inner suburban neighborhoods. The threat of displacement was a consequence of the fact that the housing commission apartments were located on what had become very desirable real estate for some within the middle and upper middle classes and had exceptionally fine views of the city.

16. The running sheet was a record the police were obligated to keep of the names and addresses of the people with whom they spoke while on patrol. The law allowed the police to collect names and addresses of people as long as the police had a justification for perceiving an individual as suspicious. This practice will be discussed in greater detail in the section entitled "Technologies of Policing."

17. It was unusual for a male officer to have a wife with a higher paid and higher status job. Many of the officers teased Drake about the fact that his wife's income kept him in a very comfortable lifestyle.

18. "Standing over" someone was a phrase police officers used to indicate intimidating someone by following that person or even physically confronting the person. It was not meant as a punishment, but seemed to be used as a way of warning individuals or a group to change their behavior in some way. Often it was a means of getting them to move their location. For instance, after a Vietnamese takeout restaurant owner repeatedly complained about drug dealing in and near her business, the Watch House keeper sent "the boys" around to "stand over" the dealers so that they would find a new location. They did this in order to help the restaurant owner feel comfortable and have a safer business. But because the officers did not

have enough information about the dealers to actually arrest them, some of the officers on patrol used more informal means of ordering the social and physical landscape, like standing over someone, in order to make Fitzroy more equitable and just.

19. The police with whom I interacted identified their shared sense of humor as something distinct about them as a profession. There was a lot of "pay out" (teasing) between police in the station. Death was very commonly joked about as well as other topics that would be considered taboo to nonpolice. I was told that one topic they were not inclined to joke about was children. I also noticed that no one joked following an incident where an officer was obliged to shoot and kill a dog that had been ordered to attack the officer by a nuffy (mentally imbalanced person) whom the officer was trying to restrain. At a social event that evening, many officers commented on how unfortunate it was that the officer had been forced to kill the dog and, rather than joke about it, they expressed anger at the owner's stupidity. This and other incidents suggested to me that officers joked more about things that happened in the past and that they were less inclined to joke about misfortunes that befell people or creatures that had no power to help themselves. In general, however, officers were less sympathetic to adults, even concerning misfortunes that they did not bring upon themselves. For instance, a car accident involving adults, even if deaths were involved, would be fair game for a joke.

20. I found it funny and a little awkward that on a number of occasions the officers I accompanied on car patrol would end up apologizing that there was not more crime to show me. Sometimes people would blame the lack of violence and "action" on the fact that it was midweek, that people's "dole" money had run out (so fewer drunks), or on the fact that it was raining. Other times I was told that I really should see the district in the height of the summer, when the heat caused people to spend more time in public spaces and caused tempers to flare. So while there certainly was enough crime to warrant a twenty-four-hour station in Fitzroy, the dystopic quality of the suburb was not necessarily an objective fact.

21. I discuss this computer system in more detail later on in this chapter.

22. In *The Image of the City*, Kevin Lynch writes about the subjective quality of people's experience of physical space (1960). People's individual perceptions, priorities, and purposes mix with the objective environment to shape their experience of the world, creating their *landscapes*. People's landscapes take into account the information they receive about the world from external sources. However, that information is limited or shaped by subjective attitudes or dispositions. One's cognitive map in turn "limits and emphasizes" what he or she perceives in the external environment. Potentially, this means that everyone lives in an individual reality. Although

some variation probably occurs on an idiosyncratic level, Lynch's empirical work on people's cognitive maps suggests that "there seems to be substantial agreement among members of the same group" (ibid., 7).

Fredric Jameson argues that structural position influences the way people interpret the physical environment around them and thereby how they construct cognitive maps of their world. He argues that we construct cognitive maps not only for our local landscapes, but also for the other landscapes in which we participate, such as the national and the international sphere (1991, 51). Jameson's work is useful in pointing out that other landscapes, such as the national and international sphere, are also produced by people in particular, situated contexts.

23. All of the incidents discussed took place with me present, unless otherwise indicated.

24. This incident occurred while I was doing a "ride along" (observing a car patrol shift) in the Carlton Police Station. Since the Carlton and Fitzroy Stations were in the same district, their practices were basically the same.

25. In December 2000 the first trial computers (removable laptops) were placed in patrol cars. The laptops were designed to allow officers to fill out police reports and check records directly. Before computers were installed in the police cars, officers had to call D-24 (central district dispatcher) in order to check records, and they had to transfer all the hard copy reports into the computer at the station.

26. I would like to thank Teresa Caldeira for suggesting Corbin's work to me and for her comments on early drafts of this ethnographic material.

27. The behavior of officers at Fitzroy was continually defying simplistic stereotypes about the police. The process of filling out forms and asking the man who had stolen a flashlight to open his mouth, for instance, could be read as very dehumanizing to the man. On the one hand, the officers certainly showed no discomfort or self-consciousness in executing the procedures involved in processing a person caught committing a crime. On the other hand, it would be a mistake to see the officers as simply bureaucrats or bullies. In this instance, for example, after leaving the station and getting back in the patrol car to continue the night's shift, Moser turned to his partner for the night and sympathized with the "poor bastard" inside. He said that he could see himself doing something stupid like putting something worthless like a cheap flashlight in his pocket on impulse. A similar empathy was demonstrated in the case of another officer whose duties included serving warrants. In making a point about another issue, the senior constable explained to me that he had tracked a man to the pub in which the man regularly drank, after the man's mother had "slagged him in" (helped the police find him). The man did not have money to post bail for himself and would therefore have to be arrested. Since the man was

very upset, the officer hung out with him in the pub (not drinking) until the man's "mate" (friend) showed up with an ATM card to provide him money for bail. While perhaps Constable Moser had been performing empathy for my benefit (which I did not think he was doing), in the main, the officers seemed to approach the people they arrested with very little moral judgment. This made the moral critique of Asian immigrants as dirty, which I discuss in the next chapter, particularly intriguing.

28. For a more detailed history of the development of Melbourne as a colonial city, see Carter 1988, chap. 7.

29. Other scholars have been more skeptical about the usefulness of Aboriginal "disorderliness" acts of defiance toward the police, questioning whether it is useful or appropriate to call them political (Moreton 1989) or to understand behaviors that seem self-destructive (drunkenness for instance) as "oppositional." See Hollinsworth 1992; Pettman 1991; Rowse 1990; and Larbalestier 1990.

30. See Brett 1997.

31. Here I am only referring to Aboriginal communities for whom traditional Dreamtime stories continue to be part of their cosmology. This would include Aboriginal people who live in traditional communities and Aboriginal people who are more integrated into mainstream Australian society but who also draw on notions of Aboriginal Dreaming in their understanding of the world. Of course some Aboriginal people do not participate in the Dreaming to any extent. That is, I am not taking Dreamtime cosmology as somehow essential to Aboriginal identity.

32. *Age,* March 8, 1995.

33. Many of the people I spoke with at the station and outside of it among other populations in Melbourne did express skepticism toward the legitimacy of the claims Aboriginal groups were making to land since the Mabo decision. This was also suggested by the popular (rural) support Member of Parliament Pauline Hanson received in 1996 when she criticized public spending on Aboriginal programs as motivated by "guilt" rather than need.

34. Here she was referring to the officers' notion of the special legal services available to Aborigines, to special mortgage rates available to them, and to examples of the abuses of affirmative action that officers cited for me on numerous occasions when discussing Aboriginal politics.

35. It would have been mainly the Labor policies of the Keating and Hawke governments the police officers were contesting since the Howard government (Liberal) did more to limit land rights claims and social service for Aborigines than his predecessors had. In formal interviews, most of the officers expressed support for the Liberal party and strongly criticized the Keating government.

## 4. THE POOR WHITE TRASH OF ASIA

1. The police often used the general category of "Asian," treating it as a unified cultural identity. So my use of this term reflects *their* category system, not my own. I have put the category of "Asian" in quotation marks to signal the constructedness of the category. But in an effort to avoid unnecessary distraction, I do not use the quotation marks throughout the rest of the text.

2. For instance, there have been Chinese in Victoria (the state in which Melbourne is located) since the gold rush at the end of the nineteenth century.

3. The Asian squad was comprised mainly of non-Asian officers; during the time of this research there was only one Vietnamese officer in the Melbourne metropolitan area. This was still the case in August 2000 when I conducted follow-up interviews in Melbourne.

4. Although members usually used the more general term of "Asian," the group with whom the police in Fitzroy interacted most was first- and second-generation Vietnamese immigrants.

5. The "caves" were the state subsidized high-rise housing commission apartments located on Brunswick Street, one block away from the Fitzroy Police Station. The Fitzroy Police were involved in policing numerous state subsidized housing units in Fitzroy; however, the "caves" were identified as having the worst crime problems. The residents of public housing in Fitzroy tended to be ethnically and racially diverse (including Anglo-Celtics) who were uniform in their low-income status. This was a popular housing option for first-generation immigrants.

6. *Age,* August 8, 1995.

7. Convicts themselves were among the minority to see their situation as an indictment against the British social and penal system. Toward the end of the nineteenth century, intellectuals such as Marcus Clarke, Price Warung, and G. A. Wood began viewing the convicts who settled Australia as victims of a capitalist class system and a brutal penal institution (White 1981).

8. Robert Hughes, in writing Australia's history as a penal colony, notes that, despite popular perception, most convicts transported to Australia were not arrested for political crimes; most had several prior convictions before being sentenced to transportation (1986, 159).

9. The move to define Australian national identity in terms of multiculturalism also has helped to qualify Australia for inclusion into the Asian region. Implicit in the idea of multiculturalism in Australia is the notion that Australia is composed of many Asians as well as people of European descent.

# Works Cited

Almond, Gabriel A., and Sidney Verba. 1965. *The Civic Culture: Political Attitudes and Democracy.* Boston: Little, Brown.

Alvarez, Robert R., Jr. 1995. "The Mexican–US Border: The Making of an Anthropology of Borderlands." *Annual Review of Anthropology* 24: 447–70.

Anderson, Benedict. 1991. *Imagined Communities.* London: Verso.

Andrews, Malcolm. 1989. *The Search for the Picturesque.* England: Scholar Press.

Ang, Ien, and Jon Stratton. 1996. "Asianing Australia: Notes Toward a Critical Transnationalism in Cultural Studies." *Cultural Studies* 10 (1): 16–36.

Appadurai, Arjun. 1996. *Modernity at Large: Cultural Dimensions of Globalization.* Minneapolis: University of Minnesota Press.

——. 1988. "Putting Hierarchy in Its Place." *Cultural Anthropology* 3 (1): 36–49.

——. 1980. "Disjuncture and Difference in the Global Cultural Economy." *Theory, Culture, Society* 7 (2–3): 295–310.

Balibar, Étienne, and Emanuel Wallerstein. 1991. *Race, Nation, Class: Ambiguous Identities.* London: Verso.

Beckett, Jeremy K. 1995. "National and Transnational Perspectives on Multiculturalism: The View from Australia." *Identities* 1 (4): 421–26.

——. 1988a. "Aboriginality, Citizenship and Nation State." *Social Analysis* 24 (December): 3–18.

——, ed. 1988b. *Past and Present: The Construction of Aboriginality.* Canberra: Aboriginal Studies Press.

Benet-Weiser, Sarah. 1999. *The Most Beautiful Girl in the World: Beauty Pageants and National Identity*. Berkeley: University of California Press.

Bennet, Tony. 1995. *The Birth of the Museum: History, Theory, Politics*. London: Routledge.

———. 1993. "The Shape of the Past." In *Nation, Culture, Text*, ed. Graeme Turner, 72–90. London: Routledge.

Berlant, Lauren. 1997. *The Queen of America Goes to Washington City: Essays on Sex and Citizenship*. Durham: Duke University Press.

Bermingham, Ann. 1994. "System, Order, and Abstraction." In *Landscape and Power*, ed. W. J. T. Mitchell. Chicago: University of Chicago Press.

———. 1986. *Landscape and Ideology*. Berkeley: University of California Press.

Bessant, Judith, Kerry Carrington, and Sandy Cook (eds.). 1995. *Cultures and Violence: The Australian Experience*. Bundoora: La Trobe University Press.

Bhabha, Homi. 1983. "The Other Question." *Screen*. 24:18–36.

———, ed. 1990. *Nation and Narration*. London: Routledge.

Birch, Tony. 1994. "The Battle for Spatial Control in Fitzroy." In *Beasts of Suburbia: Reinterpreting Cultures in Australian Suburbs*. Melbourne: Melbourne University Press.

Bird, Jon. 1993. "Dystopia on the Thames." In *Mapping the Futures: Local Cultures, Global Change*, ed. Jon Bird et al. London: Routledge.

Bird, Rose Deborah. 1992. *Dingo Makes Us Human: Life and Land in an Aboriginal Australian Culture*. Cambridge: Cambridge University Press.

Blainey, Geoffrey. 1982. *The Tyranny of Distance: How Distance Shaped Australia's History*. Melbourne: Sun Books.

Blaut, J. M. 1993. *The Colonizer's Model of the World: Geographical Diffusionism and Eurocentric History*. New York: Guilford Press.

Blunt, Alison, and Gillian Rose, eds. 1994. *Writing Women and Space: Colonial and Postcolonial Geographies*. New York: Guilford Press.

Bottomley, Gill. 1988. "Ethnicity, Race and Nationalism in Australia: Some Critical Perspectives." *Australian Journal of Social Issues* 23 (3): 169–83.

Bourdieu, Pierre. 1995. *Outline of a Theory of Practice*. Cambridge: Cambridge University Press.

———. 1984. *Distinction: A Social Critique of the Judgement of Taste*. Cambridge, MA: Harvard University Press.

Brack, John. 1968. *Four Contemporary Australia Landscape Painters*. Oxford: Oxford University Press.

Brett, Judith. 1997. "Every Morning as the Sun Came Up: The Enduring Pain of the 'Stolen Generation.'" *Times Literary Supplement* 4931 (3 October): 4–5.

Buell, Frederick. 1994. *National Culture and the New Global System*. Baltimore: Johns Hopkins University Press.

Burke, Anthony. 2001. *In Fear of Security: Australia's Invasion Anxiety*. Annandale, NSW: Pluto Press Australia.

Burke, Edmund. 1990. *A Philosophical Enquiry into the Origin of Our Ideas of the Sublime and Beautiful*. Oxford: Oxford University Press.

Caldeira, Teresa. 1996. "Fortified Enclaves: The New Urban Segregation." *Public Culture* 8 (2): 303–28.

———. 2000. *City of Walls: Crime, Segregation, and Citizenship in São Paulo*. Berkeley: University of California Press.

Carrington, Kerry. 1991. "The Death of Mark Quayle: Normalizing Racial Horror in Country Towns and Hospitals." *Journal for Social Justice Studies* 4:161–87.

Carroll, John. 1982. *Intruders in the Bush*. Melbourne: Oxford University Press.

Carter, Paul. 1988. *The Road to Botany Bay: An Exploration of Landscape and History*. New York: Knopf.

Castles, Stephen, et al. 1988. *Mistaken Identity: Multiculturalism and the Demise of Nationalism in Australia*. Sydney: Pluto Press.

Cerwonka, Allaine. 1998. "Traditional English Cottage Gardens and Modern Australian Lives." In *Australian Identities*, ed. David Day. Melbourne: Australian Scholarly Publishing.

Chambers, Deborah. 1997. "A Stake in the Country: Women's Experiences of Suburban Development." In *Visions of Suburbia*, ed. Roger Silverstone. London: Routledge.

Chan, Janet. 1996. "Police Racism: Experiences and Reforms." In *The Teeth Are Smiling: The Persistence of Racism in Multicultural Australia*, ed. Ellie Vasta and Stephen Castles. New South Wales: Allen and Unwin.

Claeys, Gregory (ed.). 1994. *Utopias of the British Enlightenment*. New York: Cambridge University Press.

Clark, Manning. 1962. *A History of Australia. Vol. I: From the Earliest Times to the Age of Macquarie*. Carlton: Melbourne University Press.

———. 1963. *A Short History of Australia*. New York: Mentor Books.

Clifford, James. 1997. *Routes: Travel and Translation in the Late Twentieth Century*. Cambridge, MA: Harvard University Press.

———. 1994. "Diasporas." *Cultural Anthropology* 9 (3): 302–38.

Commonwealth of Australia. 1991. *Aboriginal Deaths in Custody, the Final Report of the National Commissioner*. Canberra: Australian Government Publishing Services.

Cooper, Frederick, and Ann Stoler. 1998. "Tensions of Empire: Colonial Control and Visions of Rule." *American Ethnologist* 16 (4): 609–21.

Corbin, Alain. 1987. "Backstage." In *A History of Private Life: From the*

*Fires of the Revolution to the Great War,* vol. 4, ed. Michelle Perot. Cambridge, MA: Harvard University Press.

Corner, John, and Sylvia Harvey. 1991. "Mediating Tradition and Modernity: The Heritage/Enterprise Couplet." In *Enterprise and Heritage,* J. Corner and S. Harvey, eds. London: Routledge.

Cosgrove, Denis, and Stephen Daniels. 1994. *The Iconography of Landscape: Essays on the Symbolic Representation, Design and Use of Past Environments.* Cambridge: Cambridge University Press.

Cowlishaw, Gillian. 1999. *Rednecks, Eggheads, and Blackfellas.* St. Leonards: Allen and Unwin.

———. 1998. "Erasing Culture and Race: Practicing 'Self-Determination.'" *Oceania* 68 (3): 145–69.

———. 1993. "Introduction: Representing Racial Issues." *Oceania* 63 (3): 183–94.

———. 1991. "Inquiring into Aboriginal Deaths in Custody: The Limits of a Royal Commission." In "Politics, Prisons and Punishment: Royal Commissions and 'Reforms,'" ed. K. Carrington and B. Morris. Special issue, *Journal for Social Justice Studies* 4:101–15.

———. 1990. "Where Is Racism?" *Journal for Social Justice Studies* 3: 49–60.

———. 1988. *Black, White or Brindle: Race in Rural Australia.* Sydney: Cambridge University Press.

Cowlishaw, Gillian, and Barry Morris, eds. 1997. *Race Matters: Indigenous Australians and "Our" Society.* Canberra: Aboriginal Studies Press.

Creamer, Howard. 1988. "Aboriginality in New South Wales: Beyond the Image of Cultureless Outcasts." In *Past and Present,* ed. Jeremy K. Beckett. Canberra: Aboriginal Studies Press.

Cronon, William. 1996. "Introduction: In Search of Nature." In *Uncommon Ground: Rethinking the Human Place in Nature.* New York: Norton.

Crozier, Michael. 1999. "Antipodean Sensibilities." In "After the Garden?" ed. M. Crozier. Special issue, *Southern Atlantic Quarterly* 98 (4): 839–60.

Cunneen, Cris. 2001. *Conflict, Politics, and Crime: Aboriginal Communities and the Police.* Crow's Nest: Allen and Unwin.

Cunneen, Cris, and Terry Libesman. 1995. *Indigenous People and the Law in Australia.* Sydney: Butterworths.

Darian-Smith, Eve. 1993. "Aboriginality, Morality, and the Law: Reconciling Popular Western Images of Australian Aborigines." In *Moralizing States and the Ethnography of the Present,* ed. Sally Falk Moore. American Ethnological Society Monogram series, no. 5. Arlington, VA: American Anthropological Association.

de Bliji, Harm. 1992. "Political Geography in the Post Cold-War World." *Professional Geographer* 44 (1): 16–19.

de Certeau, Michel. 1984. *The Practices of Everyday Life*. Berkeley: University of California Press.

Douglas, Mary. 1966. *Purity and Danger: An Analysis of the Concepts of Pollution and Taboo*. London: Routledge.

Dunlap, Thomas R. 1999. *Nature and the English Diaspora: Environment and History in the United States, Canada, Australia, and New Zealand*. Cambridge: Cambridge University Press.

Dunn, Peter, and Loraine Leeson. 1993. "The Art of Change in Docklands." In *Mapping the Futures: Local Cultures, Global Change*, ed. Jon Bird et al. London: Routledge.

Durez, Jean. 1994. "Suburban Gardens: Cultural Notes." In *Beasts of Suburbia*, ed. S. Ferber, C. Healy, and C. McAuliffe. Melbourne: Melbourne University Press.

During, Simon. 1998. "Postcolonialism and Globalization: A Dialectic Relation After All?" *Postcolonial Studies* 1 (1): 31–47.

Elias, Norbert. 1994. *The Civilizing Process: The History of Manners and State Formation and Civilization*. Oxford: Blackwell.

Ellin, Nan, ed. 1997. *Architecture of Fear*. New York: Princeton Architectural Press.

Featherstone, Mike. 1993. "Global and Local Cultures." In *Mapping the Futures: Local Cultures, Global Change*, ed. Jon Bird et al. New York: Routledge.

Ferber, Sarah, Chris Healy, and Chris McAuliffe, eds. *Beasts of Suburbia: Reinterpreting Cultures in Australian Suburbs*. Melbourne: Melbourne University Press, 1994.

Fiske, J., B. Hodge, and G. Turner. 1987. *Myths of Oz: Reading Australian Popular Culture*. Sydney: Allen and Unwin.

Ford, Gordon. 1999. *Gordon Ford: The Natural Australian Garden*. Victoria: Bloomings Books.

Foss, Paul (ed.). 1988. *Myths of Place in Australian Culture*. Leichardt, NSW: Pluto Press.

Foster, Robert J. 1991. "Making National Cultures in the Global Ecumene." *Annual Review of Anthropology* 20:235–60.

Foucault, Michel. 2000a. "Space, Knowledge, and Power." In *Power*, vol. 3. Ed. James D. Faubion. New York: New Press.

———. 2000b. "Truth and Juridical Forms." In *Power*, vol. 3. Ed James D. Faubion. New York: New Press.

———. 1990. *The History of Sexuality*, vol. 1. New York: Vintage.

———. 1986. "Of Other Spaces." *Diacritics* 16 (1): 22–27.

———. 1980. *Power/Knowledge: Selected Interviews and Other Writings*. New York: Pantheon Books.

———. 1979. *Discipline and Punish: The Birth of the Prison.* New York: Vintage Books.

Fraser, Morag. 1999. Prologue to *Gordon Ford: The Natural Australian Garden.* Victoria: Bloomings Books.

Gibson, Ross. 1992. *South of the West: Postcolonialism and the Narrative Construction of Australia.* Bloomington: Indiana University Press.

Gilpin, William. 2003. *Observations on Cumberland and Westmoreland.* Originally published as *Observations, Relative Chiefly to Picturesque Beauty, Made in the Year 1772.* . . . London: Woodstock Books.

Gilroy, Paul. 1993. *The Black Atlantic: Modernity and Double Consciousness.* Cambridge, MA: Harvard University Press.

———. 1987. *Ain't No Black in the Union Jack: The Cultural Politics of Race and Nation.* Chicago: University of Chicago Press.

Ginsberg, Faye. 1992. "Aboriginal Media and the Australian Imaginary." *Public Culture* 5:557–58.

Goody, Jack. 1993. *The Culture of Flowers.* Cambridge: Cambridge University Press.

Gramsci, Antonio. 1989. *Selections from the Prison Notebooks.* New York: International Publishers.

———. 1971. *Reflections from the Prison Notebooks of Antonio Gramsci.* New York: International Publishers.

Gregory, Derek. 1994. *Geographical Imaginations.* Cambridge, MA: Blackwell.

Griffiths, Tom. 1996. *Hunters and Collectors: The Antiquarian Imagination in Australia.* Cambridge: Cambridge University Press.

Gupta, Akhil. 1992. "The Song of the Nonaligned World: Transnational Identities and the Reinscription of Space in Late Capitalism." *Cultural Anthropology* 7 (1): 63–79.

Gupta, Akhil, and James Ferguson, eds. 1997a. *Anthropological Locations: Boundaries and Grounds of a Field Science.* Berkeley: University of California Press.

———. 1997b. *Culture, Power, Place: Explorations in Critical Anthropology.* Durham: Duke University Press.

———. 1992. "Beyond 'Culture': Space, Identity, and the Politics of Difference." *Cultural Anthropology* 7 (1): 6–23.

Hage, Ghassan. 1998. *White Nation: Fantasies of White Supremacy in a Multicultural Society.* New South Wales: Pluto Press.

Hall, Stuart. 1996. "Ethnicity: Identity and Difference." In *Becoming National: A Reader,* ed. Geoff Eley and Ronald Grigor Suny. Oxford: Oxford University Press.

Hannerz, Ulf. 1996. *Transnational Connections: Culture, People, Places.* New York: Routledge.

———. 1990. "Cosmopolitans and Locals in World Culture." *Theory, Culture and Society* 7:237–51.

Hannerz, Ulf, and Orvar Lofgren. 1994. "The Nation in the Global Village." *Cultural Studies* 8 (2): 198–207.

Hanson, Pauline. 1996. *Pauline Hanson, The Truth*. Ipswich, Queensland: Pauline Hanson's One Nation Party.

Harley, J. B. 1996. "Deconstructing the Map." In *Human Geography: An Essential Anthology*, ed. John Agnew, David Livingstone, and Alisdair Rogers. Oxford: Blackwell.

Hartigan, John. 1997. "Unpopular Culture: The Case of 'White Trash.'" *Cultural Studies* 11 (2): 316–43.

Harvey, David. 1990. *The Condition of Postmodernity*. Cambridge, MA: Blackwell.

Hay, Roy, and Patrick Synge. 1992. *The Color Dictionary of Flowers and Plants for Home and Garden*. New York: Crown Publishers.

Herbert, Steve. 1997. *Policing Space: Territoriality and the Los Angeles Police Department*. Minneapolis: University of Minnesota Press.

Hewison, Robert. 1987. *The Heritage Industry*. London: Methuen London.

Hiebert, Murray. 1995. "The Wizard of Oz: Australia's Evans Redraws the Map of Asia." *Far Eastern Economic Review* 17 (August): 26.

Hobsbawm, Eric. 1990. *Nations and Nationalism Since 1780: Programme, Myth and Reality*. Cambridge: Cambridge University Press.

Hobsbawm, Eric, and Terrance Ranger, eds. 1983. *The Invention of Tradition*. Cambridge: Cambridge University Press.

Hogg, Russell. 1991. "Policing and Penalty." In *The Journal for Social Justice Studies* 4 (July): 1–26.

Hogg, Russell, and Kerry Carrington. 1998. "Crime, Rurality and Community." In *The Australian and New Zealand Journal of Criminality* 31 (2): 160–81.

Hollingsworth, David. 1992. "Discourses on Aboriginality and the Politics of Identity in Urban Australia." *Oceania* 63 (2): 137–55.

Hughes, Robert. 1988. *The Fatal Shore: The Epic of Australia's Founding*. New York: Vintage Books.

Human Rights and Equal Opportunity Commission. 1996. *Bringing Them Home: Report of the National Inquiry into the Separation of Aboriginal and Torres Strait Islander Children from Their Families*. Canberra: Australian Government Publishing Services.

Hunt, John Dixon, and Peter Willis, eds. 1975. *The Genius of the Place: The English Landscape Garden, 1620–1820*. London: Unwin Brothers.

Huxley, Margo. 1994. "Planning as a Framework of Power: Utilitarian Reform, Enlightenment Logic and the Control of Urban Space." In *Beasts of Suburbia: Representing Cultures in Australian Suburbs*, ed. Sarah

Ferber, Chris Healy, and Chris McAuliffe. Melbourne: Melbourne University Press.

Jackson, John Brinckerhoff. 1994. *A Sense of Place: A Sense of Time*. New Haven: Yale University Press.

Jacobs, Jane. 1996. *The Edge of Empire: Postcolonialism and the City*. London: Routledge.

———. 1994. "Earth Honoring: Western Desires and Indigenous Knowledges." In *Writing Women and Space*, ed. Alison Blunt and Gillian Rose, 169–95. New York: Guilford Press.

———. 1988. "The Construction of Identity." In *Past and Present*, ed. Jeremy K. Beckett. Canberra: Aboriginal Studies Press.

Jakubowicz, Andrew. 1984. "Ethnicity, Multiculturalism and Neo-Conservatism." In *Ethnicity, Class and Gender in Australia*, ed. Gill Bottomley and Marie de Lepervanche. Sydney: Allen and Unwin.

James, Paul. 1994/5. "Reconstituting the Nation-State: A Postmodern Republic Takes Shape." *Arena Journal* 4:69–89.

———. 1992. "Forms of Abstract 'Community' from Tribe and Kingdom to Nation and State." *Philosophy of the Social Sciences* 22 (3): 313–36.

Jameson, Fredric. 1991. *Postmodernism, or the Cultural Logic of Late Capitalism*. Durham: Duke University Press.

Jellicoe, Geoffrey, and Susan Jellicoe. 1995. *The Landscape of Man*. New York: Thames and Hudson Press.

Johnson, Louise. 1992. "Housing Desire: A Feminist Geography of Suburban Housing." *Refractory Girl* 42 (March): 40–46.

Jordon, Deidre F. 1988. "Aboriginal Identity: Uses of the Past, Problems for the Future?" In *Past and Present*, ed. Jeremy K. Beckett. Canberra: Aboriginal Studies Press.

Kapferer, Bruce. 1988. *Legends of People, Myths of State: Violence, Intolerance, and Political Culture in Sri Lanka and Australia*. Washington: Smithsonian Institution Press.

Kapferer, Judith. 1996. *Being All Equal: Identity, Difference, and Australian Cultural Practice*. Oxford: Berg.

Kearney, M. 1995. "The Local and the Global: The Anthropology of Globalization and Transnationalism." *Annual Review of Anthropology* 24:547–65.

King, Anthony. 1995. *The Bungalow: The Production of Global Culture*. Oxford: Oxford University Press.

Knight, Stephen. 1990. *The Selling of the Australian Mind: From First Fleet to Third Mercedes*. Port Melbourne: William Heinemann Australia.

Knobloch, Frieda. 1996. *The Culture of Wilderness: Agriculture as Colonization in the American West*. Chapel Hill: University of North Carolina Press.

Kumar, Krishan. 1987. *Utopia and Anti-Utopia in Modern Times.* Cambridge, MA: Blackwell.

Lal, Vinay. 1995. Review of "The Rhetoric of English India," by Sara Suleri. *Economic and Political Weekly* 4:254–55.

Langton, Marcia. 1993. "Rum, Seduction and Death: 'Aboriginality' and Alcohol." *Oceania* 63 (3): 195–206.

Larbalestier, J. 1990. Review. *Australian Historical Studies* 94:157–58.

Lardner, James, and Thomas Reppetto. 2000. *A City and Its Police.* New York: Henry Holt.

Lattas, Andrew. 1993. "Essentialism, Memory and Resistance: Aboriginality and the Politics of Authenticity." *Oceania* 63 (3): 240–67.

———. 1992. "Wiping the Blood Off Aboriginality: The Politics of Aboriginal Embodiment in Contemporary Intellectual Debate." *Oceania* 63 (2): 160–71.

———. 1991. "Nationalism, Aesthetic Redemption and Aboriginality." *Australian Journal of Anthropology* 2 (3): 307–24.

———. 1990. "Aborigines and Contemporary Australian Nationalism: Primordiality and the Cultural Politics of Otherness." *Social Analysis* 27: 50–69.

Law, Graeme. 1999. "Foreword." In *Gordon Ford: The Natural Australian Garden.* Victoria: Bloomings Books.

Lee, Christopher. 1996. "Toilet Training the Settler Subject: An Exercise in Civic Regulation." *Southern Review* 29 (1): 50–63.

Leonard, Karen. 1992. *Making Ethnic Choices: California's Punjabi Mexican Americans.* Philadelphia: Temple University Press.

———. 1997. "Finding One's Own Place: Asian Landscapes Re-Visioned in Rural California." In *Culture, Power, Place: Explorations in Critical Anthropology,* ed. Akhil Gupta and James Ferguson. Durham: Duke University Press.

Lewis, Martin, and Karen Wigen. 1997. *The Myth of Continents: A Critique of Metageography.* Berkeley: University of California Press.

Lines, William J. 1994. *An All Consuming Passion.* Berkeley: University of California Press.

Locke, John. [1690] 1980. *Second Treatise of Government.* Ed. C. B. Macpherson. Indianapolis: Hackett Publishing Company.

Lofgren, Orvar. 1989. "Learning to Remember and Learning to Forget: Class and Memory in Modern Sweden." In *Erinnern und Vergessen,* ed. Brigitte Bönish-Brednich, Rolf W. Brednich, and Helge Gerndt. Sonderdruck, Austria: Beitrage zur Volkskunde in Niedersachsen.

Low, Setha. 1997. "Urban Fear: Building Fortress America." Annual review, *City and Society,* 52–72.

———. 2000. *On the Plaza: The Politics of Public Space and Culture.* Austin: University of Texas Press.

Lynch, Kevin. 1960. *The Image of the City.* Cambridge, MA: MIT Press.

Malkki, Liisa. 1995. *Purity and Exile: Violence, Memory, and National Cosmology among Hutu Refugees in Tanzania.* Chicago: Chicago University Press.

———. 1994. "Citizens of Humanity: Internationalism and the Imagined Community of Nations." *Diaspora* 3 (1): 41–68.

———. 1992. "National Geographic: The Rooting of Peoples and the Territorialization of National Identity Among Scholars and Refugees." *Cultural Anthropology* 7 (1): 24–44.

Marcus, George E. 1998. *Ethnography Through Thick and Thin.* Princeton: Princeton University Press.

Marcus, Julie. 1991. "Under the Eye of the Law." *Journal for Social Justice Studies* 4 (July): 117–32.

Massey, Doreen. 1994. *Space, Place and Gender.* Minneapolis: University of Minnesota Press.

Mauss, Marcel. 1992. "Techniques of the Body." In *Zone Incorporations* 6, ed. Jonathon Crary and Sanford K. Winter. Boston: MIT Press.

McClintock, Anne. 1995. *Imperial Leather: Race, Gender and Sexuality in the Colonial Contest.* New York: Routledge.

McGrew, Anthony. 1996. "A Global Society?" In *Modernity: An Introduction to Modern Societies,* ed. Stuart Hall, David Held, Don Hubert, and Kenneth Thompson. Cambridge, MA: Blackwell.

Michaels, Eric. 1994. *Bad Aboriginal Art.* Minnesota: University of Minnesota Press.

Moreton, John. 1989. "Crisis? What Crisis? Australian Aboriginal Anthropology, 1988." *Mankind* 19 (1): 5–15.

Myers, Fred. 1986. *Pintupi Country, Pintupi Self: Sentiment, Place, and Politics among Western Desert Aborigines.* Washington, DC: Smithsonian Institute Press.

Nash, Roderick Frasier. 1989. *The Rights of Nature: A History of Environmental Ethics.* Madison: University of Wisconsin Press.

Nicoll, Fiona. 1993. "The Art of Reconciliation: Art, Aboriginality and the State." *Meanjin* 4:705–18.

Oelschlaeger, Max. 1991. *The Idea of Nature: From Prehistory to the Age of Ecology.* New Haven: Yale University Press.

Ong, Aihwa. 1997. "Flexible Citizenship Among Chinese Cosmopolitans." In *Cosmopolitics: Thinking and Feeling Beyond the Nation,* ed. Pheng Cheah and Bruce Robbins. Minneapolis: University of Minnesota Press.

———. 1993. "On the Edge of Empires: Flexible Citizenship Among Chinese in Diaspora." *Positions* 1 (3): 745–80.

———. 1987. *Spirits of Resistance and Capitalist Discipline*. Albany: State University of New York Press.

Ong, Aihwa, and Donald Nonini, eds. 1997. *Ungrounded Empires: The Cultural Politics of Modern Chinese Transnationalism*. New York: Routledge.

Outram, Dorinda. 1999. "On Being Perseus: New Knowledge, Dislocation, and Enlightenment Exploration." In *Geography and Enlightenment*, ed. David Livingstone and Charles Withers. Cambridge: Cambridge University Press.

Parkin, Andrew, and Leonie Hardcastle. 1990. "Immigration Policy." In *Hawke and Australian Public Policy: Consensus and Restructuring*, ed. Christine Jennett and Randal G. Stewart. South Melbourne: Macmillan.

Passaro, Joanne. 1997. "You Can't Take the Subway to the Field! 'Village' Epistemologies in the Global Village." In *Anthropological Locations: Boundaries and Grounds of a Field Science*, ed. Akhil Gupta and James Ferguson. Berkeley: University of California Press.

Pettman, Jan. 1991. "Racism, Sexism and Sociology." In *Intersexions: Gender/Class/Culture/Ethnicity*, ed. G. Bottomley, M. deLepervanche, and J. Martin, 187–202. Sydney: Allen and Unwin.

———. 1988. "Whose Country Is It Anyway? Cultural Politics, Racism and the Construction of Being Australian." *Journal of Intercultural Studies* 9 (1): 1–24.

Philpott, Simon. 2001. "Fear of the Dark: Indonesia and the Australian National Imagination." *Australian Journal of International Affairs* 55 (3): 243–71.

Povinelli, Elizabeth. 1998. "The State of Shame: Australian Multiculturalism and the Crisis of Indigenous Citizenship." *Critical Inquiry* 24 (2): 575–610.

———. 1996. "Of Pleasure and Property: Sexuality and Sovereignty in Aboriginal Australia." In *Thinking Through the Body of the Law*, ed. Pheng Cheah, David Fraser, and Judith Grbich. New South Wales: Allen and Unwin.

———. 1993. *Labor's Lot: The Power, History and Culture of Aboriginal Action*. Chicago: University of Chicago Press.

Pred, Allan. 1990. *Making Histories and Constructing Human Geographies: The Local Transformation of Practice, Power Relations, and Consciousness*. Boulder, CO: Westview Press.

Priestley, L. J. 1993. "The Mabo Case, Miracle or Monster?" Law Center of the University of South Carolina, James Madison Memorial Lecture, November 16.

Proudfoot, Peter. 1985. "Closing the Gap Between Life and Art: Arcadia and the Australian Suburb." *Transition*, July, 23–28.

Rizvi, Fazal. 1996. "Racism, Reorientation and the Cultural Politics of Asia-Australia Relations." In *The Teeth Are Smiling: The Persistence of Racism in Multicultural Australia,* ed. Ellie Vasta and Stephen Castles. New South Wales: Allen and Unwin.

Robin, Libby. 1998. "Urbanizing the Bush: Environmental Disputes and Australian National Identity." In *Australian Identities,* ed. David Day. Melbourne: Australian Scholarly Publishing.

Robson, L. L. 1965. *The Convict Settlers of Australia.* Melbourne: Melbourne University Press.

Rouse, Roger. 1995. "Thinking Through Transnationalism: Notes on the Cultural Politics of Class Relations in the Contemporary United States." *Public Culture* 7:353–402.

———. 1991. "Mexican Migration and the Social Space of Postmodernity." *Diaspora,* Spring, 8–23.

Rousseau, Jean-Jacques. 1987. *The Basic Political Writings.* Indianapolis: Hackett Publishing Company.

Rowse, Tim. 1990. "Are We All Blow-ins?" *Oceania* 61 (2): 185–91.

Ruggie, John Gerald. 1998. *Constructing the World Polity: Essays on International Institutionalization.* London: Routledge.

Rushdie, Salman. 1991. *Imaginary Homelands.* New York: Penguin Books.

Ryan, Simon. 1996. *The Cartographic Eye: How Explorers Saw Australia.* Cambridge: Cambridge University Press.

Sack, Robert. 1993. "The Power of Space and Place." *Geographical Review* 83:326–29.

Sackett, Lee. 1991. "Promoting Primitivism: Conservationist Depictions of Aboriginal Australians." *Australian Journal of Anthropology* 2 (2): 233–40.

Safran, William. 1991. "Diasporas in Modern Societies: Myths of Homeland and Return." *Diaspora* 1 (1): 83–89.

Said, Edward. 1996. "From Orientalism." In *Human Geography: An Essential Anthology,* ed. John Agnew, David Livingstone, and Alisdair Rogers. Oxford: Blackwell.

———. 1979. *Orientalism.* New York: Vintage Books.

Sassen, Saskia. 1996. *Losing Control? Sovereignty in an Age of Globalization.* New York: Columbia University Press.

———. 1991. *The Global City: New York, London, Tokyo.* Princeton: Princeton University Press.

Schaffer, Kay. 1988. *Women and the Bush: Forces of Desire in the Australian Cultural Tradition.* Cambridge: Cambridge University Press.

Scott-James, Anne. 1981. *The Cottage Garden.* London: Allen Lane.

Shapiro, Michael J. 1997. *Violent Cartographies: Mapping Cultures of War.* Minneapolis: University of Minnesota Press.

Soja, Edward. 1989. *Postmodern Geographies: The Reassertion of Space in Critical Social Theory*. London: Verso.

Stanislawski, Don. 1946. "The Origin and the Spread of the Grid-Pattern Town." *Geographical Review*, vol. 36.

Steedman, Carolyn. 1987. *Landscape for a Good Woman: A Story of Two Lives*. New Brunswick, NJ: Rutgers University Press.

Stewart, Susan. 1993. *On Longing: Narratives of the Miniature, the Gigantic, the Souvenir, the Collection*. Durham: Duke University Press.

Stoddart, David. 1986. "Geography—A European Science." In *On Geography and Its History*. Oxford: Blackwell.

Suleri, Sara. 1992. "The Feminine Picturesque." In *The Rhetoric of English India*. Chicago: University of Chicago Press.

Tambiah, Stanley J. 1985. *Culture, Thought, and Social Action: An Anthropological Perspective*. Cambridge: Harvard University Press.

Teigger, D. 1990. Review in *Australian New Zealand Journal of Sociology* 26 (2): 235–7.

Thacker, Christopher. 1979. *The History of Gardens*. Berkeley: University of California Press.

Tiffin, Chris. 1987. "Imaginary Countries, Imaginary People: Climate and the Australian Type." *Span* 24:46–62.

Tololyan, Khachig. 1991. "The Nation-State and Its Others." *Diaspora*, Spring, 3–7.

Torgovnick, Marianna. 1990. *Gone Primitive*. Chicago: University of Chicago Press.

Tsing, Anna Lowenhaupt. 1993. *In the Realm of the Diamond Queen: Marginality in an Out of the Way Place*. Princeton, NJ: Princeton University Press.

Tuan, Yi-Fu. 1996. "Space and Place: Humanistic Perspective." In *Human Geography: An Essential Anthology*, ed. John Agnew, David Livingstone, and Alisdair Rogers. Oxford: Blackwell.

Walker, David. 1999. *Anxious Nation: Australia and the Rise of Asia, 1850–1939*. St. Lucia, Queensland: University of Queensland Press.

Walling, Edna. 1952. *The Australian Roadside*. Melbourne: Oxford University Press.

———. 1948. *A Gardener's Log*. Melbourne: Oxford University Press.

———. 1946. *Gardens in Australia: Their Designs and Care*. Melbourne: Oxford University Press.

Ware, Vron. 1992. *Beyond the Pale: White Women, Racism, and History*. London: Verso.

Watts, Michael. 1992. "Space for Everything (A Commentary)." *Cultural Anthropology* 7 (1): 115–29.

White, Richard. 1981. *Inventing Australia: Images and Identity, 1688–1980.* Sydney: George Allen and Unwin.

Williams, Raymond. 1977. *Marxism and Literature.* Oxford: Oxford University Press.

Willis, Anne-Marie. 1993. *Illusions of Identity.* Sydney: Hale and Iremonger.

Wilson, Alexander. 1992. *The Culture of Nature: North American Landscape from Disney to the Exxon Valdez.* Cambridge: Blackwell.

Winichakul, Thongchai. 1994. *Siam Mapped: A History of the Geographical Body of a Nation.* Honolulu: University of Hawaii Press.

Wright, Patrick. 1985. *On Living in an Old Country: The National Past in Contemporary Britain.* London: Verso.

Zukin, Sharon. 1991. *Landscapes of Power: From Detroit to Disney World.* Berkeley: University of California Press.

# Index

ALLAINE CERWONKA is assistant professor of political science and women's studies at Georgia State University. She lived in Melbourne, Australia, for three years between 1984 and 1996, initially as an American Field Service high school exchange student and later as a Fulbright scholar at the University of Melbourne.